MW00849832

JOE WALSH

FROM THE JAMES GANG TO THE EAGLES

BY NICK THOMAS

GUARDIAN EXPRESS MEDIA

ISBN: 978-1735152325

Library of Congress Cataloging-in-Publication Data

Thomas, Nick

Joe Walsh: From the James Gang to the Eagles

Includes bibliographical references

ISBN 978-1735152325

We would like to thank the following individuals and organizations: John Mascolo; Mary Ellen Huesken; Mike Olszewski; Sigmund Vaccaro; the Akron - Summit County Public Library; and the Music Library and Sound Recordings Archives at Bowling Green State University. Additionally, we are grateful to all of the individuals who consented to our interview requests.

Please contact the publisher to report any errors or omissions. Organizations and other groups interested in purchasing quantities of this book should contact the publisher.

This is not an official or authorized work. Joe Walsh, the Eagles, the James Gang, their record companies, their managers and their representatives did not participate in the writing, editing, production or publication of this book.

Printed in the U.S.A.

TABLE OF CONTENTS

INTRODUCTION

One of the most colorful characters in the history of rock and roll, Joe Walsh has enjoyed a successful musical career for more than five-decades. With his offbeat attitude and quirky sense of humor, he earned a number of nicknames, including the Analog Man and the Clown Prince of Rock Guitar.

A much-respected songwriter and musician, Walsh first made a name for himself in Ohio as a member of the James Gang. As the group's guitar-slinging frontman, he recorded timeless classics such as "Funk #49" and "Walk Away." Later forming Barnstorm, he popularized the talk box on the rock standard, "Rocky Mountain Way."

Moving on to bigger things, Walsh joined the Eagles as the replacement for Bernie Leadon, and brought swagger as well as some much-needed showmanship to the group's live performances. Providing the soundtrack of the 1970s, the Walsh-era Eagles crafted a series of enduring classics such as "Hotel California," "In The City" and "Life In The Fast Lane." Even after joining the Eagles, Walsh maintained a solo career and enjoyed success with the autobiographical track, "Life's Been Good."

However, after the Eagles disbanded in 1980, Walsh released a series of uneven solo albums as he battled his many personal demons. When the Eagles reunited in 1994, Walsh was forced into rehab as a precondition of rejoining the group. With the music of the Eagles never falling out of favor, the group continued to fill large arenas and stadiums with multiple generations of loyal fans.

The focus of this book is on Walsh's musical career. It is not a tell-all of his much-publicized rock star antics, whether hard partying or acts of hotel destruction. This is also a book of redemption. After beating his addictions, Walsh demonstrated the power of human triumph. And after marrying Marjorie Bach in 2008, Walsh became the brother-in-law of one of his early musical heroes, Ringo Starr.

A consummate entertainer with an impressive body of recorded work, Walsh once stated: "I believe my job on this planet in this life is to work at my craft, which is music, and play guitar for people and make them happy. That's my assignment, and I know that.... It took me the first third of my life to realize it, but I know why I'm here. And I'm at peace." And in an industry where rock stars demand to be treated like royalty, Walsh stood apart as an ordinary average guy.

▶ CHAPTER 1
HOME IN KANSAS

Joe Walsh often calls himself "a guy from Ohio." In fact, many Ohioans believe he was born and raised in the Buckeye State. Emerging from the clubs of downtown Kent and joining the Cleveland-based rock group the James Gang, Walsh forever anchored himself to Northeastern Ohio and never forgot where he mastered his musical craft.

However, Walsh was actually born in America's mid-section, where he descended from hard-working Kansas stock, with both sides of his family residing in the state for multiple generations. Kansas had been carved out of the central portion of the Louisiana Purchase and achieved statehood in 1861, just three-months before the start of the Civil War.

The state of Kansas helped to shape the classic image of the rugged Wild West. While the notorious Wild Bill Hickok was a deputy marshal at Fort Riley, both Wyatt Earp and Bat Masterson were employed as lawmen in Dodge City. And in the neighboring state of Missouri, the notorious James Gang frequently crossed into Kansas to hold up a moving train or rob a bank vault.

The state later became a productive agricultural center and was known as America's breadbasket thanks to long, hot summers that were ideal for raising grains and other food crops. Located smack in the heart of Tornado Alley, Kansas also gave rise to Dorothy and her small dog Toto in the much-loved narrative, *The Wizard Of Oz.*

Walsh's hometown of Wichita was situated along the Chisholm Trail, a heavily traveled cattle-drive route. As a popular stopover and trading hub beginning in the 1860s, the city earned its first nickname – Cowtown. By 1914, oil and natural gas were discovered in neighboring Butler County. By the mid-1920s, the region was home to several oil companies and twelve large refineries. Local businessman Fred C. Koch, whose company would later evolve into Koch Industries, earned his massive wealth during this period.

As one writer observed, by the 1930s, "fortunes were being made in Wichita. Known as 'The Magic City,' it had become a magnet for risk takers, entrepreneurs, and fortune seekers of all stripes. The Texas gas-lamp salesman W.C. Coleman had established a thriving business there."

Within a few decades, the Coleman Company would dominate the outdoor recreation business.

Much of the massive profits from the oil and gas wells were invested in a brand-new industry – aviation. With its flat terrain, mild winters and central location, the region was an ideal spot for the airplane industry. Following the innovations of Orville and Wilbur Wright of Ohio, Kansas-based entrepreneurs like Clyde Cessna would help to turn the city of Wichita into "America's Air Capital." In 1917, Cessna introduced the Comet, which was the first aircraft built in the city. Competitors such as Beech Aircraft and Stearman also made Wichita their home, attracting a wide array of workers from engineers to pilots. Later, other firms arrived in the city, including Learjet, Airbus and Spirit AeroSystems.

Not surprisingly, Wichita was dotted with airfields. One of these, the McConnell Air Force Base, was established in 1941 during the early years of the Second World War. The facility previously operated as a commercial enterprise, the Wichita Municipal Airport. During the war, the city would experience another population boom thanks to a bustling Boeing plant that built the much-utilized B-29 bomber. In time, Wichita would produce more aircraft than any other city in the world, mostly light aircraft and smaller business jets. The state of Kansas would also produce thousands of pilots, the most notable of whom was Amelia Earhart, who was born in the town of Atchison. And in the 1940s, Joe Walsh's father would emerge as a skilled test pilot.

* * * * * *

Robert Newton Fidler, the father of Joe Walsh, was raised in a stately two-story, Victorian-style home on North Fairmount Street, just two blocks south of the University of Wichita, which at the time was a municipal institution. After graduating from high school in 1940, he worked for the Woodward Oil Company. Thin and hazel-eyed, he was clean-cut and looked much like a younger version of the popular bandleader of the era, Glenn Miller.

At 18-years-old in 1942, Fidler enlisted in the military. At around the same time in a town 70-miles away, fellow Kansas native and future senator Bob Dole also enlisted, and was later seriously injured during a brutal battle against a German fortification in northern Italy. Robert Fidler's own father – Alden Anderson Fidler – was drafted during World War One. Returning home, he worked as a newsreel cameraman, press photographer and projectionist at a pair of Wichita theaters. Tragically, the elder Fidler would die young, struck down by a fatal heart attack at the age of 39 in 1939, leaving behind a widow and three children.

Later, Robert Fidler and his girlfriend, Helen Alice Bowen, would both attend the University of Wichita. Studying music, Bowen was a classically trained pianist of Scottish, Irish and German ancestry. A serious-minded woman, she had long, dark hair and classic features. Her mother, Harriet Bowen, was a talented piano teacher. Her father – Floyd Palmer Bowen, Sr. – served in World War One and was stationed on the front lines amidst the wrecked farmlands of France. As a former high school athlete, he was a courier whose job was to run ten-miles, back and forth, between the command headquarters and the battlefield, where he delivered military orders. The final time he ran back to the front, the entire unit had been felled by suffocating clouds of mustard gas and there was no one to receive the orders. Returning to Kansas after the war, he worked in the banking industry.

On July 7, 1945, Robert Fidler wed Helen Bowen, who was three-years his junior, at St. James Episcopal Church. Initially, the newlywed couple stayed with Fidler's mother and her new husband. Also that year, Fidler enlisted in the Army Air Corps. In 1947, he re-enlisted for another two-years and was promoted to the rank of lieutenant.

Helen Fidler often volunteered to perform for injured soldiers at a Veteran's Administration hospital in Wichita as a member of an eleven-piece ensemble led by bandleader Dick King. Wichita had a strong jazz tradition, and the city was the birthplace of Stan Kenton, a popular big-band star.

On November 20, 1947, the only child of Robert and Helen Fidler was born at Wesley Hospital in Wichita. Joseph Fidler was named after his great-grandfather, Joseph Lewis Newton, who had passed away three-years earlier. Like millions of other post-war babies, Joe was a member of the first wave of the Baby Boomer generation.

Meanwhile, during the U.S. administration of postwar Japan, Lieutenant Fidler was shipped to Okinawa, Japan, in January 1948. The island was home to a large Army contingent and a smaller number of Navy personnel. Okinawa had been the last major military campaign of World War Two, and most of the island was still a disaster zone. All around, wrecked and burned-out military vehicles and twisted debris dotted the jagged landscape. Adding to the mayhem, Typhoon Libby would strike Okinawa in October 1948.

Excelling as a pilot in the Army Air Corps (which in 1947 became the U.S. Air Force), Fidler was a flight instructor for a new military jet built by Lockheed. Joe Walsh later discussed his father's duties in Okinawa: "He flew pre-jet, prop planes, and right when he was at his peak, jets were discovered. The F80 Shooting Star was the first real jet, and he flew that, and then the F85 Sabre." At the time, the island had just two airports: a busy one-runway airfield in the town of Naha and a military airport, Kadena, which was reserved for B-29 Superfortress bombers.

The first shipment of F-80s arrived in the Pacific region in 1948. The planes were sent to the 49th Fighter Group at the Misawa Air Base in Japan. As one military historian explained: "In the formative years of the Cold War, punctuated by the Berlin Airlift and the detonation of the first Soviet atomic bomb in 1949, the Lockheed F-80 Shooting Star was both the backbone of the new flying service and a symbol of American resolve." And with war looming on the Korean peninsula, the U.S. military needed to train a large contingent of pilots.

In January 1949, Joe and his mother arrived in Okinawa. They resided in the Bucknerville family camp. However, tragedy struck on July 22, 1949, during a routine practice run off the western coast of Okinawa. Flying over the small, uninhabited island of Irisuma Jima – which served as a military target range – 25-year-old First Lieutenant Fidler collided with another F-80 Shooting Star, which was piloted by Captain Ernest McAnulty of San Diego. During the flight, the two planes bumped wings. The newly designed airplane was difficult to maneuver and neither pilot was able to regain control of their craft. Joe Walsh explained that his father "was teaching a guy to fly, and some guy hit him.... [The pilots] had to practice where they would... come down together. The kid just hit him and wiped him out." Both pilots perished. The tragedy was reported with few details in various newspapers across the United States. Joe's parents had planned on leaving Okinawa and returning to Wichita the following January.

Years later, Walsh lamented the fact that he had no memories of his father: "I always felt kind of alone. I always wondered what he was like and what he would have thought of me." Meanwhile, Joe and his grieving mother returned to the U.S. In Wichita, young Joe struggled during this period: "In the early years, I didn't have a dad and everybody else did. I didn't have a father figure, I didn't have anybody to take me to a ballgame or play catch with, any of this stuff. I just spent all that time wondering what my dad was like." Joe's mother, who was anxious about the future, redirected her own insecurity toward her young son and became an overly strict parent.

▶ CHAPTER 2
THE MIDWEST & EAST COAST

Leaving Wichita, Helen Fidler and her son, Joe, relocated to Evanston, Illinois. Joe's mother resumed her education and worked toward earning a master's degree in musicology at Northwestern University. At the school, she met and began dating fellow student Robert Newton Walsh. A veteran of World War II, he was a member of the third team that entered Hiroshima. After a short courtship, Fidler and Walsh married in 1953, when Joe was just five.

As was the tradition at the time, Joe added his stepfather's last name and kept his birth father's surname as a middle name, so he was now known as Joseph Fidler Walsh. His mother and stepfather would later have two children, both sons. Meanwhile, Walsh's stepfather became an attorney specializing in malpractice insurance. As a high-achiever, he expected the same of his stepson. However, neither of Walsh's parents realized at the time that young Joe was suffering from an undiagnosed learning disability.

One of young Joe's memories of living in Evanston was listening to his family's radio. While getting ready for school, he was a fan of a popular morning program that was broadcast from nearby Chicago, *Don McNeill's Breakfast Club*. The show combined informal conversation with music and topical jokes.

In 1956, the Walsh family moved to Columbus, Ohio. Joe's stepfather worked in the insurance field and needed to be near the Nationwide headquarters. The capital of the Buckeye State, the city of Columbus was passionate about its local football team, *the* Ohio State Buckeyes, and its revered coach, Woody Hayes. With its Midwestern values, the city provided Joe with a sense of stability.

In Columbus, the Walsh family settled on the north side of the city in the Clintonville neighborhood, where Joe attended Crestview Elementary School. The family lived on a street of closely spaced, mid-century-style, two-story homes. Joe's homelife was marked by supportive, affectionate parents. Additionally, his stepfather made a strong effort to ensure that young Joe never forgot his birth father. Enjoying the outdoors, Joe liked to dress up as a cowboy and explore the many undeveloped spaces in his neighborhood. He would later describe this period of his young life as "vacant lots, BB gun wars, snowball fights and kick-the-can."

Thanks to his mother, young Joe was exposed to a great deal of music at home. A huge fan of classical music, his mother spent much of her free time listening to records or playing the family's piano. At age nine, Joe first heard "Adagio For Strings," which would become his favorite song of all time: "It puts me in a trance, and I can't really move until the piece is over." Joe also spent a great deal of his spare time playing the clarinet and trombone. At the encouragement of his mother, Joe also took piano lessons and became proficient on the instrument.

Then at age ten, in 1957, Joe began to explore his new love of rock and roll. He recalled: "Some of the happiest times of my life were in Columbus. I used to listen to this guy on WCOL named Dr. Bop – a famous, famous disc jockey. All he played was the great, classic, old rock 'n' roll songs." An African-American deejay, the flamboyant Dr. Bop (real name Hoyt Locke) played a mix of R&B and pioneering rock and roll during his six-hour shift.

Walsh was drawn to more upbeat rock and roll songs such as "Yakety Yak," "At The Hop" and "Chantilly Lace." He also had a fondness for doo-wop vocal hits like "Blue Moon," "Come Go With Me" and "Rama Lama Ding Dong." While Walsh was purchasing mostly 45rpm singles, he eventually bought his first full-length LP – *The Chirping Crickets* by Buddy Holly, a rock pioneer who took the electric guitar to the forefront of popular music. Walsh later recalled: "All my influences really existed between 1953 and 1960. All the pre-English Invasion rock and roll from the very beginning, and all the doo-wop and wonderful records that were made during that time period. The guitar was one of the major vehicles for all of that music."

Not surprisingly, in February 1959, Walsh was grief-stricken when he learned of the tragic plane crash near Clear Lake, Iowa, that took the lives of his early musical idols – Buddy Holly, Ritchie Valens and the Big Bopper.

* * * * * *

In June 1959, the Walshes moved again, leaving Columbus for New York City. Instead of enjoying green, open spaces, the family now lived in a congested, urban environment. The Walshes settled into a cramped, two-bedroom, third-floor apartment.

As a transplant to the city, 12-year-old Joe Walsh had no friends in his new neighborhood and had little to do during his first summer. Then, by chance, he discovered a new passion – shortwave radio. He recalled: "On the roof of my building... I found a wire leading down to the first floor. I knocked on the apartment and told the guy I wanted to know what it was, since it was the most exciting thing I'd seen since leaving Columbus. It was an antenna. He invited me in, and I saw him talk to people around the world on his radio. Soon I became an operator. His name was Jim Walden, and he saved my life." As a result of the experience, Walsh developed a lifelong interest in electronics.

On another occasion, young Joe was exposed to a new technology: "I went with my parents to visit a friend of theirs who was an 'audio engineer.' I remember talking with him about this new thing he and these other guys had been working on. He played a tape of a train... It was very loud and there were two speakers – not just one like everyone had back then. I remember being scared because it seemed like the train was coming right through the living room. I even looked out the window to see if I could see this train as it disappeared to the east. I remember him saying, 'We're going to call what you just heard 'stereo' and it's going to change recorded music from now on.'"

In New York, Walsh attended junior high at P.S. 216. Accustomed to making and losing friends on a regular basis as he moved and changed schools, Joe learned to cope by becoming the class clown. However, Walsh also suffered from a number of learning and developmental issues during his childhood. He later revealed: "I had, without knowing, attention-deficient, obsessive-compulsive [disorder], probably a little Asperger's.... Medical science had not diagnosed any of that then. You were just, 'difficult.' I was difficult. I could not complete tasks, I was all over the place." Consequently, Walsh struggled in school, but did well enough to pass his classes.

Meanwhile, Joe's musical education continued both at home and school. However, he was more interested in the music he heard on the radio. Feeding his youthful love of rock and roll, Walsh recalled listening to his favorite deejays on New York's airwaves: "Cousin Brucie, Scott Muni, Murray the K, Dan Ingram – those were the days!"

Wanting to play the songs he heard on the radio, Walsh initially acquired a ukulele. He then bought a cheap acoustic guitar. Walsh recalled: "I had a Sears, Roebuck Harmony guitar that I ordered out of the catalog. I found I could play songs a lot better on that than on a clarinet. I wasn't going to get any girls playing the clarinet."

However, it wasn't Elvis Presley but Ricky Nelson who initially motivated Walsh to hone his guitar skills. Glued to his television during the weekly episodes of *The Adventures of Ozzie & Harriet,* Walsh recalled: "It was like a serial, and every so often they would show Ricky Nelson playing at his high school dance, and of course his band involved [guitarist] James Burton, who played on most of his records." And while Joe's parents encouraged him to practice his classical instruments, he took it upon himself to master the guitar.

A few years later, Walsh acquired his first electric guitar, an inexpensive Kay Value Leader. Taking a job as a paperboy, Walsh recalled: "I always wanted an electric, but my parents didn't have a lot of money. I worked all summer and saved, which taught me the value of money. It was very frustrating, having $24 and adding three dollars to it every week, counting the weeks until I could get some equipment. My first amp was a Wollensak tape recorder. It sounded horrible, but it was the barest necessities, and I really buckled down and played and played and played."

At age 13, Walsh appeared in a school talent contest. He teamed with a fellow student to perform the theme from the film *Exodus*, an instrumental track that was a big pop hit in 1960 for Ferrante & Teicher. However, while performing in front of his classmates, Joe was terrified and began to shake.

Eventually, Joe formed an instrumental surf-music group called the G-Clefs, initially as a duo with Bob Edwards. In addition to Walsh on guitar, the group also featured a pianist, trumpet player and drummer. Walsh recalled: "Even though we could hardly play anything, we had plans to be the next Ventures. All those great instrumentals like 'Wipe Out,' 'Wild Weekend' and 'Walk, Don't Run,' were coming out, and we learned them all. We were terrible, but it was cool."

* * * * * *

After a few years in their crowded apartment, the Walsh family left the congested environment of New York City and moved 30-miles west to a house in northern New Jersey. Settling in Montclair Township, it was here that Joe's musical ambitions were firmly established. The quiet, tree-lined community was situated at the base of the First

Watchung Mountain. Home to the state's second largest university, Montclair had a strong and lively arts community that supported Joe's creative efforts. Walsh's stepfather, meanwhile, opened a legal practice in New York City.

Joe attended Montclair High School, a safe and nurturing institution. With its stately, picturesque architecture, the school was the perfect backdrop for numerous television shows and films, including the original 1950 version of *Cheaper By The Dozen*. Notable graduates of Montclair include astronaut Buzz Aldrin, NFL player Josh Allen, actress Christina Ricci and golf course architect Robert Trent Jones, Jr.

At Montclair High, Joe felt a sense of belonging for the first time in his young life: "Oh it was great, for some reason our class got along fine. My little brothers' high school was a whole different deal. I guess drugs got into high school, we didn't have drugs yet, nobody got pregnant, and basically it was pretty much our high school against other high schools.... It was a great time to grow up."

Somewhat of an athlete, Walsh joined his high school football team during his junior year. Playing the tight end position, he wore #80 on his jersey. But after suffering a game injury, he played for only one season. The following year, the Montclair Mounties football team had a perfect season and won the state championship. A true powerhouse, the team was ranked #3 in the nation, which gave Joe and his classmates a sense of collective pride.

Walsh also joined his high school marching band, originally on clarinet. Switching to the oboe, Walsh explained the advantage of playing his new instrument: "I got to get out of homeroom because the whole orchestra tunes up to an oboe. Everybody paid attention to me. I didn't even know it yet, but that's part of what I wanted out of music." Active at his school, Walsh ran for the position of class president during his junior year but was not victorious. Later, he joined a new student organization, the Radio Station Club, which was tasked with starting a student-run campus radio station.

Then on February 9, 1964, 16-year-old Joe had a life-changing experience. Catching the Beatles' debut performance on *The Ed Sullivan Show*, Joe was mesmerized by the group's energy, charisma and catchy songs. As he later recalled: "I still have a really clear image of watching them, and my parents shaking their heads left and right, and me shaking my head up and down, and that hit a spark inside me and I knew that was what I wanted to do. I thought, 'Those guys are cool,' and I'd like to do that."

Soon, Joe would regularly take a 45-minute bus ride from Montclair to New York City, where he usually headed to Greenwich Village. Drawn to the burgeoning folk and rock scenes, the underage Walsh couldn't enter any of the nightclubs. Confined to the sidewalk, he recalled: "I would stand out in front of the Night Owl [Cafe] and listen to the Lovin' Spoonful. And [Frank] Zappa was in town all the time.... And I'd go to the Peppermint Lounge and stand out front and listen to Joey Dee and the Starliters. And [Jimi] Hendrix was playing for him.... That was good enough: to be part of the scene – even though I really wasn't old enough to get in anywhere." (A few years before Hendrix joined the Starliters, the band included guitarist Joe Pesci, who later became a successful actor.)

In addition to absorbing the music emanating from the city's nightclubs, Walsh would also visit instrument stores: "I would go to Manny's Music Store and I would look at all the guitars and all the amps and dream. Didn't have money to buy 'em. And then I would take the last bus back out to Montclair." Around this time, Joe managed to land a part-time job, taking orders at a Cadillac parts center. But instead of answering the phones, he took his guitar to his workplace and played along with the radio, which led to his firing.

After the G-Clefs, Walsh joined a real, working top-40 cover band, the Nomads, as the replacement for Bruce Hoffman. Walsh recalled: "They had just dumped their bass player and asked me if I could play. I said 'sure.' I'd never played bass in my life, but I figured it couldn't be too hard with only four strings. I ended up playing bass for the Nomads most of my senior year. My parents still have a picture of me all slicked up... playing at the prom."

Based in the nearby town of Madison, the Nomads didn't play any original material – only cover versions of pop hits. Nearly every weekend, the group performed all over New Jersey. Walsh explained: "The leader of the band was the leader because his dad had a station wagon." At Walsh's first few shows, he constantly gazed at his shoes, avoiding the faces in the audience. As for the level of the band's musical proficiency, Walsh explained: "Back then, you didn't have to be good if you knew Beatles songs. And if you had Beatles boots, you were cool."

In October 1964, the Nomads were booked to play a Halloween dance at Montclair High School. The opening act was a folk quartet, the Rum Runners. After many of their performances, Walsh and the Nomads set up their instruments in someone's basement for an extended jam session in front of an audience of friends and family.

Meanwhile, Walsh noticed that his fellow bandmates drank a few beers before the shows. He soon discovered that a beer or two gave him the ability to perform more confidently in front of crowds. Walsh had found his liquid courage.

Walsh and his bandmates even managed to record a single. As he recalled: "The Nomads made a record which sold four copies, because each guy in the band bought one." However, the group disbanded after Walsh finished high school in 1965. And in his senior yearbook photo, Walsh looked distinguished in his sharp businessman's suit and short, tidy hair.

* * * * * *

One of the most notable concerts in rock history took place at Shea Stadium in New York City on August 15, 1965. Normally the home of the New York Mets, the large venue was instead packed with thousands of young, screaming Beatles fans along with 2,000 seasoned security guards. The show kicked off the group's second, full U.S. tour.

After the five opening acts finished their sets, Ed Sullivan introduced the Fab Four with the words: "Now, ladies and gentlemen, honored by their country, decorated by their Queen, loved here in America, here are the Beatles!" Perched on a temporary stage near second base, the group performed for a little over 30-minutes, starting the show with their upbeat rendition of the R&B classic, "Twist And Shout," and finishing with the frantic rocker, "I'm Down."

On the following day, *The New York Daily News* reported: "The Beatles packed Shea Stadium with 55,000-odd deliriously screaming teenagers last night – and literally had them climbing the walls.... The event was billed as a concert, but the lucky legion who managed to get inside the stadium – a good 75% of them teenage girls – couldn't possibly have heard anything but their own screams.... You couldn't even hear the planes passing overhead to and from nearby LaGuardia Airport."

In the audience were Linda Eastman and Barbara Bach, both of whom would later wed members of the Beatles. Joining 17-year-old Bach at the show was her younger sister, Marjorie. Barbara Bach was there to chaperone Marjorie, who was crazy about the band and came to the concert wearing a Beatles wig. Amazingly, also in attendance were a pair of 17-year-olds from New Jersey, Joe Walsh and his then-girlfriend, who had purchased the tickets. Decades later, Walsh and the Bach sisters realized they were seated a mere fifty-feet from each other.

Meanwhile, just one-week after the Beatles appeared at Shea Stadium, the group performed for thousands of screaming fans at Olympia Stadium, a hockey arena in Detroit. One of the teens in attendance was a young, aspiring musician named Glenn Frey.

▶ CHAPTER 3
JOE GOES TO COLLEGE

Days after attending the Beatles concert at Shea Stadium, Joe Walsh would pack his belongings – including a guitar and small amplifier – and board a train for Ohio. After arriving at a train depot in downtown Kent, Walsh emerged onto a brick street that was lined with a series of mismatched, older buildings that housed the bars and restaurants that catered to the city's large student population. Across the street from the depot was Ray's Place, a popular student hangout that served food and beer, and would soon become one of Walsh's favorite hangouts. The decaying train depot would serve its final passengers just five-years later.

Although he was a bright, inquisitive student, Walsh wasn't certain he was destined for college. Initially, he didn't want to go: "I fought with my parents, tried to tell them, 'Look, I'm a rock star here. I'm gonna be a Beatle. This is really *important.*' And they said, 'Baloney, you're going to college.' So I went."

While Walsh's parents thought it was a terrible idea for their son to pursue a career as a rock musician, not everyone in the family agreed. As Joe recalled: "My grandfather took me aside and said, 'Never mind everybody. You go ahead and go for it. Instead of regretting that you didn't, go ahead and see where it goes.' He gave me permission to be me." Additionally, Joe knew that attending a university would keep him from having to fight in the unpopular war that was raging in southeastern Asia. He later admitted that he didn't have much of a desire to go to school, but "wanted to go to Vietnam less."

Meanwhile, Walsh understood that his time in higher education consisted of more than just studying in a classroom. During his childhood in Columbus, he had witnessed the exuberance and collective spirit in the community whenever the Ohio State University's football team took the field every Saturday – especially when the opponent was the dreaded team from up north in Michigan.

However, while Joe's grades were in high school were fair, he was not destined for an institution with high academic standards like Ohio State. Just two-hours away from Columbus, Kent State University seemed like an acceptable alternative. Although he was also accepted by

Rutgers in New Jersey, he preferred to leave the state for his education. As for why Walsh had specifically selected Kent State, he later admitted: "*Playboy* [magazine] called it a country club, 'cause you didn't have to study to pass... so Kent sounded fine to me." It also helped that the tuition at Kent State was very reasonable.

Kent State University was situated several miles east of Akron. The city of Kent at the time of Walsh's arrival had a population of 23,000. The city was originally known as Franklin Mills, and named after the 19th century milling operations that were constructed along the Cuyahoga River. (The river was later pictured on the front cover of the first James Gang album.) In 1835, the notorious abolitionist John Brown arrived in the community and launched a business partnership with a prominent local businessman, Zenas Kent. Franklin Mills was later renamed Kent, after Zenas's son Marvin was successful in his effort to bring a railroad to the village in 1863.

Ultimately, it was the Kent family that convinced the Ohio legislature to establish a state-funded university in the city by donating 53-acres of prime land. In 1910, the Kent State Normal School was founded as a teachers college. The institution was renamed Kent State University following the passage of a state bill in 1935 which allowed the institution to add new departments and graduate programs. And after the end of World War Two, enrollment skyrocketed as more than 10,000 military veterans took advantage of the G.I. Bill to attend Kent State over the next decade. In 1961, a local tree-trimming company imported ten Canadian black squirrels, which became the university's mascot.

By the time Walsh arrived at Kent State in 1965, the university had dramatically expanded its academic offerings and was approaching an enrollment of 20,000 students. A college town, Kent was often considered a suburb of neighboring Akron, an industrial city whose growth was tied to the automobile industry thanks to tire behemoths like Goodyear, Goodrich and Firestone. In the early, boom years of the industry – 1910 to 1920 – Akron was the nation's fastest-growing city with a 202-percent increase in population. One of the workers drawn to the Rubber City was a little-known actor named Clark Gable. Akron native Chrissie Hynde later recalled: "Two odors... pervaded Akron when I was a kid. There was the putrid smell of burning rubber from the Goodyear factories and the fantastic aroma of the raw oatmeal coming from the Quaker Oats mill in town. You felt basic, just those smells."

However, due to its close proximity to the big metropolis just 45-

miles to the north, Akron itself was sometimes considered a suburb of Cleveland. As such, for many years Akron was the largest city in the country without its own local television news program. Consequently, the cities of Kent, Akron and Cleveland listened to the same radio deejays, attended concerts by the same musical acts and bought the same vinyl records.

* * * * * *

During the 1960s, Akron would produce only a few national music stars, most notably Ruby & The Romantics, who topped the pop charts with "Our Day Will Come." Another Akron act, Jordan Christopher & The Wild Ones recorded the first version of the garage-rock classic, "Wild Thing," a year before the Troggs released the definitive rendition of the song.

Cleveland – then the ninth largest city in the nation – had been home to a vibrant music scene ever since local deejay Alan Freed popularized the term "rock and roll" during his evening shift at WJW. And in March 1952, Freed staged what has been called the first rock and roll concert – the infamous Moondog Coronation Ball. More than 15,000 music fans arrived at a Cleveland hockey arena for a concert that ended in a riot.

After the Beatles made their triumphant debut on *The Ed Sullivan Show* in 1964, the country experienced a tidal-wave shift in popular music. The first Cleveland band to perform British Invasion-style music was the Mods, which formed in late-1963 after a female friend of the band returned from England, bringing back a Beatles single, "She Loves You," as well as a Beatles album. This was before any Ohio radio station had ever played a record by the Fab Four. Eventually, the Mods were renamed the Choir and would later score a regional hit with "It's Cold Outside." (Three members of the Mods/Choir would later join Eric Carmen to form the Raspberries.)

During the mid-1960s, the Beatles would perform twice in Cleveland. After their first appearance in 1964 – which had to be stopped by police when screaming, over-exuberant fans rushed the stage – Cleveland Mayor Ralph Locher imposed a so-called "Beatle Ban," prohibiting rock concerts at city-owned venues for the next eighteen-months. The second Beatles show, in the summer of 1966, also ground to a halt after 5,000 hysterical fans stormed the small stage, which had been erected on the infield of Cleveland Municipal Stadium during the middle of baseball season.

Another Cleveland group, the Outsiders, reached the top-10 nationally with the 1966 single, "Time Won't Let Me." Lead singer Sonny Geraci recalled: "One of the biggest thrills in my entire life was the day the first box of records came. I opened the box, and it was on the same label as the Beatles and the Beach Boys. My record looked just like theirs." Other '60s garage rock classics that emerged from Northeastern Ohio included "Nobody But Me" by the Human Beinz and "Little Bit O' Soul" by the Music Explosion.

* * * * * *

When Joe Walsh first arrived at Kent State in 1965, he had let his sandy-blond hair grow longer. In the school's yearbook photos that year, male students uniformly wore very short hairstyles. As a result, Walsh stood out from his classmates and was often targeted due to the length of his hair.

During his first two-years at the university, Walsh lived on campus at Manchester Hall. The all-male dorm housed nearly 380 students. After taking a full load of classes in his first quarter, he became less academically inclined and began focusing on his music. Originally a political science major, Walsh later switched fields: "I majored in English and minored in music." In addition, he also studied everything from electronics to welding. Walsh recalled: "I became the phantom of Kent State, taking all these weird courses that nobody could quite understand." Coming from a military family, Walsh also enrolled in two quarters of ROTC training.

Often avoiding the classroom, Walsh spent his first two-years at Kent State learning to play songs by the Beatles and other British Invasion acts. He did most of his practicing in his dorm – either on a stairway or an outdoor fire escape. During this period, he also began writing his own songs.

Walsh later recalled: "It was a very creative time to be at Kent, and I was encouraged to be creative while I was here. I'm just so grateful that I found this little place in Ohio where creative people were all together." Likewise, former Kent State student Chrissie Hynde recalled: "Kent was a cool university, famously bohemian, known for its art and cinematography departments and anti-Vietnam War stance.... I loved being in Kent. There were people walking the streets like in a real town. This was human pageantry on display where it should be."

▶ CHAPTER 4
THE MEASLES

During his first few months in Kent, Joe Walsh spent a great deal of time exploring the university campus, the streets of the somewhat hilly city and the bustling downtown, where a large number of college bars and restaurants catered to the student population and university staff. During this period, downtown Kent was home to a booming music scene with live bands playing a variety of styles – mostly folk and rock. At one point, there were 52 clubs in the small city, 25 of which featured live music. On weekends, music lovers from all parts of Northeastern Ohio – from Cleveland down to Canton – came to Kent, many arriving with fake IDs. Also drawn to the city were students from the nearby University of Akron, which lacked its own live music scene.

North Water Street in downtown Kent was the center of the city's music scene, with clubs and taverns such as Big Daddy's, Seavers and Ron-de-Vou. Clubs that featured live music on a nightly basis included the Kove, the Water Street Saloon and J.B.'s. The most legendary of these venues, J.B.'s opened in March 1966. Founded by namesake Joe Bujack, he constructed a small, brick building atop a foundation that was laid out in the 1820s, when the city was founded. Bujack recalled: "If you were in Kent in those days and you didn't go to Water Street, you really hadn't been in Kent." A native of Poland, Bujack spoke in broken English and had little actual knowledge about rock music. He just knew that a quality rock band would pack his club with paying customers. Ritch Underwood and the Majestics were the very first group to perform at J.B.'s.

Like so many young musicians around Northeastern Ohio, Walsh yearned to start his own rock band. Initially, Walsh auditioned for a number of local outfits. For a time, he was a member of a group led by a fellow freshman at Kent State who later became a powerful radio executive: "I walked in and met a skinny, blonde guy playing a Rickenbacker 12-string. We shook hands and I said, 'Hi, I'm Walt Tiburski,' and he said, 'Hi, I'm Joe Walsh,' which meant nothing to me at that time. We knocked around for a little bit, but his musical ability was so outrageous that the limitations of the band I'd formed there were too great for him. We were just interested in making a few bucks playing wherever we could scrounge up a gig. Meanwhile, he was interested in playing the music that was happening at that time." (Within just a few years, Tiburski was hired as the general manager of the Cleveland rock powerhouse WMMS.)

At the end of September 1965, Walsh formed his own group, the Measles. The band's name was suggested by a janitor at Kent State. The group was assembled in Manchester Hall by Walsh and another dorm resident, Mike Williams, who sang and played the tambourine. Buddy Bennett, who, like Walsh, hailed from New Jersey, was hired as the drummer. Larry Lewis, a student from nearby Field High School, was the rhythm guitarist, and Walsh played the lead guitar – a cherry red, electric Guild Starfire V.

Over their first year, the Measles went through a number of lineup changes. In April 1966, Mike Williams would be forced from the group. Another original member, bassist Chas Madonio, eventually quit to join the Majestics, which at the time were earning more money. Although Walsh had set his sights on Bobby Sepulveda as a replacement, Sepulveda wasn't interested. Already a member of an in-demand working band, Sepulveda was hesitant to even audition for the Measles. But after hearing the Measles' three-part vocal harmony on a rendition of the Beatles' "You've Got To Hide Your Love Away," Sepulveda quit his group on the spot to join the Measles. With his formal background in music, it was Walsh who had taught his bandmates the art of harmonizing – something that came in handy when he later joined the Eagles. And although Walsh provided the lead vocals on a few songs, Lewis and Sepulveda were the main singers in the band. As the Measles amassed a growing fanbase, the group hired a sound man, JT Rieder.

The Measles often performed at J.B.'s as well as a few other clubs around Kent. The group played cover versions of top-40 rock hits, mostly by British Invasion acts like the Rolling Stones, the Animals and, especially, the Beatles. Although the Measles were not initially a guitar-driven band, Walsh's skills on the instrument attracted a growing legion of fans. What had set the Measles apart from their competition was Walsh's ability to play intricate solos. With his oversized hands and long fingers, he had a physical advantage over his peers. On songs like the Beatles' "And Your Bird Can Sing," Walsh was able to simultaneously play both the lead and rhythm guitar parts.

The first mention of the Measles in the university newspaper came on February 18, 1966, with the announcement of an upcoming performance in the Student Union building. It was a holiday, President's Day, so the group had a good turnout. On April 1, another on-campus appearance by the group was promoted in the university newspaper: "Tomorrow evening a bunny will be given to some lucky person at the Bunny Hop at Olson Cafeteria (8:00 p.m. – Midnight). Come and dance to the swinging music of the Measles and the distinguished voice of D.J. Ron Davison." The Measles also played outside of Kent and were the opening act at the Canton Auditorium for Sam the Sham & the Pharaohs and Paul Revere & The Raiders. Around this time, Walsh was in search of a new guitar and drove to Manny's Music in New York City. After making his purchase, Walsh spent a few days at his parents' home in New Jersey.

Soon, the Measles were regularly performing at the largest nightclub in downtown Kent, the Fifth Quarter. Joe Shannon, the club's owner, recalled: "Joe worked. We paid them minimum union scale, and on a Saturday they'd pull about 1,500 people into the place. They played the old time rock. Top-40 stuff. He was one of the few people that had the knack." In a matter of just several months, the Measles were the second-most popular rock band in Kent, right behind a well-established, older act, the Counterpoints.

Instead of returning home to New Jersey at the end of his freshman year, Walsh stayed in Kent over the summer break because he wanted the Measles to rehearse and reach the next level of musical proficiency. In fact, he would remain in Kent every summer while attending Kent State. (Walsh, however, did make it back home for Thanksgiving and Christmas.)

As a serious student of music, Walsh spent much of his time devouring a diverse variety of guitar styles from gypsy jazz legend Django Reinhardt to blues master Elmore James. However, Walsh was initially unaware of the original blues pioneers until after he arrived in Kent. Instead, he first emulated a number of second-generation, blues-inspired guitarists like Eric Clapton, Peter Green and John Mayall. As Walsh later admitted: "I studied the blues through their translation. I studied the blues through white English guys!"

At Kent, Walsh began using his electronic skills to improve the sound of his guitars – what he called "hot wiring." He explained: "I removed the tone condenser and capacitor in [my] Telecasters, so as to make the forward pickup hotter. I made the Telecaster pickups stronger by winding wire around the magnets and made them more sensitive by winding smaller wire (and consequently more of it) around the pickup. I also took the chrome covering off the humbucking pickups on Gibson guitars and put different tubes in amplifiers to make them louder." And after discovering that Vox had introduced Super Beatle Amps, Walsh asked a friend to build what were dubbed "Super Measle Amps," which at six-feet tall towered behind the band.

In the fall of 1966, the Measles added Ritch Underwood from the Majestics on guitar, which now permitted Walsh to occasionally play his new Farfisa Compact Organ – an inexpensive instrument that was heard on a number of 1960s garage-rock classics like "Wooly Bully," "96 Tears" and "Double Shot (Of My Baby's Love)." Underwood had been invited to join the Measles by the group's then-manager, Joe Basile.

Despite the Measles' growing popularity around Kent, the group didn't always receive the respect it deserved. Underwood recalled that on occasion, "people treated Joe Walsh like crap when he played here. The same thing happened to Eric Carmen when he started in Kent. People used to throw things at Devo when they used to play at J.B.'s."

On September 3, the Measles appeared at Chippewa Lake – a small but popular amusement park located in a rural community, one-hour west of Kent – for what was billed as a Teen Fair. The headlining act, the McCoys, had scored a hit the previous year with "Hang On Sloopy." Also on the bill were Harvey Russell and the Rogues, a local group signed to Roulette Records that had scored a regional hit with "Shake Sherry." With Walsh sporting a Beatles haircut and wearing a collarless, Beatles-style suit, the Measles performed for more than 20,000 teens.

Then on October 8, Walsh attended a concert at Memorial Gym on the Kent State campus. The show was headlined by Jay & The Americans and featured the Blues Project as the opening act. Little could Walsh know that he would be playing on that same stage as a solo artist in just a few years. And at the end of October, the Measles performed at the Eastway Ballroom on the Kent campus – along with a rock band from Youngstown, the Pied Pipers – this time for a Halloween party.

Although the club owners in Kent still demanded that rock groups stick with top-40 material, Walsh and the Measles began infusing their own stamps on the hit songs they played, whether adding a few blues riffs or layers of psychedelia. Then in early-1967, the Measles entered a local studio to record some original material. However, the sessions at the Akron Recording Company were unproductive.

Soon after, the group's producer, Bill Palmer, helped the Measles hook up with a music production company that was headed by the notorious team of Jerry Kasenetz and Jeffrey Katz, who were affiliated with Buddah Records. Kasenetz and Katz – also known as the Super K Production Company – oversaw a number of pop and bubblegum-style hits by the Ohio Express, the Music Explosion and the Lemon Pipers, all of whom hailed from Ohio. Not surprisingly, Kasenetz and Katz considered Ohio a hotbed for musical discoveries. At an audition in New York City, the Measles recorded four songs. Not happy with the Measles' psychedelic-based sound, Kasenetz and Katz decided to pass on the group.

However, two songs from the audition were soon released. The B-side of the 1967 top-40 single, "Beg Borrow And Steal" by the Ohio Express, was actually a Measles track. Renamed "Maybe," the Walsh composition was originally titled "I Find I Think Of You." Also that year, the Ohio Express' debut album included a second Measles track, "And It's True," which was written by Bobby Sepulveda. Ironically, Sepulveda, who was in the military at the time, recognized the two songs when someone in his Army barracks played the album.

An impatient Walsh became frustrated by the musical limitations of the Measles and began to contemplate a new career strategy. Although the group was a big draw in Kent, Walsh was growing uneasy about playing in a top-40 cover band. With his musical tastes evolving, Walsh was drawn to bluesy, British rock bands like Cream and the Yardbirds.

As a result, Walsh quit the Measles in the spring of 1967. Afterward, he began sitting in with a number of local bands, including the Chancellors and the Turnkeys. Meanwhile, shortly before forming Glass Harp, guitarist Phil Keaggy was in a band called the New Hudson Exit and wanted to hire Walsh. However, Keaggy's bandmates felt that Walsh's guitar playing was too flashy for the group.

Meanwhile, Walsh teamed with Dan Klawon and Dave Burke – former members of the Cleveland band, the Choir – to form the short-lived act, the Power Trio. Also during this time, Walsh was joined by three other local musicians for a cameo appearance in the award-winning, avant-garde film, *Akran*. The project was directed by Richard Myers and was shot in various locations around Northeastern Ohio, including Kent.

As the lead guitarist of a popular band, Walsh had the opportunity to meet many women. And in 1967, the 20-year-old guitarist would marry for the first time. His young bride, Marjorie, was also a local student. However, the young couple would divorce just three-years later. Over the next few decades, Walsh would repeatedly demonstrate his propensity for quickly falling in love.

As for the Measles, Ritch Underwood joined the Navy for a two-year stint and was replaced by a returning Chas Madonio. Two of Underwood's bandmates also went into the military. A new lineup of the Measles without Walsh or Underwood continued to draw large crowds around Kent, especially at the Fifth Quarter. The group subsequently added a female singer, Mary Sterpka, who earned the nickname, Mary Measle. Then in 1970, the group temporarily changed its name to Lacewing and subsequently recorded a poor-selling, psychedelic-pop album for Mainstream Records. Although the group's popularity would wane over time, drummer Buddy Bennett would maintain a version of the Measles until finally calling it quits in 1977.

▶ CHAPTER 5
THE JAMES GANG

When Joe Walsh first arrived in Kent in 1965, the local youth bought 45rpm records and carried portable, battery-powered transistor radios. Top-40 AM radio was king, and most Kent State students listened to WHLO or WAKR from Akron or WKYC from Cleveland. A pair of low-power top-40 stations out of Cleveland, WIXY and WHK, could barely be heard in Kent. On the other hand, 50,000-watt powerhouse CKLW out of Windsor, Ontario, was a major player all over Northeastern Ohio during this period. Although CKLW broadcast from Canada, it was located in the Detroit metro area and targeted listeners in the United States. It was on this station that Walsh was exposed to Motortown rock acts like Ted Nugent, Bob Seger and Terry Knight and the Pack, and also heard about an influential nightclub in Detroit called the Grande.

However, by 1968, popular music was evolving and moving toward a harder edge. Instead of 45s and AM radio, rock music was moving toward album tracks and free-form or underground radio. And unlike typical AM radio fare, songs on FM rock stations were not limited to three- or four-minutes in length. That same year, albums outsold 45rpm singles for the first time in history. And with the release of the groundbreaking album *Sgt. Pepper's Lonely Hearts Club Band*, the Beatles made history by issuing no singles from a hit album.

Despite the fact that less than ten-percent of consumers in Northeastern Ohio – or anywhere else in the country – owned FM radios during the late-1960s, the popularity of the Album-Oriented Rock (AOR) format was quickly growing. In Cleveland, AOR caught on in a big way, initially with WNCR. However, it was another station, WMMS, that soon dominated the airwaves in Northeastern Ohio and was responsible for breaking dozens of acts in the U.S. from David Bowie to Rush.

*　　*　　*　　*　　*　　*

In 1966, drummer Jimmy Fox formed the James Gang. Originally a trumpet player, he had switched to drums after catching a performance by jazz legend Max Roach at a small nightclub. The son of a professional violinist, Fox started taking music theory classes at the Cleveland Music School Settlement at just eight-years-old. While still in high school, he was a member of the popular Cleveland band, Tom King and the Starfires. Fox played drums on the group's regional hit, "Stronger Than Dirt." Shortly after the Starfires evolved into the Outsiders, Fox left the group. But after the Outsiders scored a national hit in 1966 with "Time Won't Let Me," Fox briefly returned for the sessions of their debut album. He also joined the Outsiders on their first national tour, which included an appearance on the NBC television show, *Hullabaloo*.

The roots of the James Gang were in Columbus, not Cleveland. As Fox explained: "I was going to Ohio State and I had a band there with a guy named Ronnie Silverman. We got Richard Shack in the band too. I got kicked out of Ohio State and I moved back to Cleveland." After leaving Columbus and returning to Northeastern Ohio in 1966, Fox attended the Cleveland Institute of Music and, later, Kent State University.

In the fall of 1966, Fox formed the James Gang. As he recalled: "So, Ronnie Silverman and I got a bass player named Tom Kriss; he was the younger brother of a guy I played [with] in all these greaser bands... back in high school. Tom brought [keyboardist] Phil Giallombardo in the band, because he was his friend. So, we had four guys, but we needed a lead guitarist." The James Gang held auditions and initially hired guitarist Greg Grandillo, who was with the band only briefly. (Grandillo later joined the group Rainbow Canyon and recorded two albums for Capitol Records in the early-1970s. The group's first album was produced by Jimmy Fox.) Grandillo's replacement, Dennis Chandler, took over the lead guitar duties.

Soon after, Chandler also left the James Gang and was replaced by John "Mouse" Michalski, who was previously a member of the West Coast garage-rock band, the Count Five, which had just scored a top-40 hit with "Psychotic Reaction." The Count Five had imploded after the group's teenage members refused to quit high school in order to make public appearances.

However, as Fox explained, the James Gang were looking to hire another local guitarist: "There weren't any bands, less lead players, who were playing Yardbirds stuff back in 1966. We had heard of this Glenn Schwartz guy who was in a band called the Pilgrims before he got drafted. But Glenn was in the Army then."

*   *   *   *   *   *

Glenn Schwartz had grown up listening to blues records, not a common activity in the conservative, middle-class suburb of Euclid. But this was Cleveland, where Alan Freed was playing music for black and white listeners alike. A talented musician who took guitar lessons beginning at age ten, Schwartz had initially joined a series of polka groups in the early-1950s. Later drawn to rock and roll, he joined his first notable local band in the late-1950s, Frank Samson and the Wailers.

Later, as a member of the Pilgrims – a Sandusky-based British Invasion-style group – Schwartz scored a local hit with the single, "Plymouth Rock." But when Schwartz was drafted into the Army in 1964, the Pilgrims lost a promised recording contract with Motown Records. While serving on a military base in England, Schwartz reportedly received some lessons from guitar virtuoso Jeff Beck.

After returning to Cleveland, Schwartz yearned to restart his music career. At the time, he was married and had a young son, and needed to earn a living. Initially, Schwartz auditioned for a 12-piece show-band. Learning about Schwartz's plans, Fox took the opportunity to meet the fabled guitarist at the audition. The two men talked about music, and Schwartz was asked to join Fox's group. Schwartz hesitantly agreed to attend a James Gang performance at the English Grille in Cleveland. Impressed with the band's energy and sound, Schwartz jumped onstage and played his signature tune, the Yardbirds' classic, "Jeff's Boogie." Schwartz had wanted to join an established group that could play blues-rock and, in 1967, he didn't have many options. Unhappy with Fox's decision to hire Schwartz, guitarist John Michalski left the band.

Schwartz, who was significantly older than the other members of the James Gang, brought a new level of musical sophistication to the group's sound. With his sharp goatee and bright, psychedelic clothing, he also stood out from his more conservatively dressed bandmates. In one early press photo, two members of the band donned traditional blazers while another member wore a formal necktie.

Butch Armstrong, a veteran Cleveland musician, later recalled: "I was thirteen-years-old and the first time me and my friends saw Glenn, we all thought he looked like Jesus. We didn't know his name so we just called him Jesus. He had hair down to his shoulders and wore sandals. And I remember he had the biggest hands in the world! There was a sound going around back then, something Clapton and the Stones were introducing to music and we just couldn't figure out how they did it. We couldn't get the licks right. Then we saw Glenn Schwartz and he knew how to do it and he created that sound right in front of us! He used his fingers with the whammy bar and that was it! He became God to us in that moment." In early-1967, three members of the James Gang, including Schwartz, were joined by a few other musicians, including Bill "Mr. Stress" Miller, for a performance at the Coffeehouse in the city's University Circle district. The sessions were belatedly released in 2016 as *The Schwartz-Fox Blues Crusade*.

In June 1967, Ronnie Silverman was drafted into the Army and left the James Gang. The previous month, the group had placed a classified ad in *The Cleveland Plain Dealer*: "The James Gang wants a singing rhythm guitar player." Silverman was replaced by Bill Jeric, who was a big fan of the James Gang. After joining the group, Jeric was given a number of guitar lessons by Schwartz. That summer, the James Gang recorded the demo, "Long Hair Soulful," and auditioned to appear on an NBC television special. Unfortunately, nothing came of either endeavor.

Nonetheless, the James Gang continued to garner a strong reputation for their musicianship and stage antics. *Scene* magazine, a local music publication, reported: "Like Hendrix and the Who, Glenn wanted to give audiences a show that would leave them stunned. During a solo, Glenn would throw his legs over Jeric's shoulders, then play guitar hanging upside down, as Jeric swung his torso. 'I'd bang his head against the stage,' says Jeric. 'He loved it when I drew blood.' On one such occasion, opening for Cream at Detroit's Grande Ballroom, the underdog James Gang earned an encore – no small feat, considering that backstage, Eric Clapton was waiting for his turn." And as Fox recalled: "People danced to the James Gang, but we were never in our minds a dance band."

Meanwhile, during a tour stop in Los Angeles, Schwartz had a life-changing experience when he stopped to listen to a street preacher on the fabled Sunset Strip. Schwartz was mesmerized by the preacher's message and became a born-again Christian soon after. As *Scene* reported: "Some friends say that Glenn was tripping on acid when he had his spiritual awakening. Others say that his world was simply spinning too fast: the drugs, the traveling, the exhilaration of success. He needed something to ground him."

In late-December 1967, Schwartz abruptly quit the James Gang. In fact, he left both the band and Cleveland due to a number of reasons. He had financial problems – including unpaid alimony – and was AWOL from the military.

Schwartz returned to California and began hanging out with notable rock artists such as Jimi Hendrix and Janis Joplin, neither of whom took Schwartz's religious zeal seriously. In fact, Joplin was openly hostile toward Schwartz whenever he launched into a sermon.

In Los Angeles, Schwartz also began performing in the city's famed nightclubs. Meanwhile, he reportedly turned down an invitation from Duane Allman to join the Allman Brothers Band. Instead, Schwartz accepted an offer to join Pacific Gas & Electric, a blues-rock band led by vocalist/drummer Charlie Allen. The group took its name from a local utility company. Soon after forming, PG&E was performing at the Fillmore West as the opening act for a number of leading rock acts including Jefferson Airplane and Santana. PG&E bassist Brent Block recalled: "We were blown away by Glenn's talent. I had a very hard time keeping up with him.... Glenn was also an acrobat of sorts. Glenn thought nothing of jumping off stacks of amplifiers and rolling around on stage. One night at the Cheetah Club, I saw him roll off the stage, fall maybe twenty feet, and he never missed a note!"

* * * * * *

After the departure of Glenn Schwartz, the James Gang needed to hire an equally talented replacement. It didn't take long. Jimmy Fox recalled: "Our last gig with Glenn was on a Sunday night and the next day there was a knock on my door – it was Joe Walsh. I hadn't even thought of him, but I knew if there was one guitarist in this whole town who could fill Glenn's shoes, it was Joe Walsh.... He said, 'You guys need a guitar player?' Of course, he was in the band right away." Walsh and Schwartz were good friends and had often jammed together for hours at a time. During these informal sessions, Walsh learned much from the older and more experienced Schwartz.

The new lineup wasted no time in preparing for their first public performance, just two weeks later. As Fox recalled: "We played with Joe and he learned 30 songs at our first rehearsal; Jerik was knocked-out." The group's rehearsals took place in suburban Cleveland at the home of Fox's parents.

In January 1968, the James Gang played a sold-out, on-campus show for 1,000 students at the Eastway Cafeteria. Walsh was dressed in tight jeans, Beatle boots, a bright, flower-print jacket, a vest and a floppy, oversized hat. And just like his predecessor, Walsh closed his early James Gang gigs with the blues-rock classic, "Jeff's Boogie." Meanwhile, the opening band, the T.P. Waterhouse Jug Band, ended its set with the group's guitarist smashing his instrument into the floor of the stage.

Walsh enjoyed this period of his music career: "I was joyous and carefree. I didn't have a lot of the responsibilities that you get later on in life.... But more importantly, it was totally supported. There were places to play, lots of people came and you didn't have to be that good." However, as much fun as Walsh was having, the members of the group were struggling financially: "We were starving, and it was down to survival and we were testifying."

The James Gang would experience some more lineup changes. As Fox recalled: "Phil [Giallombardo] was having troubles at home and he was showing up late for gigs. I fired him one night on stage – showed up two hours later for a three-hour job. Soon after that Bill Jeric got pissed because his amps rolled out of his van when he was driving on the freeway; he just quit and went to California. Jerik was replaced by Ronnie Silverman, who had just returned from the military. In addition to playing rhythm guitar, Silverman also provided the lead vocals.

On May 11, 1968, the James Gang opened up for Cream. Staged at the 2,600-seat Akron Civic Theater, the concert featured a number of local opening acts including an all-girl, local rock group, the Poor Girls. The following day, Cream would perform at the Music Hall in Cleveland.

With the James Gang enjoying growing popularity, Walsh was mentioned for the first time in *The Cleveland Plain Dealer* on July 26, 1968. Then, four-months later, he was mentioned for the first time in *The Daily Kent Stater*, with a writer commenting: "The James Gang have carried their blues-oriented sound throughout Ohio as well as many other Midwestern cities and towns."

When the James Gang performed in downtown Kent, Chrissie Hynde would often travel from Akron to see the band. Underage and in high school at the time, she would tell the doorman that she was Walsh's cousin. (Hynde's older brother, Terry, was a student at Kent State and would form the Numbers Band in 1970.) Another local fan who followed Walsh was future MTV veejay Nina Blackwood: "I'd have my dad chauffeur me and my girlfriends around to various teen clubs in Northeastern Ohio to hear the James Gang play."

*   *   *   *   *   *

When Joe Walsh first arrived in Kent and began performing in nightclubs, he did what comes naturally to college students – he had a few beers before shows. He especially liked how alcohol took away any jitters or stage fright that he might develop when playing in front of a boisterous audience. Eventually, he would start throwing back a few post-concert shots of tequila to relax and celebrate the night's performance.

And later, Walsh progressed to harder stuff: "In my early 20s, I discovered cocaine, and that was it – my problem was solved. I could write and finish a song. I felt like Superman onstage, and I played that way. I thought cocaine and alcohol was the combination, and it was just a kid trying to feel better. And I chased that initial solution to my problems for 30 years or so." Walsh would later point out that cocaine and Ritalin – a prescription drug used to treat Attention Deficit Disorder – were in the same family of drugs and had similar effects on the brain.

▶ CHAPTER 6
THE POWER TRIO

The James Gang unexpectedly became a trio before a performance at the Grande Ballroom in Detroit. The legendary venue had opened in October 1966 as a 17-years-and-older concert club and was an important stop for both local and touring rock acts. The club's owner, deejay Russ Gibb, wanted to replicate what he had experienced while visiting the Fillmore Theater in San Francisco.

The Grande had great acoustics with its high ceiling and solid wood floor. However, with no ventilation or air conditioning, the club usually got hot and steamy during concerts, especially during the summer months. The smell of burning incense was often in the air, and abstract psychedelic images were projected onto a screen behind the stage. In the absence of a liquor license, patrons simply sneaked in their own intoxicants. Although the venue had a legal occupancy limit of around 1,500 people, sometimes twice as many concertgoers were packed into the rectangular, second-floor ballroom. (The first floor of the building housed a variety of retail businesses.) In October 1968, the Detroit-based hard-rock band, MC5, recorded their seminal live album at the Grande, *Kick Out The Jams*.

On June 9, 1968, the James Gang were scheduled to perform at the Grande as an opening act for Cream. The night before the show, Joe Walsh and his bandmates got into a big argument. While enroute from Kent to Detroit, Jimmy Fox stopped to telephone his missing bandmate, Ron Silverman, the group's lead singer and rhythm guitarist. During their conversation, Silverman announced he was quitting the group and would not be making the trip.

Arriving at the Grande, the three remaining members of the James Gang decided to play the show as a trio and were hoping the audience wouldn't react too negatively. The band members were broke and were counting on the performance fee to buy gas for the drive home.

A terrified Walsh realized he had to assume the lead vocal duties due to the fact that his two bandmates were far worse singers. However, since Walsh didn't know all the lyrics to the songs he was about to perform, he planned on singing the first verse and then playing an extended, improvised guitar solo. Afterward, he would finish the song by either repeating the first verse or singing the last verse. Walsh recalled: "We figured we'd pick some Traffic or Spencer Davis or something. I knew most of the words."

Walsh was also forced to learn how to play rhythm and lead guitar at the same time – something that Jimi Hendrix had mastered in his three-piece band. Walsh recalled: "I was one of the guitarists. And I was put in a position where all of a sudden I was the lead singer, and I had to figure out how to do both. That has had a big effect on the way I developed. I had to figure out a style. If you play rhythm guitar, there's nobody playing lead, and if you play lead, you really notice that the rhythm guitar has stopped."

To the amazement of Walsh and his fellow bandmates – drummer Jimmy Fox and bassist Tom Kriss – their plan worked perfectly. Walsh recalled: "We thought 'oh well this'll be the last job.' It was a make it or break it night and we were deadly scared. It was purely experimental on stage that night, three guys trying to get together what five guys normally did." Fox remembered: "Each time we played another number, the crowd roared. We got higher and higher, and we even did 'Foxy Lady' [by Jimi Hendrix]. They loved it." Instead of being booed off the stage, the trio played for two hours and played six encores! After receiving three standing ovations, the band realized they had accidentally stumbled upon a winning formula. Fox recalled: "When we came off the stage, [Detroit artist manager and booking agent] Jeep Holland said: 'If you assholes break up, you are crazy!'"

After the show, Eric Clapton of Cream shook Walsh's hand and praised the band's strong determination. One audience member who was particularly impressed by the group's inspired performance was a teenager named Doug Fieger, then a member of an emerging local group, Sky, and later the founder of the power-pop group, the Knack. Years later, Walsh would name the Grande Ballroom as his favorite place to perform.

* * * * * *

After their triumphant performance in Detroit, the three remaining members of the James Gang began to contemplate the future of the group. Before making a decision, Jimmy Fox and his former bandmate Tom Jeric took a trip to California to catch a performance by Glenn

Schwartz's new band, PG&E. Meanwhile, a homesick Joe Walsh traveled to New Jersey for a visit with his family.

After a two-week break, the James Gang agreed to soldier on as a trio. During this period, power trios in rock music were quite rare. There were only a few successful American power trios at the time, most notably Grand Funk Railroad and Blue Cheer. (The Jimi Hendrix Experience consisted of one American and two Brits.) However, there were inherent problems to playing in a group with just three musicians on the stage. As Walsh observed: "A three-piece group is a risk, 'cause if you have a bad night, you really do. If you have a bad night with a five- or six-piece group, you can cover it up."

Over the next year, the James Gang employed the formula they crafted at the Grande. They started playing the first verse of a well-known song such as "The Pusher" by Steppenwolf. Then they would launch into an original, extended jam. Lastly, the group would close with the last verse of the song. It was these original, improvised jams that became the basis of the new James Gang sound. And instead of playing cover songs, the group began emphasizing their own material.

With Walsh still unsure about his future in a three-piece band, fate seemed to intervene in his life. In August 1968, he was offered a spot in the Human Beinz, a Youngstown-area pop-rock band that had scored an upbeat, top-10 hit earlier that year with "Nobody But Me." He was invited to join the band by the group's manager, Tommy Shannenberger, following the departure of singer/guitarist, Dick "Richard" Belly. Walsh began practicing with the group in preparation for an upcoming tour. However, Belly had a change of heart and returned to the group, leaving Walsh the odd man out. A few months later, Belly quit again and the band disintegrated.

* * * * * *

Meanwhile, in September 1968, Glenn Schwartz returned to Cleveland with his new band, Pacific Gas & Electric, for a performance at a small nightclub, La Cave. The group's new track, "Get It On," was a hit on local FM radio. Then, two-months later, the group returned for a pair of shows as the opening act for Jefferson Airplane, who were making their debut appearance in Cleveland. The shows were emceed by WMMS deejay Doc Nemo.

In December 1968, after releasing a pair of poor-selling albums,

PG&E was invited to perform at the Miami Pop Festival, which featured like-minded hard-rock acts such as Canned Heat, Iron Butterfly, Steppenwolf and an early lineup of Fleetwood Mac. On the first day of the three-day music festival, Schwartz famously proclaimed his religious faith and disdain for drugs in front of 80,000 sun-soaked spectators.

After receiving spectacular reviews in a variety of publications, PG&E was signed by Columbia Records. The following year, the group released its breakthrough album. But just as the single, "Are You Ready," was climbing up the charts enroute to the top-20, Schwartz declared he was quitting the group and leaving the music industry. A close friend said of Schwartz, "People were doing a lot of drugs out there and Glenn was an acid casualty. So he quit the scene and turned to religion."

Tired of the temptations on the rock and roll road, Schwartz left PG&E in mid-1970. He subsequently turned down an offer of $50,000 from his record company to stay with the group. Instead, he returned to Cleveland, where he formed a duo with his brother, Gene. After a couple years of performing locally as the Schwartz Brothers, Glenn Schwartz joined a local blues band led by Robert Lockwood Jr. – a local guitarist who was schooled by the legendary 1930s bluesman, Robert Johnson.

Schwartz subsequently joined a local Christian rock group, the All Saved Freak Band, which was an evangelistic arm of an Ohio religious sect, the Church of the Risen Christ. In the early-1970s, Schwartz and the group often performed in a downtown Kent nightclub. Schwartz's life during this period was chronicled in the book, *Fortney Road: Life, Death, and Deception in a Christian Cult*. In all, Schwartz would record four albums with the group before quitting in 1980.

Later, he continued to play his blues-rock music while preaching the gospel at a handful of Cleveland clubs, sometimes with his brother, Gene. Despite encouragement and aid from local musicians, Glenn Schwartz was never able to again achieve any level of success.

▶ CHAPTER 7
THE JAMES GANG GET SIGNED

Beginning in 1969, producer Bill Szymczyk (pronounced sim-zik) began playing a major role in the career of Joe Walsh – first as a member of the James Gang, later as a solo artist and lastly as a member of the Eagles. Szymczyk once stated, "I'm a professional listener. I listen and I react. I never was a musician, so I don't bring any preconceived prejudices to the table; I don't favor the guitar over the keyboard, and so forth. I just listen and try to figure out if I have anything I can bring to a song."

Szymczyk was raised in a small tourist town along the eastern shore of Lake Michigan, about 100-miles northeast of Chicago. During his youth, he became fascinated with electronics and built a rudimentary crystal radio. Attaching an antenna to the metal box-spring of his bed, he heard a distant station out of Nashville, WLAC, and was exposed to blues and R&B music for the first time.

At 17-years-old in 1960, Szymczyk enlisted into the U.S. Navy. He was able to finish high school by taking correspondence courses. He recalled: "It was the height of the Cold War at the time. Our arch-enemy, the Russians, supposedly had submarines everywhere, loaded with missiles ready to attack us. So the Navy had put a premium on finding recruits with very good ears, to become SONAR operators. As soon as they inducted you, they gave you an audiometer test to check your hearing. The people who scored in the top five-percent they sent directly to SONAR school. They didn't ask you; they just sent you, whether you liked it or not. I guess I had pretty good ears, because in the next six months they crammed about three years' worth of college-level electronics knowledge into me."

While in the military, Szymczyk also took a course in radio and television production. Then after his discharge, he applied to the Media Arts program at New York University. Before his classes started, he found a job in the city's fabled Brill Building. During the golden age of rock music in the 1950s and early '60s, hundreds of hit songs were written, arranged and recorded in a conveyer-belt fashion by both amateur and experienced talent in what became known as the Brill

Building Sound.

Although Szymczyk was initially hired to sweep floors and fix broken equipment, he spent his first day watching a recording session by the famed songwriting team of Carole King and Gerry Goffin. Deciding that he didn't need a college education, Szymczyk was soon earning $70 a week manufacturing acetate copies of newly recorded songs, which were shipped across the country to various artists and record labels.

Due to his strong electronics background, Szymczyk was eventually hired as a recording engineer. At Regent Sound Studios in New York City, he worked with a new state-of-the-art, four-track system and was tasked with churning out hundreds of demo records. At one of his early assignments, he supervised a live, stage recording of a young comedian named Rodney Dangerfield.

Then in 1967, Szymczyk met songwriter and producer Jerry Ragavoy, who had previously written a number of hits, including "Time Is On My Side" and "Piece Of My Heart." After constructing a new recording studio called the Hit Factory, Ragavoy hired Szymczyk as the chief engineer. A number of classic albums would be recorded at the legendary studio complex including *One Trick Pony* by Paul Simon, *Emotional Rescue* by the Rolling Stones, *Songs In The Key Of Life* by Stevie Wonder and *Double Fantasy* by John Lennon and Yoko Ono. Szymczyk later admitted: "If anyone taught me how to be a producer, it was Jerry Ragavoy. I saw how he handled musicians, how he chose songs, how he got performances out of people. The kinds of things you can only learn by being and working with someone closely for months and months on end."

Later, Szymczyk was offered a job as a staff producer at Paramount Records, a subsidiary of ABC. Although the move would mean a dramatic reduction in pay, he understood what a position at a major record company would mean for his career. At the label, Szymczyk shocked his bosses when he asked to produce veteran blues guitarist, B.B. King. Although ABC reluctantly agreed to the request, the label would first need King's consent.

In 1968, Szymczyk produced King's album *Live & Well*, which featured the R&B hit, "Why I Sing The Blues." With ABC's blessing, Szymczyk teamed with King for a second project, *Completely Well*. The album spawned King's career-defining hit, "The Thrill Is Gone," which, at Szymczyk's insistence, paired the electric bluesman with a string section. Szymczyk recalled: "The energy was there. B.B. started playing the song riff in that minor key.... It fell into its groove in minutes. I was freaking out, that's how good it was."

Proving to ABC Records that he possessed the necessary skills to craft hit records, Scymczyk was given permission to sign and produce rock acts. He recalled: "I had a friend of mine who used to be a roommate in New York, named Dick Korn, who had moved to Cleveland and was working as the manager/head bartender at this rock club called Otto's Grotto. It was in the basement of the Statler Hotel. He said, 'Man, [there's] a bunch of great acts coming through here. You've gotta come and check some of them out!' So I started going to Cleveland, and in the course of three or four visits, a band called the Tree Stumps – which was an awful name – came through. The lead singer was Michael Stanley, and I really liked his tunes and his voice. I signed them and changed their name to Silk."

Released in 1969, the album, *Smooth As Raw Silk*, charted on *Billboard* for just one-week. Szymczyk was unhappy with the album and later stated that it "died a death it deserved." However, Szymczyk would work with Stanley a few years later.

Szymczyk returned to Cleveland and scouted for another band to sign. The first time he heard the James Gang at the Hullabaloo Club in the suburban community of Mentor, he assumed the booming trio was actually a five-piece band. Later, after a James Gang show at Packard Music Hall in Warren, Ohio, Szymczyk offered to record the group. Signing with BluesWay Records (a subsidiary of ABC-Paramount), the James Gang received a modest $2,000 advance. Ironically, the James Gang had previously mailed dozens of copies of their demo record to numerous labels – including ABC-Paramount.

In early-1969, the James Gang hired a new manager, Mike Belkin, one of two brothers who operated Belkin Productions, a fledgling concert promotion company in Northeastern Ohio. Previously, Belkin had refused to manage the James Gang because the group was unsigned at the time.

* * * * * *

Still residing in Kent, Joe Walsh moved around often: "I must have lived in practically every house in that town one time or another." Walsh and his young wife also spent a year living in a farmhouse, just south of Kent in rural Brimfield Township. With Walsh practicing for hours at a time, his neighbors could hear his blaring guitar. One of Walsh's neighbors – a few houses down the road – was drummer Joe Vitale.

* * * * * *

In January 1969, Bill Szymczyk took the James Gang to the Hit Factory in New York City. The group's debut album, *Yer' Album*, was recorded over a one-week period. The project cost just $7,000 to make. The album's tracks revealed the band's varied influences – West Coast folk-rock, hard rock, jazz and even classical music – all within a blues-rock, jam-band framework. One track, "Funk #48," began as a warm-up exercise before the band's performances.

The James Gang had little original material and were forced to record some of the more popular songs from their live shows. The best of the album's three remakes was the Stephen Stills composition, "Bluebird," which was dramatically different than the original rendition by Buffalo Springfield. For whatever reason, the James Gang's recorded version did not include the intro that Walsh usually performed during the group's concerts. Another remake, a nine-minute version of the Yardbirds' classic "Lost Woman," included lengthy solos by each of the group's three members.

Lastly, the 12-minute track, "Stop," was a Jerry Ragavoy/Mort Schuman composition. Szymczyk was able to convince Ragavoy to play piano on the track. The song was originally recorded by soul singer Howard Tate, but made more famous by Al Kooper and Mike Bloomfield on the breakthrough, blues-rock album, *Super Session*. The James Gang's rendition of the song was a perfect vehicle for Walsh's fastbreak guitar skills.

* * * * * *

In between the short period when the album was finished and before it was released, a deeply unhappy Tom Kriss wanted to quit the group. The normally reserved and quiet bassist unloaded his feelings at a band meeting, during which he expressed a strong distaste for the direction of the group's music. Kriss recalled: "Walsh was getting into more Neil Young type stuff of music and I wanted to stay with the Jeff Beck style."

After Michael Stanley turned down an offer to join the James Gang, Jimmy Fox turned to Dale Peters – who at the time was a member of the popular Cleveland act, E.T. Hooley. Coincidentally, Peters had earlier replaced Fox in a Columbus-area band. Peters was a former star athlete who nearly quit high school after he was invited to join a minor league baseball team, the Rochester Redwings, an affiliate of the Philadelphia Phillies. But after suffering a serious knee injury that required surgery, his dream to go professional came to an abrupt halt. Just like Joe Walsh, Peters was born in Wichita, Kansas.

A few days later, Peters was invited to sit in with Walsh and Fox for an audition. A perfect match for the group, Peters was hired that same day. Informed by Fox that the band had found a replacement bass player, Kriss expressed deep relief. However, just two-weeks later, Kriss had a change of heart and tried to rejoin the band, telling Walsh and Fox that it was a huge mistake to quit. However, at this point it was too late. (Kriss would subsequently team with drummer Joe Vitale in the Kent-based rock group, Sheriff.)

Yer' Album was released at the end of March. The front cover featured the three members of the James Gang standing in front of a waterfall in downtown Kent. In the album's liner notes, Szymczyk wrote: "This recording was mixed to be played at the highest possible volume, and not to be listened to on stereo headphones until after three times in the speakers."

The album was a moderate seller that received widespread airplay on album-rock radio. *The Cleveland Plain Dealer's* music writer Jane Scott wrote: "Cleveland's own James Gang is coming across like Gangbusters today with guitar, bass and drums. Their first album, *Yer' Album*, on BluesWay (ABC) is a sell-out in all the local stores. The group's hit, 'I Don't Have The Time,' is here, the one that was No. 1 in Erie, Pa. But the whole album is very good. I particularly liked 'Take A Look Around,' written by guitar player Joe Walsh."

Soon after, the James Gang began touring around the country, which meant fewer club gigs in Northeastern Ohio. During his travels, Walsh was able to feed his guitar-collecting hobby. Long before acquiring rare guitars was a serious and expensive business, Walsh purchased a number of vintage instruments, which at the time were reasonably priced: "The fun for me was being on the road and going to a little pawn shop or music store – not a big chain like Guitar Center but an actual little music store – and seeing what they had, and collecting guitars that way. And then opening them up to see why they sounded the way they did."

*　　*　　*　　*　　*　　*

On July 20, 1969, a man walked on the moon for the very first time. Millions of Americans were glued to their television screens as Neil Armstrong uttered the historic words: "One small step for man, one giant leap for mankind." However, in Cleveland, thousands of blues-rock fans were attending a concert by Led Zeppelin at the Musicarnival, an outdoor venue covered by a huge, round tent. A last-minute replacement, the James Gang opened the show. Reportedly, Jimmy Page took notice of Joe Walsh's skills on the guitar.

After the concert, Walsh convinced Page and his bandmate Robert Plant to drive down to Kent for an impromptu, late-night jam session. Arriving at J.B.'s, the three men jumped onto the stage and joined the scheduled band, Voo Doo, which included Joe Vitale on drums. Within twenty-minutes, J.B.'s was packed well past its legal capacity, drawing perhaps several-hundred fans, with hundreds more standing on the stairs and outside on the sidewalk. The performance lasted 90-minutes. The club's owner, Joe Bujack, was unaware that Page and Plant were members of a high-profile rock band, and asked them if they would be available to play on Thursday nights. After they broke down laughing, Page and Plant politely turned down Bujack's offer. (Years later, when asked about the surprise J.B.'s show, Walsh claimed he had no memory of the event.)

*　　*　　*　　*　　*　　*

On November 2, 1969, the James Gang opened for Sly & the Family Stone on the campus of Youngstown State University. However, the local fire marshal cut the concert short due to overcrowding. Several hundred people without tickets had stormed into the 3,000-seat arena. Backstage after the concert, Joe Walsh met guitar virtuoso, Jimi Hendrix.

Later that month, the James Gang entered the newly built Record Plant complex in Los Angeles to record their second album, *The James Gang Rides Again*. Produced by Bill Szymczyk, the project was completed in just a few weeks. Jimmy Fox recalled: "We went to L.A. with one song. It was an old classic story about how you have a lifetime to prepare for your first album and six months to prepare for your second. Boy, were we victims of that. On the other hand, we were just stupid enough to think we could pull it off anyhow. We were the first band to record at the Record Plant. They were still shoveling dirt out of the place." A few weeks later, the band finished the album at the *other* Record Plant studio in New York City. During the sessions, the James Gang ran into Stevie Wonder and Marvin Gaye, both of whom were recording their own albums.

In early-1970, the James Gang added a lead vocalist, Kenny Weiss. Fox and Weiss had gone to grade school together. Walsh was growing tired of playing the guitar and singing at the same time, and welcomed the idea of hiring a singer.

Meanwhile, after ABC Records merged with Dunhill in late-1969, Szymczyk was sent to the company's new offices in Los Angeles. Arriving on New Year's Day in 1970, he was given his first assignment – supervise the music for a surrealistic, rock and roll-themed, Western film, *Zachariah*. The James Gang contributed two songs to the film – an instrumental track, "Laguna Salada," and "Country Fever," which featured Weiss on lead vocals.

The members of the James Gang were also asked to appear in the film. However, shortly before the flight to Mexico where the film was being shot, Walsh and the group's manager Mike Belkin decided to fire Weiss. Subsequently, an enraged Weiss sued the band for millions of dollars. The lawsuit was eventually settled for less than $1,000. (Weiss later attended Ohio State University and became a psychologist.)

Shot in Mexico, the oddball film included appearances by the James Gang, the New York Rock & Roll Ensemble, the anti-establishment rock band Country Joe & The Fish and jazz artist Elvin Jones. During the filming, Walsh became friends with a young, then-unknown actor, Don Johnson. Walsh later recalled: "It was hot; it was probably about 110 by nine in the morning. But no, it was great, Don Johnson and I got to be buddies a long time ago. He's a good guy and just being around a movie set and seeing how it's made came in handy later on."

In the film, the James Gang portrayed a saloon band. During the performance of the song, "Country Fever," Walsh attempted to lip-synch Weiss' vocals. Released in 1971, *Zachariah* recouped only half its cost.

* * * * * *

Meanwhile, Chrissie Hynde was now enrolled at Kent State and was old enough to legally visit the nightclubs in downtown Kent. She later wrote in her autobiography: “The James Gang played regularly at J.B.’s and I would sit on the floor at the feet of Joe Walsh and bask in our very own world-class guitar hero right there where I could reach over and touch his tennis shoes if I wanted to.”

▶ CHAPTER 8
MAY 4TH AT KENT STATE

On April 4, 1970, the James Gang headlined a dance on the Kent State campus – the annual Spring Fling. One of the opening acts was Lacewing. A reviewer for the student paper observed that the crowd at Memorial Hall "was enthralled by Joe Walsh and his guitar. His hypnotizing voice and enthusiasm kept everyone in somewhat of a stupor." Meanwhile, exactly one-month later, multiple students would be maimed or injured and four would die, just a few-hundred feet from the site of the dance.

*   *   *   *   *   *

The opposition to the Vietnam War was at the core of the counterculture movement on America's college campuses during the late-1960s. The first anti-war protest on the Kent State campus occurred on April 14, 1965, with protesters carrying signs that read "Yankee Come Home" and "U.S. Constitution Guarantees Free Assembly." In his comprehensive history of the university, author William H. Hildebrand wrote: "Kent had its first political demonstration since the isolationists' march thirty years earlier. Staged at noon for maximum effect, it took place in front of Bowman Hall, where campus police had cordoned off a ten-foot-square area. Sixteen picketers – nine students and seven professors – walked in a circle surrounded by a crowd of several hundred mostly hostile students. The students' placards denounced American involvement in Vietnam.... Violence had marred such protests on many other campuses, but, aside from verbal abuse (catcalls and shouts of 'draft dodgers'), the only violence that day in Kent was some water-filled balloons flung at demonstrators. The picketing stopped after an hour."

By 1970, the anti-war protests around the country had intensified. And on April 20, when President Richard Nixon announced that he was expanding the war and sending forces into neighboring Cambodia to attack elements that were aligned with North Vietnam, students launched massive protests at nearly 440 U.S. universities. And weeks before the May 4th tragedy, there was widespread unrest at other campuses around the state of Ohio, most notably at Ohio University in

Athens and Ohio State University in Columbus.

Meanwhile, the trouble at Kent State started on Friday night, May 1, when reveling protesters decided to take over a main downtown street. As *Time* magazine reported, "One irate motorist gunned his car's engine as if to drive through the dancers. Some students climbed atop the car, jumped on it, then led a chant: 'One-two-three-four, we don't want your war!' A drunk on a balcony hurled a bottle into the street – and suddenly the mood turned ugly. Students smashed the car's windows, set fires in trash cans, began to bash storefronts. Police were called. Kent Mayor LeRoy Satrom had ordered a curfew, but few students were aware of it. Police stormed into bars after midnight, turning up the lights, shouting 'Get out!' Some 2,000 more students, many of whom had been watching the Knicks-Lakers basketball game on TV, were forced into the street. Police and sheriff's deputies pushed the youths back toward the campus, then fired tear gas to disperse them." Playing at J.B.'s that night was Lacewing, whose performance was cut short.

With a large demonstration planned for Saturday, alarmed authorities at Kent State attempted to diffuse the situation by quickly setting up various on-campus activities such as poetry readings, films and a concert. A performance by a pair of bands – Lacewing and Joe Vitale's new group Marblecake – was planned at the Tri-Towers dormitory complex. However, Vitale and his band were stopped enroute to the show, with protestors smashing glass bottles in front of their vehicle and threatening to destroy the band's instruments. Later in the evening, a rowdy crowd attempted to stop Lacewing's performance at Tri-Towers. Although there were a few clashes and tense moments, the performance was eventually allowed to continue. However, a large number of the concertgoers left with the protestors and headed for the university's aging ROTC building.

As *Time* magazine reported: "Saturday began quietly. Black student leaders, who had been demanding the admission next year of 5,000 more blacks to Kent State [up from the 1970 total of 600], and leaders of the mounting antiwar sentiment on campus talked of joining forces. They got administrative approval to hold a rally that evening on the ten-acre Commons at the center of the campus. There, despite the presence of faculty members and student marshals, militant war protesters managed to take complete charge of a crowd of about 800, many still smarting from the conflict of the night before. They... attacked the one-story Army ROTC building facing the Commons. They smashed windows and threw lighted railroad flares inside. The building caught fire." With a large cache of weapons and ammunition stored inside the building, there were numerous explosions over the next hour.

The bedlam intensified. As *Time* explained: "Without bothering to consult Kent State authorities, Mayor Satrom asked for help from the National Guard. Governor James Rhodes, still engaged in his tough – and ultimately unsuccessful – campaign for the Senate nomination, quickly ordered Guardsmen transferred from points of tension in a Teamster strike elsewhere in Ohio. Within an hour, about 500 Guardsmen, already weary from three nights of duty, arrived with fully loaded M-1 semiautomatic rifles, pistols and tear gas."

On Sunday, Joe Walsh returned from an out-of-state trip and found the campus and the downtown district in a high state of tension. Meanwhile, Governor Rhodes arrived in Kent and chose not to close the campus. Instead, he banned campus demonstrations and declared a state of emergency.

Then on Monday – the fateful date of May 4th – the unthinkable happened. *Time* reported: "It seemed that the campus atmosphere had settled. Shortly after noon, nearly 1,000 protestors had gathered to challenge and harass the young Guardsmen. In addition to the active protestors, another 2,000 spectators kept their distance as they watched the unfolding tragedy. Then the outnumbered and partially encircled contingent of Guardsmen ran out of tear gas. Suddenly they seemed frightened. They began retreating up the hill toward Taylor Hall, most of them walking backward to keep their eyes on the threatening students below.... When the compact formation reached the top of the hill, some Guardsmen knelt quickly and aimed at the students who were hurling rocks from below. A handful of demonstrators kept moving toward the troops. Other Guardsmen stood behind the kneeling troops, pointing their rifles down the hill. A few aimed over the students' heads.... Within seconds, a sickening staccato of rifle fire signaled the transformation of a once-placid campus into the site of a historic American tragedy."

Kent State student and Devo co-founder Gerald Casale described the scene as he stood near Taylor Hall: "We had no idea there was live ammunition in those guns. We didn't know what the hell they were doing. They were at a one-row kneel and one row standing, like in the Civil War. This guy in a gas mask, he gave a signal and bang!, they shot live rounds into the crowd, like a duck shoot. Some of the kids – they had nothing to do with the protest at all, they just happened to be coming out of the journalism building to see what was going on. It changed absolutely everything." Another member of Devo, Bob Lewis, was also a spectator to the tragedy. But unlike Casale, Lewis was in a safer spot.

Chrissie Hynde, who was standing off to the side, remembered: "The grassy, rolling common was teeming with students, I'd never seen it so packed. Then I heard the 'tatatatatatatatatat' sound. I thought it was fireworks. An eerie silence fell over the Commons.... The quiet felt like gravity pulling us to the ground. Everything slowed down and the silence got heavier. Minutes passed – and nothing. Then the sound of the siren. An ambulance was cutting its way into the crowd."

Joe Walsh was within several-hundred feet of the shootings, but did not directly witness the incident. He recalled that upon hearing gunfire, "everybody stopped dead in their tracks, knowing what it was, but asking each other what that sound was anyway. I got to the site 30 seconds after it happened. People started to scream and cry. I even saw a National Guardsman throw down his gun and sob." Walsh personally knew two of the four students who were killed that day, Jeffrey Miller and Allison Krause.

Meanwhile, the campus was completely shut down and remained closed for a month. But while the war in Southeast Asia continued to rage, the Kent campus eventually re-opened. However, most of the university's students didn't return in the fall. British singer Elton John later recalled, "When I first went to America... I remember playing Kent State University... after the students were killed there... and it was a really strange feeling – really odd."

Two lasting memories emerged from the shootings – the image of a hysterical 14-year-old runaway named Mary Ann Vecchio leaning over the body of a dead student, and the passionate and angry protest song, "Ohio," by Crosby, Stills, Nash & Young. After viewing photographs of the tragedy in *Life* magazine, Neil Young wrote the lyrics of the song while staying at David Crosby's home near San Francisco. Rushing to a Los Angeles studio, the foursome recorded the track in just a few takes. The song was delivered to Atlantic Records within 24-hours and released as a single a week later. Although the song was widely banned by top-40 radio, it still received a great deal of airplay.

A few weeks later, Crosby, Stills Nash & Young arrived in nearby Cleveland for a concert sponsored by the city's AM powerhouse, WIXY. The following day, the band was joined by deejays from a local FM station, WNCR, for a morning trip to the scene of the fatal protests.

Distressed upon his arrival at Kent State, Young stared in disbelief at the near-empty Commons area. A few months later, on September 9, the James Gang performed in McLean, Virginia, to raise money for the Kent State Student Medical Fund.

Another consequence of the downtown riots came in the form of a city-wide referendum on the ballot in November 1970. The residents of Kent were asked to decide whether or not to prohibit live music from bars within the city limits. The so-called "entertainment ban" was defeated by a margin of 3,350 to 2,222.

It would take three-decades for the enrollment at Kent State University to recover to pre-May 4th levels. As for the CSN&Y song "Ohio," it continues to receive airplay on rock and oldie stations around the Buckeye State.

* * * * * *

In the wake of his experience on May 4th, Walsh knew he had to leave Kent State: "After that, I didn't look at college the same. Being at the shootings really affected me profoundly. I decided that maybe I don't need a degree that bad." Walsh's bandmate Jimmy Fox was just 13 credit hours short of earning his music education degree when he also quit school. Chrissie Hynde also left Kent State and went hitchhiking around Canada. With many talented musicians fleeing from Kent, the city's fabled music scene took a major hit.

On May 7, Walsh was relieved to be out of Kent when he went back on the road with the James Gang. A few days later, the band performed two shows at the Ocean Ice Palace in Brick Township, New Jersey. After the shows, a weary Walsh visited his parents and tried to reflect on what had happened in Ohio.

▶ CHAPTER 9
JOE RIDES AGAIN

Joe Walsh owed some of his early success to Pete Townshend of the Who, who befriended the James Gang after a show in Pittsburgh. At the concert, the James Gang were the last-minute replacement for an act that had cancelled. The concert took place shortly before the release of the group's second album, *The James Gang Rides Again*.

A local journalist reported: "The Who played its one and only theater show in Pittsburgh with the James Gang (led by Joe Walsh) opening, and despite the Woodstock buzz, it was not covered by the local papers – an indication perhaps of how the Who was seen as a second-rate British import. This was the second leg of a U.S. tour playing *Tommy*, and by this point they were doing almost the entire rock opera, along with songs like 'I Can't Explain' and 'My Generation,' with a 'Tommy' reprise inserted. The Who had matured beyond being instrument-smashing lunatics and were more focused on the demands of the songs."

Jimmy Fox recalled: "The Who came in before our set was finished. Pete Townshend went up front to listen to us. Afterwards he called us into the dressing room and said we were just fantastic. It mushroomed from there." Townshend took a specific interest in Walsh, with whom he felt a musical kinship. Soon after, Townshend spoke to the group's manager, Mike Belkin, and invited the James Gang to tour with the Who. Beginning with a show on June 20, 1970, in Houston, the James Gang would open up for the Who approximately two-dozen times over the next few weeks.

On June 27, the Who and the James Gang played a show at Public Hall in Cleveland. Tickets were $5 in advance and $6 on the day of the show. For the most part, the concert went well. The James Gang went on first and were well received. However, a then-little-known folk singer named James Taylor followed. Taking the stage with an acoustic guitar, he destroyed the high energy in the room. Afterwards, the Who reinvigorated the audience. During the show, Townshend smashed a Gibson SG guitar on the floor of the stage.

After the concert, Mike Belkin took members of the Who and the James Gang to dinner at Captain Frank's, a seafood restaurant in downtown Cleveland, near the East Ninth Street Pier on the shore of Lake Erie. Enroute to the restaurant, the Who's drummer, Keith Moon, jumped from the wooden pier into the lake, which at the time was heavily polluted. Helped by Dale Peters, Moon was pulled out of the water. When Moon joined his bandmates for dinner, his white shirt and pants were now black and filthy. According to Belkin: "If Dale hadn't been walking by, Keith would have never come around. Keith was happy, having fun, couldn't have cared less, he was soaking wet, sat down as if nothing had happened." On the following day, Belkin threw a picnic for the members of both bands. They arrived at a farm owned by the father of Jimmy Fox's fiancee. (In 1972, Townshend would sing about Cleveland on his solo track, "Sheraton Gibson.")

* * * * * *

In July 1970, the James Gang released *Rides Again* – a half-electric and half-acoustic album. The project, which was the first to feature Dale Peters on bass, spawned the group's first top-40 hit, "Funk #49," which was essentially recorded live in the studio. However, Walsh was not particularly happy with the song's lyrics. The track was an expanded version of a warm-up exercise, much like the song's predecessor, "Funk #48."

Another standout track, "The Bomber" (also known as "The Bomber: Closet Queen/Bolero/Cast Your Fate To The Wind"), featured a portion of a well-known Maurice Ravel piece, which would cause legal troubles for the band. Walsh had included approximately 85-seconds of Ravel's "Bolero" because his mother was a huge fan of the composer. However, the group learned that according to French copyright laws, the band could not record just a portion of the piece. Consequently, "Bolero" was deleted from the track after 30,000 of the albums had already been pressed.

Another notable track, the instrumental "Asshtonpark," was titled after Assheton Gorton – the good-natured production designer on the set of the film, *Zachariah*. The acoustic piece, "Ashes, The Rain & I," was inspired by a classical music class Walsh had taken at Kent State. The track featured a twenty-piece string section arranged by Jack Nitzsche. (In 1999, the song would be sampled by Fatboy Slim on his hit single, "Right Here, Right Now.")

With their growing success, the James Gang were targeted by a number of detractors in the rock press. However, Jimmy Fox insisted: "Sure we all listened to a lot of different musicians, but regardless of what the press said, once we got together we never tried to be like Grand Funk or Cream. That's the obvious comparison because it's guitar, bass and drums. And we were aware that 'Closet Queen' sounded like Zeppelin about an hour after we cut it, but when we went to cut it we weren't. We just knew it sounded good and we were happy with it."

Rides Again reached the *Billboard* top-20 and gave the James Gang their first certified Gold Album. More importantly, the breakthrough album cemented the band's position on album-rock radio.

* * * * * *

On August 6, 1970, the James Gang appeared at the Festival of Peace concert, which was staged at Shea Stadium in New York City, where just 15-years earlier Joe Walsh had attended a Beatles concert. With 50,000 music fans in attendance, it was largest audience the James Gang had ever seen. Other performers on the bill included Janis Joplin, Steppenwolf, Paul Simon, Creedence Clearwater Revival, Johnny Winter, Miles Davis and Herbie Hancock. Also on the bill were Pacific Gas & Electric, which at that point were without guitarist Glenn Schwartz. Then, a couple days later, the James Gang performed at the Goose Lake International Music Festival in southern Michigan, this time for a whopping 200,000 concertgoers.

Meanwhile, the Who invited the James Gang to tour across Britain for two-weeks in October. Although Walsh accepted the invitation, the James Gang had also been offered opening slots by a pair of top-tier rock acts, Led Zeppelin and the Moody Blues. Just two-days before the James Gang were due to leave for England, the group played a Friday night, hometown show at the Plato nightclub. Present at the performance was Jimmy Fox's new wife, Kent State student Diane Bieder.

Meanwhile, Pete Townshend continued to praise the James Gang. In a 1970 column for the British music magazine, *Melody Maker*, he wrote: "Joe Walsh is definitely one of the best guitarists in rock that I've come across. His playing makes my neck tingle like only Jimi Hendrix has affected it before. He doesn't move much... but his playing reaches heights that to my mind have only been reached before by the Claptons, Pages and Hendrixes of this world." Townshend also predicted that the James Gang would garner a strong fanbase in Britain. However, despite

Townshend's glowing praise, the James Gang would never score a pop radio hit in the U.K.

The tour marked the British premiere of the Who's groundbreaking rock opera, *Tommy*. Mike Belkin, the James Gang's manager, flew to England in order to watch over Walsh and his bandmates. At each stop on the tour, the James Gang recorded a daily report for broadcast on the Cleveland radio station, WNCR. Townshend made a guest appearance on one of the reports.

The trek across Britain did not always go well. As Walsh recalled, "We were supposed to be the new heavy metal wonders from the United States." At one early show, Dale Peters' amp went out during the first song, as Townshend watched from the side of the stage. And at the London Palladium, Walsh was stricken with a bacterial infection and began throwing up onstage. The exuberant audience thought it was a planned part of the show.

Meanwhile, during the tour, Walsh would learn *other* kinds of lessons from the Who's notorious drummer. As Walsh recalled: "Keith Moon decided that he liked me and that we should stay up for the entire tour. He taught me the basics of hotel damage, blowing stuff up and anarchic chaos in general. He was my mentor."

Rock journalist Dylan Jones once stated that Moon had set the bar for audacious behavior in rock and roll: "The Who's perpetual-motion machine of a drummer was long established as the quintessential rock 'n' roll reprobate, a man who would go out drinking on a Friday night, come back the following Wednesday and then ask his long-suffering girlfriend, 'Why didn't you pay the ransom?' This is the man who once drove his car through the glass doors of a hotel, who then drove all the way up to the reception desk, got out and asked for his room key. His antics were considered so outrageous that he made Keith Richards, Jim Morrison and Ozzy Osbourne all seem like mischievous altar boys."

And in a conversation with his friend John Lennon, Moon described how he once redecorated a room: "I decided my hotel room would look better with the furniture nailed to the ceiling. It was a major undertaking... I got the roadies, and we started with the bed. Then we glued down the pillows, sheets, and blankets. We turned the bed upside down, hoisted it up on our shoulders, and drove some big spikes through it into the ceiling. It was a true joy to behold. We did the bureau next – of course, we took the drawers out first. We glued the lampshade to the lamp before we glued that to the bureau. We also had to glue the chairs.

They proved the most slippery and difficult. But we did not stop until the job was done. It was such an improvement."

Moon also gave Walsh his first taste of rock and roll pharmaceuticals. As Walsh later explained: "I have fond memories of him catching me after a show and forcing me to take two white crosses [speed] in my mouth and looking under my tongue to make sure I'd swallowed them and then downing it with some brandy. I was with him about a week after that. We ran together. I rode with him in that crazy Rolls-Royce he had. We would get off the freeway and take local roads with the Beach Boys blaring away." One night in London, Moon challenged Walsh to a drinking contest – a competition that lasted a full eight-hours. In the aftermath, Walsh admitted to a reporter: "At around 8 a.m. I had to stop, and by 10 a.m. I'd slid under the chair unconscious."

Although the members of the James Gang had enjoyed their first overseas tour, they sometimes felt out of their element. Additionally, some of the venues were small and had wobbly stages that were barely able to support the band's gear. Jimmy Fox said at the time: "I'll be honest, though. We were all ready to go back home after a couple of days. We wondered what the hell we were doing here." Conversely, Walsh stated: "Europe made me a little more mature, made me feel a bit more like a man of the world, instead of a dummy from Ohio."

* * * * * *

After returning to Cleveland, the James Gang made a radio appearance to discuss the highlights of their tour across Britain. While back home, the group performed at a pair of local clubs, Cyrus Erie and the Mentor Rock Shop. Later, at a West Coast concert as the opening act for the Steve Miller Band, a *Los Angeles Times* reviewer labeled the James Gang a less-commercial version of the Midwest rockers, Grand Funk Railroad: "Led by Joe Walsh.... they play at a volume several decibels above the pain threshold and give Walsh all the time he wants to show off with electronic effects."

On December 29, the James Gang would play their last-ever show at their former home-base in Kent, J.B.'s, with Glass Harp as the opening act. The James Gang no longer needed to play college bars. And even though the James Gang were now an established hit act with multiple radio hits and two charting albums, the group's performance fee at J.B.'s never increased. Walsh and the James Gang would close the year with an appearance in front of 30,000 concertgoers at Maple Leaf Gardens in Toronto on a bill with Rare Earth, Chilliwack, Steel River, Sha Na Na and headliner Johnny Winter.

Also in December 1970, Walsh's divorce from his first wife was finalized. The following year, Walsh would marry Stefany Amaro. Walsh had met his second wife while she was attending Boston College. They married a month after her graduation. Later, the couple welcomed a daughter, Emma Kristen. Walsh truly enjoyed being a father and spent as much time as he could with his bright-eyed, blond-haired, little girl.

▶ CHAPTER 10
THIRDS: A FINALE

After touring with the Who and releasing a pair of critically-acclaimed albums, the James Gang had finally earned some respect in the music industry. Shortly before the release of the group's third album, Dale Peters stated: "For so many years we played second and third to other people to get the exposure and now we're getting our own shows. Our music hasn't changed a lot but we've got a little harder, a little tighter, more exciting."

In April 1971, the James Gang issued their final studio album, *Thirds*. Mostly recorded at the Record Plant in Los Angeles, the album was completed at the Cleveland Recording Company. While Bill Szymczyk was the primary producer, the members of the James Gang also received co-producer credit.

The album was highlighted by the guitar-driven single, "Walk Away." Although failing to reach the top-40, the song became a standard on album-rock radio. Walsh achieved the fuzztone sound on the track by turning all of the knobs on his guitar to "10," as a tribute to Pete Townshend.

The second single, "Midnight Man," featured the backing vocals of Mary Sterpka and Bob Webb, both of whom had joined the Measles following Walsh's departure from the group. Joe Walsh had written the song about a former girlfriend from Akron. Another track, "White Man/Black Man," featured the backing vocals of the Sweet Inspirations, a female vocal group that had backed Elvis Presley at many of his Las Vegas shows. Walsh had composed another track, "It's All The Same," after reading J.R.R. Tolkien's fantasy classic, *The Hobbit.*

* * * * * *

The James Gang continued their heavy touring schedule throughout 1971, crisscrossing the country in a station wagon. That same year, the prestigious Carnegie Hall in New York City had finally embraced rock and roll. Suddenly, the venue began booking bands such as Poco, the Allman Brothers Band, Chicago, Elton John, Frank Zappa, Pink Floyd, the Kinks, T. Rex and others.

On May 15, the James Gang made their Carnegie Hall debut. A subsequent album, *Live In Concert*, featured seven songs from the performance. Released in September, the guitar-heavy project was considered one of the most sonically flawless albums of the era. Joe Walsh's carefully balanced pairing of his Les Paul guitar and Marshall amp was hailed by fellow musicians. The set was highlighted by an 18:20 version of the Yardbirds track, "Lost Woman." Unfortunately, missing from the live album were tracks like "The Bomber" and "Funk #49" as well as a cover of Chuck Berry's "Johnny B. Goode." (The night before their Carnegie Hall show, the James Gang performed in South Orange, New Jersey. Although the band had planned on recording the concert, a vandal had cut all the wires between the stage and an outdoor sound truck.)

On June 22, the James Gang performed at the Overton Park Shell in Memphis. After the concert, the group made a pilgrimage to Graceland. Dale Peters told a British journalist at the time: "We're big Elvis Presley fans. He's very big in America again, he's been consistent all these years, which is very hard to do. We went to his house in Memphis but we didn't get in. He's surrounded by his family and his cousin took us round the grounds. He's got iron bars on the windows, which is a shame."

Meanwhile, Walsh was mentioned in *Rolling Stone* for the first time in July 1971, in a review of the James Gang album, *Thirds*. A critic wrote: "By no exertion of the imagination are [the] James Gang the greatest rock and roll band ever to walk the face of the earth or anything (although some maintain that they are the greatest rock and roll band ever to have walked the face of Cleveland, Ohio), but they are capable of some nice little treats every now and then." The reviewer also called the track, "Midnight Man," a "ripoff" of the Beatles' classic, "Nowhere Man." Walsh's name would not grace the magazine's pages for another two years. Also in July, the James Gang traveled to Europe for a brief tour. The trio would perform in the Netherlands, France, Scotland and England.

* * * * * *

Joe Walsh was growing increasingly unhappy with the limitations of playing in a three-piece group. He also feared being typecast as a hard-rock guitarist. Deciding to leave the band, Walsh gave his notice to Jimmy Fox and Dale Peters. Fox later explained: "The way that Joe left the band was in such a nice, painless way that I could almost cry when I think back. He said, 'I Gotta leave, but I'll stay until January.'" After a grueling touring schedule of 300 gigs per year, Walsh amicably left the James Gang at the end December 1971.

Not surprisingly, Fox and Peters wanted to continue the James Gang. After Walsh's departure, Fox telephoned Pete Townshend for some career advice. Townshend suggested that Fox and Peters take a much-deserved break for several months before deciding their next move. Fox told *Rolling Stone*, "Pete Townshend told us to just find a kick-ass replacement, so we thought, 'Well, we'll just get another guitar player.' We were too stupid to understand the ramifications of Joe leaving.... But Joe Walsh isn't just a guitar player. He's a singer, a songwriter and more specifically a personality."

After leaving the James Gang, Walsh was asked to join the British rock group Humble Pie as the replacement for outgoing guitarist Peter Frampton, who would soon launch a very successful solo career. Jerry Shirley, the group's drummer, recalled: "So there we were with an album that... heavily featured two guitar players playing off each other, and now we only had one. It was time to start figuring out what sort of guitarists were out there, and whether or not they would fit in. Our first choice was Joe Walsh, who had just left the James Gang, or was about to. [Our manager Dee Anthony] called Mike Belkin, the promoter from Cleveland, Ohio, who we had worked for many times, and who was also Joe's manager. He presented the offer to Joe, but Joe gracefully declined, as he was putting his Barnstorm and solo projects together and wanted to see them through to fruition. On reflection, I think Joe made the right choice – he had great success as a solo artist and, later, mega-success when he joined the Eagles. Musically speaking, it would have made for an astonishing lineup with Joe in Humble Pie, although I suspect that hotel chains across the U.S. would have run for cover."

Walsh gave the offer to join Humble Pie some serious consideration, despite the fact that both his manager and record label were against the move. As Walsh recalled: "That was something I really wanted to do.... but I just couldn't." Additionally, Walsh also considered joining Bad Company, but that also fell through.

Several months after Walsh had left the James Gang, Fox stated: "[Walsh] was very, very tired with bein' on the road, and he felt he had his own music to explore. Joe had a lot of varied interests, he was very good at a whole lot of different kinds of music. I imagine that whatever he comes up with will be softer.... He was tired of bouncing ideas off the same two heads for years and years, he wanted some new things." Walsh agreed with Fox's assessment: "When I left the James Gang, I wanted a fresh start.... Nobody really understood why I quit the James Gang, because we were doing really well, but I didn't want to be in a three-piece rock and roll band anymore. I thought I was painting myself in a corner, in terms of being a musician. And I wasn't really crazy about being a grandparent of heavy metal!"

Meanwhile, Fox and Peters expanded the James Gang to a quartet with the addition of singer Roy Kenner and guitarist Dominic Troiano. Fox and Peters first heard Troiano at an Eric Clapton concert in Cleveland. However, Troiano wasn't a good fit for the high-energy, blues-oriented rock group. Fox explained: "We found he was more into R&B and soul and he didn't like to play loud. He just wasn't right for the band. One day he said, 'I'll save you guys the trouble of firing me. I'll leave.'" Troiano subsequently joined the veteran Canadian band, the Guess Who.

Then coincidentally, Walsh telephoned Fox and asked if the James Gang could use a new guitarist. Walsh suggested Tommy Bolin, who was then a member of the Colorado-based rock band, Zephyr. Joining the James Gang in August 1974, Bolin appeared on the group's next album, *Bang*, the first release on their new label, Atlantic Records.

But without Walsh at the helm, the James Gang were never able to replicate their early success, and would disband after recording two more albums. Before the group disbanded, Fox was hired by Eric Clapton as a session player on his hit album, *461 Ocean Boulevard*. Still yearning to salvage the James Gang, Fox rejected Clapton's invitation to join his backing band.

* * * * * *

As for who was a more talented guitarist – Joe Walsh or Glenn Schwartz – Hank LoConti, the founder of the Cleveland-based Agora nightclub chain, offered an opinion: "I think the James Gang was just a raw music group, period. Whether it was Joe Walsh or Glenn Schwartz, the guitar was strong. Glenn Schwartz was as good as or better than Joe Walsh, but Joe was a better songwriter, and I think that's what they needed. I think he is one for the ages. He went on to become a legitimate musical legend, and he never got a bigger hat size."

* * * * * *

Joe Walsh never forgot Pete Townshend's kindness at a time when the James Gang needed a career boost. Walsh once declared: "I like to give people equipment and stuff. For me, it's a kind of payback. Anyone who is an influence or hero for me, I'm always concerned with how I can balance the karma."

Meanwhile, in late-1970, Townshend had gifted Walsh an ARP Odyssey synthesizer, which was a then state-of-the-art instrument. Intrigued, Walsh spent three-weeks exploring the potential of the device and would use it on his next album.

Soon after, a grateful Walsh reciprocated by giving Townshend some vintage musical equipment – a 1959 Gretsch 6120 and a 1959 Fender Bandmaster amp. Townshend recalled: "I never really got into old guitars until Joe Walsh rang me up one night and said, 'I've got something for you,' because we buy one another presents. He buys me old concert amps and I buy him synthesizers and we have become very good friends. Anyway, he said, 'I've got something for you,' and I said 'What?' and he said, 'A 1959 Gretsch.'"

After inspecting the guitar for a few seconds, Townshend recalled his initial reaction: "I said, 'Great, cheers, man.' I was being polite. I opened the case and it was bright orange and I thought, 'Ugh! It's horrible, I hate it.' I went home and went into my studio and plugged it in and it totally wrecked me out, it's the best guitar I've got now."

Townshend employed the guitar and amp combo on his next album, which was produced by Glyn Johns. Townshend admitted: "I used that guitar on every track on *Who's Next*, it's the best guitar I've ever had. It's the finest guitar I've ever owned, it's the loudest guitar I've ever owned. It is so loud, man, it whips any pickup that I've ever come across. It's maybe six or seven times louder than anything I've come across."

Although Townshend adored the instrument, the inevitable finally occurred in October 1973. According to his bandmate John Entwistle: "Pete always seems to smash the guitars he loves, somehow. He [destroyed] a nice Gretsch that Joe Walsh had given him. He really liked it, but he lost his temper on [the British television show] *Top Of The*

Pops and broke the neck off. He's since had it repaired. But for the most part, the stuff that Pete trashed was readily available ordinary gear that was plentiful and replaceable." Townshend was in a poor mood that day and had smashed the instrument at end of a performance of the Who track, "5:15."

Previously, Walsh had sold another guitar – this one to Jimmy Page. Walsh recalled: "When the first [Led Zeppelin] album really took off, Jimmy was still playing the Telecasters that he played in the Yardbirds. He was looking for a Les Paul and asked if I knew of any, 'cause he couldn't find one that he liked." At the time, Walsh owned two rare Les Paul guitars – one of which he had purchased in Akron: "In those days, Les Pauls weren't god awful expensive, they were just kind of hard to find. You had to go into the basements of music stores and pawn shops. I happened to have two, and one I liked better than the other, so I kept my best one and gave him the other, which had a slightly smaller neck."

Walsh flew to San Francisco, where Led Zeppelin were touring to promote their debut release. In May 1969, Page finally played the Les Paul onstage for the first time during a concert at the Rose Palace in Pasadena. Usually referred to as his "Number One," Page embraced the 1959 Les Paul Standard, which he famously played on the album, *Led Zeppelin II*. In fact, Page would use the instrument on every future Led Zeppelin album and concert, as well as during his stint with the 1980s group, the Firm.

⯈ CHAPTER 11
ROCKY MOUNTAIN WAY

On the morning of February 9, 1971, the ground rumbled across Southern California. The San Fernando Earthquake – a magnitude 6.6 tremor – spawned widespread damage and caused at least 64 deaths and 2,000 injuries. Bill Szymczyk, who was living on a hillside in Los Angeles at the time, was horror-struck by the force of the natural disaster. Looking out his window, he watched the violent swaying of his neighbor's swimming pool. Concerned about his pregnant wife and young daughter, he decided right then to move out of the state. As for a destination, he joined another employee at ABC Records, Larry Ray, in moving to Denver. Before leaving, both men quit their jobs.

Just eight-days later, Szymczyk was living in Colorado. He was so profoundly affected by the quake that he had left California without taking his possessions. Instead, he had the items packed and shipped. In the mile-high city of Denver, 28-year-old Szymczyk and Ray, age 31, joined forces to launch their own record company. While waiting for his business partner to hustle up some funding, Szymczyk found a job at KMFL, Denver's progressive-rock radio station. Hired as a fill-in deejay on nights and weekends, he cherished the freedom to play whatever he liked.

Ray quickly managed to secure financing and a distribution deal with Gulf+Western, an entertainment conglomerate that operated Paramount Pictures. In the spring of 1971, Szymczyk and Ray launched Tumbleweed Records. Working out of a rented two-story house, east of downtown Denver, the label hired a dozen workers. There was a constant party atmosphere at the label and money was freely spent. Tumbleweed's artist roster included mostly singer-songwriters, few of whom were well-known except for bluesman Albert Collins and former doo-wop singer Dewey Terry.

* * * * * *

In February 1971, Joe Walsh accepted Bill Szymczyk's invitation to relocate from Ohio to Colorado. Walsh welcomed the change of scenery as well as the chance to reflect on his career options. He settled near the small town of Nederland, which at the time had a population of just 600. The town's most notable attraction was a mining museum, which housed historical artifacts from the late-19th and early-20th century, when huge loads of silver were dug out of the ground. Much of the silver was shipped to the U.S. mint in Denver, where the metal was used to manufacture coins.

Walsh was joined in Colorado by his wife and baby daughter. Their hilltop home was nearly 9,000-feet above sea level and was situated on the foothills of the snow-topped Rocky Mountains, near the Continental Divide. Located nearby was the picturesque Barker Meadow Reservoir. Shortly after settling into his new residence, Walsh contacted drummer Joe Vitale, who at the time was living in Canton.

* * * * * *

Joe Vitale first met Joe Walsh in 1968 at Meyer's Lake Park in Canton, after a James Gang show at the park's large ballroom. While Vitale clearly remembered their first meeting, Walsh did not. (Just 16-years earlier, deejay Alan Freed was banned from staging rock and roll concerts at the ballroom after unruly concertgoers damaged the building.)

Taking drum lessons since the age of six in his hometown of Canton, Vitale worked with numerous instructors. Although Vitale's father was a professional musician, he was also a barber. At one point, the elder Vitale gave one of his customers free haircuts in exchange for his son's drums lessons. For a brief period, the Vitale family lived in Florida, where young Joe joined a youth orchestra.

Returning to Canton, Joe Vitale began his professional music career as a drummer in his father's polka band, the Tony Vitale Trio. This was the early-1960s, when tens of thousands of factory workers across Northeastern Ohio spoke Slovenian, Polish and a host of other Eastern European languages at home. Polka was big business at the time, and Cleveland's polka king, Frankie Yankovic, was considered a major star. But Vitale later admitted: "That was not fun at all, to be 15 and playing polka with your dad."

Although Vitale was a huge Beatles fan, he was originally a disciple of Dino Danelli, the drummer of the Young Rascals. Later, Vitale emulated the styles of Keith Moon and John Bonham. Also during his teens, Vitale spent many hours playing baseball with one of his neighbors – future New York Yankees star Thurman Munson.

Vitale's first big break came at the 1965 Magnolia Homecoming Festival, just south of Canton. Vitale's polka band and a local garage-rock group called the Echoes were scheduled to play on the same day. When a member of the Echoes couldn't make the gig, Vitale was asked if he would fill in on drums. After impressing the Echoes with his musical skills, Vitale was asked to join the band: "It was the greatest day of my life. I remember putting my drums in my car and driving on Route 62 to Cholley's Rollatorium (a roller rink where the Echoes rehearsed). I was in heaven."

Soon after, the Echoes were renamed the Chylds, patterning the spelling of their name after the Byrds. In a matter of months, the Chylds emerged as one of the two most popular bands in Canton. Vitale recalled: "We had to turn down work, we had so many bookings. In the summer, we were playing five or six shows a week. We'd each get $10 to $12 a night for playing three hours. I made enough to pay for two years of college and a couple cars." The Chylds also began opening up for a series of national acts including the Buckinghams, the Standells, the McCoys and Mitch Ryder. In 1967, the Chylds opened up for the Beach Boys at the Akron Civic Theater.

Recording a few singles, the Chylds garnered some local radio airplay around Canton and Akron. Later signing with Warner Brothers, the group recorded "Psychedelic Soul," with the single gaining national momentum and almost hitting *Billboard's* Hot 100. But after two of the group's members left in early-1968, the Chylds soon disbanded.

Meanwhile, Vitale had graduated from Lehman High School in 1967 and then attended a small Canton college for two-years. He then relocated to Kent and joined a series of bands including, for a short period, a post-Walsh version of the Measles.

The first time that Walsh and Vitale interacted as musicians in Kent, there was a bit of tension. In 1969, Walsh strolled into the Kove and watched Vitale, who was onstage at the time. As Vitale recalled: "He was disgusted by the way I played drums standing up."

Eventually, the two musicians became good friends and often discussed rock music while eating hamburgers at Lujan's restaurant, just east of the Kent State campus. They also talked about forming a band together in the future. Oftentimes over the next year, Vitale would be playing at the Kove at the same time that Walsh was performing next-door at J.B.'s. As Vitale recalled: "We'd both be playing in bars then jam after our gigs. I'd call him a hippie and he'd call me a greaser."

Eventually, Vitale formed his own band, Voo Doo, which played mostly original material. Later, he formed another band, Sheriff. Then after a midweek performance in front of just two-dozen spectators at J.B.'s, Vitale was approached by Chip Killinger – the former manager of Glass Harp – and asked if he wanted to join Ted Nugent's backing band, the Amboy Dukes. Soon after, Nugent invited Vitale to the Electric Lady Studios in New York City for an audition.

Thrilled to leave the bar scene, Vitale was touring around the country for the first time in his life. He later recalled: "I sure lost a lot of weight and got a lot of chops doing that. We were mega-rock. It was great to work with him, though. I needed that." However, Vitale's stint in Nugent's backing band would last just six-months. Vitale felt he wasn't a good fit for the booming, metal-driven band.

Near the end of August 1971, Vitale would have a fateful encounter with a friend from Kent. Ted Nugent and the James Gang were on the same bill at the Dome, a 3,500-seat venue in Virginia Beach. After the concert, Vitale was asked by Walsh to join a new group he was forming. Just two-weeks later, Vitale parted with Nugent under friendly circumstances. Vitale later recalled: "I had spoken to Ted after me and Joe Walsh talked about putting something together. Ted was wonderful. He said, 'That's great. You guys should be in a band together.' There was no weirdness or nothing. It was all real friendly and loving. He rooted for us and actually came to a few of our shows after we got started." After leaving Nugent's band, Vitale returned to Canton and anxiously waited a full four-months for Walsh's telephone call.

* * * * * *

Finally, in early-1972, Joe Vitale was invited to join Joe Walsh at his home in Nederland. Shortly after arriving, Vitale was met by a major snowstorm, and the van that was transporting his music gear from the airport was buried under three-feet of snow. In that part of Colorado, snow could fall six-months out of the year. Two-months would pass before Vitale was able to retrieve his drum kit from the snowbound van.

Instead of making music, Walsh and Vitale initially spent their time on their hobbies. Walsh sat in front of his ham radio, chatting with fellow operators from around the globe. The two men also built model airplanes and shot model rockets into the cold sky. Eventually, at Bill Szymczyk's urging, Walsh began writing songs for his new band, which he named Barnstorm.

Signing with ABC-Dunhill Records, Barnstorm began working on their debut album in the spring of 1972, with deep snow still on the ground. On the first day of the sessions, one of the mixing boards in Walsh's newly built home studio started filling the room with smoke. Throwing the still-smoldering 24-track board into a snowdrift, the three men abandoned the idea of recording at Walsh's home. Szymczyk suggested they move the sessions to the Record Plant in Los Angeles. Then after recording two tracks – "Birdcall Morning" and "Home" – Walsh, Vitale and Szymczyk decided to return to Colorado. While in Los Angeles, Walsh would meet the members of the Eagles for the very first time.

After returning to Colorado, Barnstorm added bassist Kenny Passarelli, who was recommended to Walsh by guitarist Tommy Bolin. (Passarrelli and Bolin were close friends and former bandmates.) Formally trained on the trumpet, Passarelli had performed with a local music troupe at the inauguration of President Lyndon Johnson. Switching to the bass at age 15, Passarelli later attended the University of Denver on a music scholarship. Although he was planning to enroll in law school, Passarelli changed his career plans after an offer to tour with guitarist Stephen Stills. But after contracting hepatitis, Passarelli was sidelined for six-months and was unable to join Stills on the tour.

Meanwhile, Szymczyk suggested finishing the Barnstorm album at a recording studio that was under construction a mere three-miles from Walsh's home. The studio was situated on a 4,000-acre spread, formerly known as the Van Vleet horse ranch. The scenic ranch was surrounded by grand meadows, untouched forests and spectacular mountain peaks, and was the setting for four motion pictures including the 1966 remake of *Stagecoach*.

The Caribou Ranch studio was owned by 26-year-old James William Guercio. A native of Chicago, Guercio was a former Los Angeles-based musician who got his start in Dick Clark's traveling rock and roll revues. Guercio later emerged as a hit producer and worked with bands like Blood, Sweat & Tears and Chicago.

Guercio hired audio engineer Tom Hidley to design the studio. An expert in the field, Hidley had also designed the state-of-the-art Record Plant in Los Angeles. Guercio explained why he constructed his studio so far from the music industry hubs in New York and Los Angeles: "They'd unionized the studios. I couldn't touch a button. They heard I was cueing stuff so they put a union steward in and threatened to fine me. I was 19 and I just said, this is not the creative process." However, Colorado was actually Guercio's backup location. He explained: "In 1968 I had been up in Billings and Bozeman [Montana] and found a real pretty ranch. We went into this bar; I had kinda long hair. I think it was in Big Fork. These guys said, 'You're buying that ranch and building a studio? We'll give you a haircut with a chain saw.' You can't make that up. It was like *Deliverance*."

Meanwhile, Guercio was hesitant to allow Barnstorm to work in the studio, which was still under construction. Guercio was leaving for a few months to direct a film starring Robert Blake, *Electra Glide In Blue*. Eventually, Guercio had a change of heart and allowed Walsh and his group to record their debut album at the partially finished studio.

The actual recording studio was located on the second floor of a large, three-story barn. The unfinished ground level still had a dirt floor and a row of weathered horse stalls. The third floor would soon be converted into a musician's lounge with a pool table and bar. However, at the time, the building lacked both running water and bathroom facilities. Szymczyk explained: "We were on our own. There was no maintenance guy. No studio manager. Nothing. The buildings were there but they hadn't been refurbished. There was a mess hall from when it was a working ranch but there was no one there to cook. We showed up with our lunch." Eventually, Guercio would build a number of cabins on the property to give visiting musicians a place to stay.

▶ CHAPTER 12
ARRIVAL OF BARNSTORM

Joe Walsh and Barnstorm began recording at Caribou Ranch in April 1972. Bill Szymczyk urged Walsh to take a more Beatlesque approach. Walsh had other ideas. He toned down his hard-rocking guitar and took a more introspective, singer-songwriter direction.

With a good mood permeating the sessions, the project was quickly recorded. The trio of Walsh, Kenny Passarelli and Joe Vitale were augmented in the studio by Paul Harris on piano, Al Perkins on steel guitar and Chuck Rainey on bass guitar. During the sessions, Walsh experimented with a host of electronic wizardry including a fuzzbox and a high-end Leslie 122 speaker. Walsh also utilized the ARP Odyssey synthesizer given to him by Pete Townshend on the tracks, "Mother Says" and "Here We Go."

Taking occasional breaks, Walsh and Vitale often went into Nederland for drinks at the town's only watering hole, the Pioneer Inn. As the Caribou Ranch grew in popularity, a number of notable artists knocked back drinks at the bar, including John Lennon, Rod Stewart, Carole King and Waylon Jennings. Oftentimes, Walsh went behind the bar and poured drinks for his friends.

Eventually, Vitale and Passarelli decided to share an apartment in Boulder, which was a 30-minute drive down a steep and curvy canyon road. Unlike Nederland, Boulder had slightly better weather and a more agreeable altitude of 5,400-feet above sea level. Before the release of their debut album, Barnstorm played a few nightclub gigs in Boulder and Denver. The band performed a variety of old rock songs as well as some James Gang tracks.

Released in October 1972, the album, *Barnstorm*, was a moderate success, peaking at #79 on *Billboard's* sales chart. The front cover featured a photo of a dilapidated barn near the Caribou Ranch. On the back cover, Walsh thanked the owner of J.B.'s nightclub in Kent, Joe Bujack. The album's lone hard-rocking track, "Turn To Stone," was a hit on album-rock radio. Co-written by Walsh and Terry Trebandt, the song was about Richard Nixon and the Vietnam War as well as one of the victims of the Kent State shootings, Allison Krause. (Walsh later re-

recorded the song on his 1974 solo album, *So What.*) Another highlight of the album was the contemplative track, "Birdcall Morning." And at the end of another track, "Giant Bohemoth," a message was tapped out in Morse code.

Soon after, the group hit the road and played all over the country, sharing bills with the J. Geils Band, Kiss, Jimmy Buffett and REO Speedwagon. In October 1972, Barnstorm played six shows at the tiny Bitter End nightclub in New York City. Walsh recalled: "We were playing pretty much anything we could, just to be able to play and be able to pay for the equipment. It wasn't particularly from choice, but it was good."

In 1973, Szymczyk worked with Rick Derringer on his debut solo album, *All American Boy,* which spawned the hit single, "Rock And Roll, Hoochie Koo." Walsh would play guitar on two of the album's tracks.

* * * * * *

After parting with his Cleveland-based manager, Joe Walsh signed with Irving Azoff. Over the next decade, Azoff would play a major role in shaping Walsh's career. A native of Danville, Illinois, Azoff dropped out of the University of Illinois at age 22 in 1970 in order to work in artist management. Although Azoff had originally planned on going to medical school, that all changed at age 17 after he watched a performance by the Yardbirds at the Indiana Beach amusement park, an hour south of Chicago.

According to Cameron Crowe, within a few years, Azoff was "running the affairs of eighty-six artists (like the Buckinghams and the Cryan' Shames) and promoting them across five states. Suddenly, a group could make or break on whether Azoff put them on his circuit." However, Azoff moved his operation to Los Angeles after authorities in an upper-crust Chicago suburb raided one of his shows and arrested many of the concertgoers. Arriving in Los Angeles, Azoff initially signed with the Heller-Fischel booking agency.

Meanwhile, Walsh crossed paths with Azoff during a tour stop in Los Angeles. Barnstorm was headlining at the Whisky a Go Go on the Sunset Strip for a full week in February 1973. The two men had first met a few years earlier when Walsh was a member of the James Gang. As Walsh recalled: "Out of nowhere, Irving came up, saying he believed in me. He was a booking agent and wanted to at least keep me working until I could straighten my career out.... He was the only guy I'd talked to who had answers. I just gave him everything, completely trusted him and said, 'Help.'"

Soon after, Azoff helped Walsh sort out a myriad of legal matters. Additionally, Azoff also began managing Walsh and booking shows for Barnstorm. Not initially prepared to operate his own management firm, Azoff joined GR Management, which represented a number of leading artists. The company was headed by a pair of music industry heavyweights, Elliott Roberts and David Geffen, and boasted a growing number of notable rock and folk acts on its roster.

When an opportunity arose to strike out on his own, Azoff quit GR Management to form his own firm. He quickly earned a reputation in the music industry. Nicknamed "Big Shorty" and "The Poison Dwarf" due to his diminutive height and forceful personality, Azoff was a firebrand who aggressively protected the interests of the artists he represented. Azoff proclaimed at the time: "People keep saying I'm just lucky, that my artists would have been successful anyway. I still have this driving obsession to prove to people that I have something to do with my artists' success."

Don Henley would later describe Azoff in fairly dramatic terms: "He's Napoleon with a heart. But I'm always awed because he's screaming at some guy twice his size and never gets his face crushed for it. I think it helps that people are shocked at this short, deceptively *cute*-looking guy who goes to the top floor of a building, and just explodes on some guy for his incompetence."

▶ CHAPTER 13
THE SMOKER YOU DRINK

After the success of the debut Barnstorm album, a number of musical acts began streaming into rural Colorado to record at the Caribou Ranch, beginning with Elton John, Blood, Sweat & Tears and Chicago. Danny Seraphine, a founding member of Chicago, recalled: "The experience of recording in Colorado was radically different from working at an established studio in New York or Los Angeles. These facilities were expensive and restrictive. When the band booked studio space, we were there for a certain amount of time at a set hourly rate. As soon as we walked into the building, the meter started running. Up at the Caribou Ranch, there were no scheduling conflicts. Chicago had total freedom to work as long as we wanted at our own pace, and being so far removed from the hustle and bustle of New York or Los Angeles, the band stayed focused and concentrated on writing and recording."

However, the visiting musicians quickly discovered that their instruments made different sounds at nearly 8,000-feet above sea level. Additionally, the frozen climate posed other challenges. One musician said of the winter snowscape: "We loved the mountains but were shocked to find five-foot snow drifts and below freezing temperatures. We would need to wear parkas and snowshoes to walk from our mountain style log cabin down to the studio. And when we got there, it took ten minutes just to get our breath back."

By this time, the studio had installed a highly prized, custom-built Neve-8016 German mixing console. According to Dave Grohl of Nirvana and Foo Fighters: "The Neve boards were considered like the Cadillacs of recording consoles. They're these really big, behemoth-looking recording desks; they kind of look like they're from the Enterprise in Star Trek.... and to any studio geek or gear enthusiast it's like the coolest toy in the world."

* * * * * *

Joe Walsh and Barnstorm began working on their second album in late-1972. Walsh wanted to add a keyboard player to the band. Although the position was initially offered to Tommy Stephenson, Walsh instead enlisted a musician recommended by Stephenson – Rocke Grace. A native of South Dakota, Grace was just 21 at the time.

Most of the album's tracks were recorded at Caribou Ranch. Oftentimes, Walsh's young daughter, Emma, slept on the floor of the studio while the musicians played nearby. During this period, the Walsh family relocated to nearby Boulder. As various musicians passed through their home, Walsh's wife grew weary of the intrusions and at one point wouldn't let an unknown singer-songwriter named Dan Fogelberg sleep on their couch.

The second Barnstorm album, *The Smoker You Drink, The Player You Get*, was released in June 1973. The front of the album pictured a British-made Sopwith Snipe fighter plane from World War One with French markings. As for the album's unusual title, Walsh came up with the phrase at a party during a conversation with jazz guitarist Howard Roberts, whom Szymczyk was producing at the time. Vitale explained that Walsh "kinda laughed about album titles that had all this deep meaning and all that, so he thought he would just pick a title that would create havoc... You know, 'What does this mean?' And it doesn't mean anything. It was just one of those Joe Walsh funny things."

The album was highlighted by the raucous track, "Rocky Mountain Way," which was mostly written by Walsh. The song came about after Szymczyk instructed Walsh to write something featuring a slide guitar. Walsh had first started playing slide guitar after the sudden death of Duane Allman in 1971. Walsh had first met Allman when the James Gang and the Allman Brothers were on the same bill. Walsh later recalled: "Duane Allman had showed me open E tuning and given me a Coricidin bottle, the glass bottle slide that he used. So I had been practicing slide guitar for a long time. And 'Rocky Mountain Way' was really my coming out song on slide, having learned all that Duane taught me and practiced for a year. That was my 'Hey, I play slide too!' song." Vitale added: "It was the first recording that Joe had ever played the slide on. Go figure – it turns out to be his biggest song."

Szymczyk and Walsh had their first-ever fight during the sessions for the track. As Szymczyk recalled: "[We] had our first falling out, and he decided that he wanted to produce himself, so he brought the band down... to [Criteria Studio in] Florida. This was when we were all living in Colorado. So he... worked with [producers] Ronnie and Howie Albert, and at the time they did that track... and he didn't have any words for it, but it was great, a slow shuffle blues. They brought it back to Colorado.... The track and the overdubs were done maybe a year apart – it was one of the first tracks he started, and one of the last ones we finished for that album."

Meanwhile, Walsh struggled to write lyrics for the song. Finally, while mowing his lawn and admiring the nearby Rocky Mountains, Walsh had a sudden flash of inspiration. Rushing off his riding mower, he ran to his home and wrote down the lyrics, which he later described as a celebration of his life up to that point. Walsh explained: "I always felt 'Rocky Mountain Way' was special, even before it was complete. We had recorded that before I knew what the words were going to be, but I was very proud of it.... I got kind of fed up with feeling sorry for myself, and I wanted to justify and feel good about leaving the James Gang, relocating, and going for it. I wanted to say, 'Hey, whatever this is, I'm positive and I'm proud,' and the words just came out feeling that way, rather than writing a song out of remorse. It turned out to be a special song for a lot of people. It's an attitude and a statement. It's a positive song, and it's basic rock 'n' roll, which is what I really do."

Additionally, "Rocky Mountain Way" marked Walsh's first use of a talk box, a device that synthesized the sound of his voice. The instrument was invented by Bill West, a Nashville-based electrical engineer and steel guitarist who was a member of Pete Drake's band. In 1964, Drake had first used West's talk box on the country/pop hit, "Forever." After the session, the talk box was placed on a shelf in West's garage. Several years later, the device found a new user.

During the 1970s, whenever Walsh was in Nashville, he made sure to visit the home of West and his wife, country music star Dottie West. On one occasion, Bill West had a gift for Walsh – the dust-covered talk box previously used by Drake. Walsh, who was always intrigued by odd musical gadgets, was shown how to use the device. However, Walsh later determined that the talk box was not loud enough for a rock band. Taking the device to Bob Heil, the owner of Heil Sound, Walsh asked if it could be modified to increase the volume. Not long afterward, Heil began manufacturing an improved version of the talk box.

In the fall of 1973, "Rocky Mountain Way" was a significant hit on both top-40 and album-rock radio. Consequently, Barnstorm was invited to perform on both *Don Kirshner's Rock Concert* and *Midnight Special*, which was hosted that week by Richard Pryor. Unfortunately, Pryor introduced the band as the Barnstormers.

The album's second single, "Meadows," was a only minor hit on pop radio but became an album-rock staple. Walsh had started writing the melodic, mid-tempo track while in the James Gang. Also on the album, Joe Vitale provided the lead vocals on two tracks, "Bookends" and "Days Gone By." Another track, "Midnight Moodies," was written by Rocke Grace.

The Smoker You Drink peaked at #6 on the *Billboard* sales chart, giving Walsh his first top-10 album. At the time, Walsh was running low on cash and was considering quitting his music career. He had financed both Barnstorm albums with his James Gang earnings and was nearly broke. But after the success of "Rocky Mountain Way," he was able to keep paying his band. Without the hit, it's likely that Walsh would have disbanded Barnstorm and returned to Cleveland.

Also in 1973, Walsh played the slide guitar on the REO Speedwagon album, *Ridin' The Storm Out*. A live version of the album's title track was later a hit for the group. The song was inspired by a concert in Boulder, Colorado, during a major blizzard.

* * * * * *

Peter Frampton used a talk box on his 1976 smash album, *Frampton Comes Alive!* At the time, Walsh insisted: "I taught Peter how to use the talkbox, and he never even thanked me!" However, in his autobiography, *Do You Feel Like I Do?*, Frampton claimed he was first introduced to the talk box in the summer of 1970, while working on George Harrison's solo album, *All Things Must Pass*. At the sessions, Frampton chatted with one of the other guest musicians, Nashville-based guitarist Pete Drake.

During a break in the sessions, Drake demonstrated the talk box. As Frampton recalled: "He got out this metal box, put it on the edge of his pedal steel [guitar], plugged this in here and that in there. Then he got a plastic tube out, a clear plastic tube, and fixed it onto this new-fangled gadget. He then put the tube in his mouth and the pedal steel started singing to me. The sound is coming out of his mouth. And I'm going, 'Holy crap.'"

In 1973, Frampton received one of Heil's improved talk boxes as a Christmas present. And like Walsh, Frampton mesmerized audiences when he utilized the device in concert: "After I'd learned how to use it, the first number I used it on live was 'Do You Feel Like We Do.' And that first time we did it was the most incredible experience, because it got everybody's attention immediately. It felt like the whole audience instantly moved forward twelve inches. The connection between me and the audience got much closer straightaway." Over his lengthy career, Frampton would use the talk box on just three songs.

* * * * * *

After Barnstorm finished the sessions for *The Smoker You Drink, The Player You Get*, Tommy Stephenson had a change of heart and agreed to join Barnstorm, just as the group was preparing to go on the road. The band now had two keyboard players. In the summer of 1973, Joe Walsh and Barnstorm went on a short, co-headlining tour with Stephen Stills. At the end of the shows, Walsh would join Stills, his former neighbor in Colorado, for a pair of duets. During the tour, bassist Kenny Passarelli would play in both bands. After backing Walsh, Passarelli would change his clothes and then join Stills' band.

In July, Barnstorm appeared at the Winterland ballroom in San Francisco as the opening act for the Doobie Brothers and the New Riders of the Purple Sage. As *Rolling Stone* reported: "Several hours before showtime, Joe Walsh sat in nervous anticipation on the edge of his motel room bed, 'I am *so* excited about tonight,' he blurted. 'I just want to go out there and... *kill* 'em.'" A young Cameron Crowe reviewed Barnstorm's performance: "Walsh's guitar wailed and his voice soared. The set had been flawlessly paced. Pete Townshend has said many times that Joe Walsh was his favorite contemporary guitarist. Let us just say that Townshend saved face that evening. Walsh did kill 'em."

Then in August, Barnstorm returned to the Cleveland area for a show with the Guess Who at Blossom Music Center. However, when Walsh and his band left the stage after their allotted time as the opening act, the over-enthusiastic audience rioted, causing damage to the venue. And at the end of 1973, Joe Walsh appeared on NBC's New Year's Eve special along with the Pointer Sisters, Billy Preston and Tower of Power. The program was hosted by comedian George Carlin.

Remarkably, Walsh and the members of Barnstorm suffered three airplane mishaps within a two-month period in 1973. The first near-disaster occurred shortly after take-off in Denver. Minutes after leaving Stapleton Airport, one of the plane's engines blew up, which also destroyed the hydraulic system controlling the craft's brakes. The plane initially went into a nose-dive, but the pilots were eventually able to regain control. However, the craft went off the runway into a ditch. No one aboard was injured. Shaken up, the band decided to drive to their gigs for the next few months.

* * * * * *

Meanwhile, Bill Szymczyk was still operating his label, Tumbleweed Records. In 1973, he signed Michael Stanley, who at the time was working as a regional manager of an Ohio record store chain. On the album, Stanley was joined by a number of guest players such as Joe Walsh, Joe Vitale, Rick Derringer and Todd Rundgren.

The album, *Michael Stanley*, garnered radio airplay with the ballad, "Rosewood Bitters." Walsh said of the track: "I've always loved that song. I think it's about getting comfort out of sadness. Kind of being at peace with yourself, with the road behind you you've traveled down. It's melancholy, but it's still remembering the good things. All in all, things balance out." (In 1985, Walsh would record "Rosewood Bitters" for his solo album, *The Confessor*.)

In early-1974, Walsh convinced his old friend in Cleveland, David Spero, to quit his job as a deejay at WMMS in order to manage Stanley's new group. (Spero would later manage a host of notable acts including Harry Nilsson, Nicky Hopkins, Sam Moore, Dickey Betts, Survivor and the solo careers of J.D. Souther and Don Felder.)

Ultimately, Tumbleweed Records would spend nearly $1.5 million and release just nine albums over a two-year period before Gulf + Western decided to pull the plug. Over its short existence, the label would never manage to place a song on the top-40 charts.

Meanwhile, on March 16, 1974, Michael Stanley appeared on the television show, *Don Kirschner's Rock Concert*. The performance was billed as Michael Stanley's Super Session and featured musical guests such as Joe Walsh and fellow Barnstorm members Joe Vitale and Bryan Garofalo. Amazingly, this was Stanley's first public performance since December 1969.

Then on June 23, Walsh performed for an audience of 40,000 at the World Series of Rock, which was staged at Cleveland Stadium. Also on the bill were the Beach Boys, Lynyrd Skynyrd and REO Speedwagon. A reviewer said of Walsh's performance: "Cleveland's most talented native son in rock returned with a vengeance. His tight, talented backing group is possibly the best line-up Walsh has played in since the James Gang."

Although Walsh would often help his many musician friends, he was not always generous with his time. In author Evie Nagy's book, *Freedom OfChoice*, she chronicled Walsh's meeting with two acquaintances from Ohio who had formed the avant-guard rock group, Devo: "In 1974, Mark [Mothersbaugh] and Jerry [Casale] drove out to L.A. to try to get a demo tape into the hands of labels. Exploiting a Kent State connection, they stayed on soon-to-be Eagle Joe Walsh's floor, hoping the fellow Ohioan would get what they were about and lend them a hand. 'Halfway through the first song on the demo tape, he ran into the other room,' says Mark. 'Him and this other guy with really long hair, they're in the dining room smoking a joint, trying to stifle laughter.'"

Meanwhile, in early-1974 at the Record Plant in Los Angeles, Walsh would meet two of his musical idols for the very first time. During some informal sessions, John Lennon was rehearsing a number of songs that he was planning to include on his upcoming album, *Walls And Bridges*. The recording sessions for Lennon's album were scheduled to begin in the summer, and he wanted some reactions to the songs from his fellow musicians. Also present at the studio was Ringo Starr as well as a number of other rock heavyweights. Decades later, when Walsh and Starr were asked about their first meeting, neither had any recollection of their encounter at the Record Plant. And during this period, Walsh played guitar on Ray Manzarek's second post-Doors solo album, *The Whole Thing Started With Rock & Roll Now It's Out of Control.*

* * * * * *

In the spring of 1974, Joe Walsh suffered a terrible personal tragedy that would impact his emotional state for decades. Walsh was due to return to Colorado from the West Coast on April 1. Earlier that day, his wife, Stefany, was driving their daughter, Emma, to pre-school near their home in Boulder when their car was struck by a drunk, elderly driver who ran a stop sign at the intersection of 9th and Spruce Streets. The impact caused Walsh's car to spin around and hit a fence on the other side of the road.

Emma, who less than a month away from turning 3-years-old, sustained massive head injuries and was taken off life support later that day. Walsh recalled: "At the hospital, there were no signs of brain activity. The doctors made me aware of donor situations, and I made the decision to turn the machine off. They put her on ice and took her away. One kid got her corneas; another got her kidney. And I've had to live with the decision to turn the machine off. That's one reason why I named my next solo album *So What* and why I joined the Eagles. I just wasn't strong enough to pursue a solo career. It's also the reason I went into self-abuse for a long time, having to live with that and hating myself." Walsh's wife suffered broken ribs and was in a coma for weeks.

Walsh kept the news of his daughter's death out of the newspapers. As a result, few of his friends knew about his loss. Consequently, Walsh had to deal with the tragedy on his own. Additionally, his record company did not give him any time off to grieve or heal. Walsh's wife later explained: "The accident kind of did us in. We divorced shortly afterward."

Just five-months earlier, on December 11, 1973, Walsh had suffered another loss when his paternal grandmother, Dora Joy Woodward, passed away at the age of 74. Joe had spent every summer at her home in Wichita during the first 12 years of his childhood. Many years later, Walsh would admit: "I'm not afraid to die. But I'm afraid of the people I love dying."

* * * * * *

With Barnstorm disbanding and his marriage ending, Joe Walsh moved to Los Angeles in May 1974. Ultimately, the Rocky Mountains were not a good match for a Midwesterner like Walsh. He later explained: "I was totally down and out in Colorado. Couldn't get any gigs.... and the IRS was auditing me three years running. My manager didn't even care."

Although Joe Vitale remained in Walsh's band, he decided to move back home to Canton: "It was great out in Colorado at first, but then it got to be a drag. So we moved back home." Vitale would fly to Los Angeles whenever Walsh needed him in the studio.

After returning to Ohio and briefly working with Michael Stanley, Vitale yearned to record a solo album. At his small, four-track, home studio, Vitale recorded several demos that he shopped around to various record labels. Signed by Atlantic Records, Vitale released the album, *Roller Coaster Weekend*, in late-1974. Vitale wrote all eleven songs and was aided on the sessions by a talented trio of guest guitarists – Walsh,

Rick Derringer and Phil Keaggy. However, the album was not a commercial success. Later, a portion of one of the album's tracks, "Falling," was used in the Walsh song, "At the Station," which appeared on his album, *But Seriously, Folks.*

Wanting to promote *Roller Coaster Weekend,* Vitale formed a touring band that included Barnstorm veterans Kenny Passarelli and Tommy Stephenson as well as former Measles bandmate Bob Webb. Before hitting the road, the Joe Vitale Band (alternatively known as Madman) held their practices in Kent. In November 1974, Vitale opened for Aerosmith at Firestone High School in Akron. And amazingly, Vitale also opened for the Rolling Stones. Around this time, Passarelli received an invitation to join Elton John's band. Parting with Vitale, Passarelli would appear on John's chart-topping album, *Rock Of The Westies,* which was recorded at the Caribou Ranch.

Soon after, Vitale would join Stephen Stills and Neil Young in the Stills-Young Band. Vitale would subsequently tour with the reformed Crosby, Stills, Nash & Young. (Eventually, Young would part with his bandmates as he had done in the past.) Vitale would tour with Crosby, Stills & Nash, on and off, for the next 35-years.

CHAPTER 14
JOE SAYS SO WHAT

Joe Walsh began working on his first solo album in the fall of 1973. The sessions were interrupted a few months later by the tragic death of his daughter. An emotional wreck at the time of the album's release, Walsh gave the project an appropriately wry title, *So What*. The cover featured a photo of a despondent Walsh wearing a black scarf and a pair of vintage aviation goggles.

The album was produced by Walsh, Bill Szymczyk and John Stronach. Oftentimes, Walsh was the only musician in the studio. The album – which featured the Barnstorm lineup on just two-tracks – portended a major change in Walsh's career, with some of the backing vocals provided by three members of the Eagles. Additionally, Don Henley wrote the lyrics for one of the tracks, "Falling Down."

The uneven album mirrored Walsh's state of mind at the time. *Rolling Stone* writer Bud Scoppa gave the album a positive review: "As he's moved westward – from the East Coast to Ohio to Colorado to Los Angeles – Joe Walsh has assimilated one regional style after another. Walsh's appealing and extremely well-made third solo album, *So What*, attests to his varied background."

The album was highlighted by an updated version of "Turn To Stone." On the track, Tommy Stephenson played an electric organ while Walsh played a traditional church organ. Released as a single, it reached only the lower half of *Billboard's* Hot 100, but enjoyed heavy airplay on album-rock radio. Walsh also revisited his love of classical music with a rendition of Maurice Ravel's "Pavane For The Sleeping Beauty." The moody track featured a vintage Mellotron as well as both Moog and ARP synthesizers. As Walsh recalled: "It's really strange because we recorded it on Halloween night and there was a full moon and the song came out really spooky. I did that all on synthesizer. I went and got the [original] record and listened to it, and I memorized it and worked it out on piano."

Walsh had written another of the album's tracks, "All Night Laundry Mat Blues," when he was a student at Kent State. Walsh recalled: "I just used to sit down and play guitar in the laundromat and have 20 washers going at the same time." Dan Fogelberg was a guest guitarist on the track.

However, the most touching song on the album was a tribute to his daughter, "Song For Emma." Walsh explained that the track originally featured the guitarwork of Jimmy Page: "Jimmy came down one night and played a guitar part on 'Song For Emma' which was ridiculous. It was incredible. But you won't recognize it because there's no guitar on the track! I feel rotten about that because we decided that it should just be strings and drums and me, no electric anything. So Jimmy's guitar part didn't get used and I hope it doesn't make him too sad." Another track, "Help Me Thru The Night," was written about a woman Walsh had met in Los Angeles who had helped him deal with Emma's tragic death.

Meanwhile, Walsh's previous manager, Mike Belkin, sued ABC, two of its executives and Irving Azoff in California Superior Court for "interfering with the management relationship between Joe Walsh and Belkin." According to the complaint, Walsh had signed a contract that gave Belkin a percentage of the rocker's earnings from music publishing, recordings and other related ventures until July 1975.

* * * * * *

In the summer of 1974, Joe Walsh reunited with his friend Keith Moon, who was working on a solo album, *Two Sides Of The Moon*, at the Record Plant in Los Angeles. At the time, Walsh was finishing *So What* in an adjoining studio. A huge fan of West Coast surf music, Moon had hoped to emulate the sound of the Beach Boys and other mid-1960s rock acts. Moon was joined at the sessions by Rick Nelson, Harry Nilsson, Jay Ferguson, John Sebastian, Spencer Davis, surf-guitar legend Dick Dale and Ringo Starr, who had come up with the album's title. Moon drummed on only three of the tracks, but provided all of the lead vocals. Walsh appeared on half of the songs and played guitar and an ARP synthesizer on a new rendition of the Who classic, "The Kids Are Alright."

Not surprisingly, the sessions dragged on because of the constant diversions in the studio. Recording engineer Gary Ladinsky remembered: "You'd get something done for an hour, and then it's a party scene. Eventually, you clear out the studio and you might do something for another half an hour, and then people wander out, and you realize, 'I guess the session is over.'"

*   *   *   *   *   *

In 1974, Joe Walsh produced an album by 23-year-old Dan Fogelberg. Mentally drained from the demands of his busy solo career, Walsh enjoyed working with a fellow singer-songwriter: "Here was this really humble kid, undiscovered, with these wonderful songs, and finely crafted songs. And I brought him out to Los Angeles to try to help him do an album, and our whole community kind of took him under our wing." The project was Fogelberg's second album. His debut release had failed to chart.

Under Walsh's guidance, Fogelberg would take a more rock-oriented approach. Fogelberg explained: "It was a perfect match, working with Joe. He got involved entirely on the basis of [my first album] *Home Free* and proved indispensable throughout. Joe allowed me my freedom in the studio, but still supplied very capable direction." Additionally, Walsh performed on ten of the album's eleven tracks.

Walsh had become comfortable in the producer's chair after closely working with Bill Szymcyck over the previous several years. As Walsh recalled: "Bill and I got very tight, probably because besides the music, I've always been very technically oriented. Bill taught me a lot and he is the reason I could produce Fogelberg. I became an apprentice and eventually his first black belt." Szymcyck remained at the sessions as an engineer until Walsh felt confident enough to work on his own.

Released in October 1974, *Souvenirs* reached the top-20. The album spawned Fogelberg's first top-40 hit, "Part Of The Plan," which featured Walsh on guitar and Graham Nash on harmony vocals. Subsequently, Fogelberg's little-noticed debut album found new interest among fans and was later certified Platinum.

*   *   *   *   *   *

In late-1974, Walsh began assembling a band for a solo tour. He hired bass player Bryan Garofalo who had replaced Passarelli in the waning moments of Barnstorm; drummer Ricky Fataar who spent some time working with the Beach Boys; and a pair of keyboardists – Paul Harris, an old friend from Walsh's tenure with the James Gang; and David Mason, who had once worked in a Florida band with a teenage Tom Petty. However, it took the newly assembled group some time to master Walsh's growing body of work, and their live performances were sometimes not up to Walsh's high standards.

▶ CHAPTER 15
THE RISE OF THE EAGLES

The Eagles emerged from the Southern California singer-songwriter tradition of the late-1960s and early-1970s, which was centered in the Laurel Canyon enclave of Los Angeles. Rooted in the American troubadour tradition, the era gave rise to the creative talents of solo artists such as Joni Mitchell, Gram Parsons and Jackson Browne as well as groups such as the Byrds, Buffalo Springfield, the Mamas and Papas and Crosby, Stills, Nash & Young.

As the most successful American musical act of the 1970s, the Eagles proved that great melodies, memorable lyrics and sharp musicianship were the keys to success and career longevity. Without having to rely on intricate stage shows, lasers, fog machines, fancy costumes or production tricks, the Eagles garnered a loyal legion of fans who consistently filled vast stadiums and purchased tens-of-millions of the group's records. The ambitious nature of the group's members also played a role in the Eagles' success.

* * * * * *

It was Bob Seger who convinced a young Glenn Frey to leave Detroit and head to the West Coast in the late-1960s. Previously, Frey had played acoustic guitar and provided background vocals on Seger's breakthrough hit, "Ramblin' Gamblin' Man." Taking Seger's advice, Frey landed in Los Angeles. As Frey later explained: "We all watched the sun set in the West during every night of adolescence and thought about some day coming out here. It all seemed so romantic... the *Life* magazine articles about Golden Gate Park and the Sunset Strip; the whole love and peace thing. And the music: the Beach Boys, Byrds, Buffalo Springfield. It was definitely the archetype of the most beautiful place in the world."

In Los Angeles, Frey met a number of like-minded musicians who were all fighting to make it in the music business. He soon formed Longbranch Pennywhistle along with his roommate, songwriter J.D. Souther. In 1969, the duo recorded an album for a tiny label, Amos

Records, which was founded by former rockabilly artist Jimmy Bowen. During this period, another struggling singer-songwriter, Jackson Browne, teamed with Frey to compose the future Eagles hit, "Take It Easy."

Frey was drawn to the bustling music scene at the Troubadour nightclub in West Hollywood. There, he met Texas native Don Henley, another transplant who had also signed with Amos Records. Henley was previously a member of a local country-rock band called Shiloh that was mentored by Kenny Rogers. Henley, who studied English and philosophy at North Texas State University, utilized his academic background when writing song lyrics and would later refer to himself as "an educated redneck." Soon after, Frey and Henley would begin a musical partnership.

In 1971, Frey and Henley were discovered by record producer and artist manager John Boylan, who hired both musicians to back singer Linda Ronstadt. Her road band was rounded out by Randy Meisner – a native of Nebraska who had been a member of Poco – and Bernie Leadon, a veteran musician who had been a member of a pair of pioneering country-rock bands, the Flying Burrito Brothers and Dillard & Clark. As an informal backing band with an often-shifting lineup, all four future members of the Eagles performed together behind Ronstadt only one time – at a show staged at Disneyland.

Meanwhile, artist manager David Geffen was beginning to make a name for himself in the music industry. In 1971, Geffen was trying to convince Atlantic Records honcho Ahmet Ertegun to sign 22-year-old singer-songwriter Jackson Browne: "I went to Ahmet again and I said, 'I'm telling you, this guy is good. I'm the guy who brought you Crosby, Stills and Nash. I'm doing you a favor.' And he said, 'You know what? Don't do me any favors.' I said, 'You'll make millions with him.' And he said, 'You know what? I got millions. Do you have millions?' I said, 'No.' He said, 'Start a record company and you'll have millions. Then we can all have millions.'"

Geffen went on to launch Asylum Records along with his business partner Elliot Roberts. Surprisingly, Ertegun provided a large chuck of the label's initial financing. After starting the company and signing Jackson Browne, Geffen had more good fortune: "As it happened, Souther and Frey were living upstairs from Jackson Brown in a duplex in Silver Lake. They were broke. Jackson Browne came to me and said, 'I want you to sign them. They're really good and they're broke. They can't pay their rent.' So, to be a hero to Jackson Browne, I signed them. I encouraged John David Souther to be a solo artist and I encouraged Glenn Frey to put a group together. Glenn would come to me with each new member, and he would say, 'Can I make a record now?' And I'd say, 'No, not good enough yet.' Finally it was, and that was the beginning of the Eagles." In addition to signing with Asylum, the Eagles were also managed by Geffen and Roberts.

Around this time, comedian Steve Martin described a discussion he had with Frey at the Troubadour: "One night I was lingering in the bar and talking to Glenn Frey, who was just leaving his duo, Longbranch Pennywhistle. He said he was considering a name for his new five-man group. 'What is it?,' I said. He said, 'Eagles.' I said, 'You mean, *the* Eagles?' And he said, 'No, Eagles.'"

However, before Geffen was able to sign the Eagles, he had to buy out Frey's contract from Amos Records, which cost a mere $5,000. Geffen then began polishing the group's image and instructed the members to start writing songs. In August 1971, the Eagles were shipped to Colorado in order to solidify their stage show. At a small club in Aspen called the Gallery, the band was billed as Teen King and the Emergencies.

Meanwhile, Frey convinced Geffen to hire Glyn Johns to produce the debut Eagles album. The following month, the band performed at a college hangout in Boulder called Tulagi. As the club's owner recalled: "About eight people came each night, but the band was brilliant. Glyn Johns would take notes, and after each show they'd go back to the bar and talk about it. It was tremendous. And they literally went to London right after that and produced their first record."

Frey was brimming with confidence at the time: "We had it all planned. We'd watched landmark country-rock bands like Poco and the Flying Burrito Brothers lose their initial momentum. We were determined not to make the same mistakes. This was going to be our best shot. Everybody had to look good, sing good, play good and write good. We wanted it all. Peer respect. AM and FM success. No. 1 singles and albums. Great music. And a lot of money."

However, the members of the group began bickering right away. As *Rolling Stone* reported: "It was hell from the start. [Bernie] Leadon and [Randy] Meisner both resented the united front of Henley and Frey but couldn't get together in their opposition. Hardly a day passed that someone wasn't sulking. They called themselves the Eagles, which pleased Frey because he thought it sounded like a street gang."

In February 1972, the Eagles arrived in chilly and damp England, far away from the endless sunshine of Southern California. At Olympic Studios, Glyn Johns barred the group from drinking or taking any kind of drugs. After the sessions, the members of the band spent their nights relaxing and having a few drinks inside a small apartment. That was the band's daily routine for the duration of the sessions.

Recorded over a two-week period, the group's debut album, *The Eagles*, was released on June 1. The first single, "Take It Easy," was issued in May 1972. With its easygoing, country-pop flavor, the song gave the Eagles their first top-40 hit. The group subsequently scored a pair of followup hits with "Witchy Woman" and "Peaceful Easy Feeling." Henley said of the Eagles' early success: "Some of it you can't explain. You can call it fate, you can call it dumb luck. But you can also give yourself credit for putting yourself in a certain place at a certain time.... We're pretty good musicians, but there's more to it than that. There's the work ethic, the perseverance, just hanging in there, going out on stage when you're sick and you don't feel like it."

Meanwhile, in early-1972, Warner Communications acquired Asylum, which was combined with Elektra Records as Elektra/Asylum. In the process, Geffen and Roberts both received $2 million in cash and $5 million in Warner stock. However, the members of the Eagles were troubled by the change in the ownership of the label. They were also unhappy about the fact that Geffen controlled the publishing rights to the group's songs, which would eventually be worth tens-of-millions of dollars. (In 1977, the Eagles would sue Geffen in an attempt to regain the copyrights and would receive an out-of-court settlement.)

In early-1973, the Eagles released *Desperado*, their first concept album. Recorded in London and produced by Glyn Johns, the album focused on themes of the old American West. Although two of the tracks became album-rock classics – the touching ballad "Desperado" and the country-tinged "Tequila Sunrise" – the project failed to spawn any top-40 hits.

Meanwhile, with Geffen and Roberts busy running Elektra/Asylum, they needed to trim the number of artists they were managing. In the summer of 1973, Irving Azoff saw an opportunity: "Geffen told the Eagles they could leave, but I don't think they anticipated I would take 'em. They were pissed." Azoff subsequently launched his own firm, Front Line Management. In addition to the Eagles and Joe Walsh, Azoff was soon overseeing the careers of Steely Dan, Boz Scaggs, Jimmy Buffett and Dan Fogelberg.

Later that year, the Eagles were in London to record their third album, *On The Border*. Unhappy with Glyn Johns' opposition to the Eagles' decision to take a more rock-oriented approach, the group wanted to hire a new producer. Frey explained the band's primary disagreement with Johns: "I didn't mind him pointing us in a certain direction. We just didn't want to make another [wimpy] L.A. country-rock record. They were all too smooth and glassy. We wanted a tougher sound." As Johns recalled: "Glenn and Don wanted a harder rock sound, and as they were not what I considered to be a rock band, I tended to hang on to what I thought was their forte, the harmony vocal sound and country-rock approach to what they were doing."

During a break in the sessions, the group visited with Walsh and listened to his Barnstorm album, *The Smoker You Drink, The Player You Get*. Impressed with the crisp, rock-oriented sound, the Eagles wanted to know who had produced the album. After flying back to Los Angeles, the Eagles requested an informal meeting with Walsh's producer, Bill Szymczyk, at a steak house next to the Record Plant.

Szymczyk recalled: "The Eagles were interviewing producers to do their *On The Border* album. I was somewhat hesitant when both Joe Walsh and Irving Azoff said to me, 'You've got to talk to the Eagles.' I didn't want to make country records; I wanted to make rock records. They said, 'Well, they want to rock!'" However, Szymczyk still needed some more convincing: "Walsh told me I should produce the Eagles and learn all about harmony. Up until then I'd only worked with single singers."

Eventually agreeing to work with the Eagles, Szymczyk recalled: "They started the third record with Glyn in London and had completed most of it when they decided to work with me. They were willing to start all over. I agreed, but on one condition: that I check with Glyn and that he was OK with it. He was one of the producers I had looked up to for a long time. I called him in London and I guess the feeling was mutual, because he said 'Better you than me, mate!'" The Eagles would release just two tracks from the sessions in London – "Best Of My Love" and "You Never Cry Like A Lover."

After joining the Eagles in the studio, Szymczyk initially produced the upbeat track, "Already Gone." He stated at the time: "Working with the Eagles was an experience, an education. It's hard working with the

Eagles in the sense that everybody is such a perfectionist." During the sessions, Szymczyk suggested that the group hire a rock-oriented session guitarist. Subsequently, Don Felder was brought in to provide some slide-guitar on the track, "A Good Day In Hell." (Felder had gone to high school with Bernie Leadon in Gainesville, Florida.)

At the session, the Eagles were impressed with Felder's guitar skills and, on the following day, asked him to join the group. Felder recalled: "I was blown away that a great band like the Eagles would ask me to join. 'This is terrific,' I was thinking, and then I got to the studio for *On The Border*. Bernie was bouncing off the wall, and Randy was threatening to quit every week. I thought, 'What have I done? I just joined a band that's breaking up!' It was like walking around with a keg of dynamite on your back with the fuse lit, but you don't know how long the fuse is." Felder became an official member of the group in January 1974.

At the completion of the sessions, Szymczyk headed to England and played a test pressing of the album for the group's former producer: "I went to Glyn's house for dinner and everything, after which we played the album. We were about eight bottles of wine into it, and I said to him, 'Well, how did I do?' and he said, 'I'm not really sure I like that.' But that was OK." However, Johns would later reflect: "They returned to America with a new manager and the intent of changing their producer. In retrospect, it was absolutely the right decision. I was standing in the way of what they wanted to achieve, and the most important role a producer has to play is to help and facilitate, not hinder, exactly that."

Released in March 1974, *On The Border* spawned three hit singles, "Already Gone," "James Dean" and the Eagles' first chart-topper, "Best Of My Love." The album reached the top-10 and would eventually sell two-million copies in the U.S. Nevertheless, none of the first three Eagles albums were exceptionally strong sellers.

▶ CHAPTER 16
BEFORE JOE JOINED

Joe Walsh had a busy and fruitful year in 1975. Now calling Los Angeles his home, Walsh was quickly embraced by the local rock community. Enjoying a sense of belonging he hadn't felt since his days in Kent, Walsh made a number of close friends. Talented, quick-witted, outgoing and not stricken with rock star arrogance, it was hard not to like him.

Hitting the road in mid-February, Walsh launched a five-week solo tour. In March, he made a triumphant return to the Kent State campus for a homecoming concert. A writer in the student newspaper declared: "Joe Walsh is coming back to Kent a bona fide star." However, Walsh told the writer: "Basically I'm the same dude." In an ad for the concert, Walsh was dressed as a Spanish conquistador – in black clothing and a wide-brimmed bolero hat.

A few days before the show, Walsh revealed: "Sometimes it feels like a million years since I've been here. Sometimes I feel very old and depressed. When I do flash back to Kent, it makes me happy." For the concert, Walsh was backed by Ricky Fataar, Bryan Garofalo and David Mason. Not surprisingly, the opening act for the hometown show was the Michael Stanley Band.

However, this was not a typical concert at Kent State's Memorial Hall. A music critic wrote: "You could tell it was a big night when you observed miles of cars crawling toward the [Kent] campus, rivaling the big Blossom Music Center traffic jams. Mobs swarmed the doors, while others who hadn't been fast enough to get tickets for this sell-out performance tried to break in the windows. It was an exceptionally aggressive concert audience and there was much pushing, shoving and shouting." Another critic reported: "Walsh appeared on stage in a white silk tuxedo and black top hat he had rented that afternoon in a Kent shop. Usually he plays in jeans, a t-shirt, just whatever he is wearing. But for Kent he wanted something special."

During his performance, Walsh revisited the tragedy of May 1970. A reviewer wrote: "Then came the song the crowd had anticipated. 'Ohio' brought back five years of memories in only five minutes of song.

It was an emotionally draining performance for everyone in the gym."

Several hours after the concert, Walsh and his bandmates barely avoided serious bodily harm when their small airplane nearly crashed shortly after takeoff. As *The Cleveland Plain Dealer* reported: "A light plane bound for Dayton, carrying the Joe Walsh rock group, nosedived at Kent State University Airport last night after trying to take off in heavy snow. None of the occupants were injured." Walsh recounted: "We were in a Twin Cessna taking off, and something went wrong and the pilot thought it was best to put it down. This was right when the runway ran out, and we just went off into the wilderness and landed on a football field."

Earlier in the day, the plane had been towed onto the runway because of the heavy snow. But during the tow, the pin holding the front wheel came off. With the wheel dropping off during takeoff, the pilot frantically attempted to return to the runway. After the plane came down, Walsh could smell fuel and smoke, and joined his bandmates as they rushed from the craft. In the aftermath, Walsh decided to remain in Kent for another two days.

On April 19, Walsh performed at the Shrine Auditorium in Los Angeles. A reviewer described the encore of the well-received show: "The audience response was incredibly receptive and when Walsh returned for a second time he brought a surprise with him. From the wings of the backstage entrance launched a colorfully adorned Elton John who joined in on an impromptu version of the Beatles' 'Get Back.'"

Meanwhile, ahead of the release of the Eagles' fourth album, *One Of These Nights*, the group went on a tour with Walsh as the opening act. Walsh also appeared onstage with the Eagles as a "special guest," which served as an informal audition. The tour began in the spring and would go into the summer. However, Bernie Leadon was hesitant about joining his bandmates on the road. Although Leadon eventually agreed to go on the tour, it was beginning to look like a foregone conclusion that he would soon be replaced by Walsh.

On May 19, the Eagles released the title track of their album, *One Of These Nights*. It became their second number-one hit. The album, which was produced by Bill Szymczyk, would spawn two more hits, "Take It To The Limit" and "Lyin' Eyes." Around this time, Eagles drummer Don Henley began dating a member of Fleetwood Mac, Stevie Nicks – who had just broken up with her bandmate, Lindsey Buckingham. Henley and

Nicks got along well and their relationship would last two-years. After their breakup, Nicks briefly dated Henley's frequent songwriting partner, J.D. Souther.

In June, Walsh and the Eagles both headed to London for a performance at Wembley Stadium that was headlined by Elton John. At the time, John was at his commercial peak with a string of chart successes. At the show, he debuted *all* the tracks from his new album, *Captain Fantastic And The Brown Dirt Cowboy*. However, another opening act, the Beach Boys, nearly stole the show. The all-day concert attracted a sell-out crowd of 72,000. According to reports, John was a fan of Walsh's music, but was uneasy around him due to his reputation as a prankster. Consequently, John tried to avoid Walsh at the concert. Walsh's performance came during the afternoon and was well received by the British audience.

After returning to the United States, Walsh hit the road for a solo tour. After a few shows, drummer Paul Harris fell ill and was replaced by Joe Vitale. During the tour, Walsh often crossed paths with the Eagles. Walsh was a surprise guest at an Eagles show in Dallas, where he performed just one song. Then at an Eagles concert on September 21 in Cincinnati, Walsh again made an appearance. After the main portion of the show, Walsh came onstage during the encore and played several of his best-known hits. And on September 28, Walsh performed for 50,000 fans at a rock festival at Anaheim Stadium, on the same bill as the Eagles, Jackson Browne and Linda Ronstadt.

A month later, Joe Walsh again opened for Elton John, this time at a pair of shows at Dodger Stadium in Los Angeles. Walsh was joined by guest guitarist Don Felder, who had backed Walsh at a number of shows earlier in the year.

* * * * * *

On November 20, Joe Walsh celebrated his 28th birthday. For the occasion, Irving Azoff bought Walsh a chain saw. It was a gift he deeply appreciated and would use on future occasions. Later, when touring as a member of the Eagles, he took it on the road just in case his hotel room needed some redecorating. However, Walsh explained: "I had a chain saw for a while. I didn't really use it but once or twice. If you have a chain saw in a hotel, you don't really need to use it. Just having it, usually you get your point across."

* * * * * *

On November 26, 1975, Joe Walsh performed at the Santa Monica Civic Auditorium. Billed as Joe Walsh & Friends, the show was filmed for an upcoming episode of *Don Kirshner's Rock Concert.* Walsh was accompanied by a large band that included Don Henley, Don Felder and Glenn Frey in what would be a preview of the new Eagles lineup. The three Eagles members demonstrated their unmatched vocal harmonies on the performance of the track, "Help Me Thru The Night."

Six of the tracks from the concert were subsequently issued on the album, *You Can't Argue With A Sick Mind.* The project was released at the height of the disco era and, as a joke, featured a mirrored disco ball on the front cover. Originally scheduled for release in January, it was delayed until March. There were two cover songs from the concert that were not included on the album – a hard rock rendition of the Beatles' "Get Back" and an extended version of the Spencer Davis Group's classic, "Gimme Some Lovin'."

The brief 35-minute album was a surprise hit that reached the top-20, and gave Walsh his first chart entry in Britain. A *Billboard* reviewer wrote: "Good live set that captures Walsh and his distinctive brand of rock 'n' roll perfectly." This was Walsh's final album for ABC Records.

* * * * * *

In December 1975, a trio of nightclubs from Joe Walsh's tenure at Kent State burned to the ground – the Kove, Pirate's Alley and the Water Street Saloon. The blaze, which was caused by a malfunctioning space heater, also destroyed the instruments belonging to two bands that were scheduled to perform – one of which included the brother of Chrissie Hynde. J.B.'s, located next door to the three clubs, was undamaged.

▶ CHAPTER 17
JOE JOINS THE EAGLES

In the aftermath of the breakup of Barnstorm, a painful divorce and the loss of his daughter, Joe Walsh needed a sense of stability and routine in his life. Additionally, he was not happy being the leader of a band. Walsh had grown weary of the time-consuming responsibilities of hiring and firing musicians, managing a payroll, writing music and organizing recording sessions. Instead, he wanted to be part of a group – preferably an established act that had already achieved some level of success, and the Eagles fit the bill.

However, a number of Eagles insiders were concerned that Walsh might be a poor fit due to his unpredictable nature. In particular, Don Henley feared that Walsh's strong personality might cause additional conflicts within the band: "When we brought Joe in he definitely helped the band. But I think Joe had the attitude that *he* was doing *us* a favor. In fact, his career was in really bad shape at the time. He wasn't getting anywhere. It was a shot in the arm for his career, certainly, and he was a little reluctant about it. I think he was almost ashamed of it for a while; I think he would make excuses for it. Then later on he became a little more gracious about it, but he always kept his little corner, his career, separate."

Similarly, producer Bill Scymczyk initially thought it was a terrible idea to add Walsh to the group, but he would eventually change his mind: "I had very little to do with it, and as a matter of fact, I was not a great fan of the move." Conversely, Walsh's biggest cheerleader in the Eagles was Glenn Frey, who welcomed another skilled guitarist to the band: "We knew a year before Bernie left that Joe was gonna replace him.... We checked around. And there was only one guitar player for the Eagles."

* * * * * *

By 1975, Bernie Leadon had grown increasingly disillusioned with the Eagles' musical transformation away from country-rock and toward mainstream rock. Leadon was also unhappy with his shrinking role in the group's decision-making process. Constantly battling the united front of Frey and Henley, Leadon felt like the odd man out in his own group. Leadon had another complaint: "I kept asking: 'Are we going to rest next month?' I wanted to get in shape before the age of thirty so I would have a chance at the rest of my life. I was afraid something inside of me was dying."

As tensions increased, Leadon threatened to leave the band at the end of the *One Of These Nights* tour. However, before Leadon was able to quit, he was fired. On December 12, 1975, Eagles manager Irving Azoff announced that Leadon had left the Eagles and would be replaced by Joe Walsh. Azoff blamed Leadon's departure on his dislike of touring. Leadon was the last original member of the Eagles to join the band and the first to leave.

When Azoff had first approached Walsh about joining the Eagles, he was very open to the idea. As the manager of both Walsh and the Eagles, Azoff realized it was the perfect solution should Leadon ever leave the band. And when that actually happened, the vacancy needed to be quickly filled. Walsh had been at the top of the replacement list because of his talent as a musician, history of success, lack of ego and easygoing demeanor.

As a natural-born showman with a strong stage presence, Walsh also brought a new visual element to the group's live performances. Additionally, he would bring something else to the Eagles – a sense of humor. Walsh recalled: "Those guys were about as much fun as Henry Kissinger when I first joined. I gave them a rock 'n' roll mentality – loosened them up, got them partying and laughing." Randy Meisner explained: "In some ways we were a little too stiff on stage. We just stood there on stage and didn't do a lot of dancing, not much entertaining. We thought, 'Our music is the entertainment. We don't want to show off.' Playing our music was the most important thing.... We all wanted to be kind of low-profile anyway."

Walsh viewed his membership in the Eagles as a solid financial move. However, despite the fact that he was now an official member of the group, he was not considered a full partner. A year earlier, the members of the group had organized as a formal company, Eagles Ltd., with the articles of incorporation filed in the State of California. All four original members, as well as new arrival Don Felder, were given an equal share of the company. During the lifetime of the Eagles, no additional members were added to the corporation. Consequently, when

Walsh was hired, he had limited rights within the group.

However, Walsh accepted the fact that he was a newcomer in a successful, established band: "I joined their band. They call the shots, that was the agreement when I came in, and it's the way it always will be. It's best when the four of us are all nodding yeah, or it's three against one, and the one guy is saying, 'Well, ya know.' But ultimately it's Glenn and Don's band. It's a democracy with two dictators." Additionally, Walsh reached an agreement that allowed him to continue his solo career while with the Eagles. And with the group's propensity for excessive revelry, Walsh certainly fit right in with his new bandmates.

*   *   *   *   *   *

The Eagles earned a reputation as workhorses on the concert road. That's where they made the bulk of their earnings. The band had a large, loyal following that would fill large concert halls and stadiums. Barry Fey, an influential concert promoter, stated: "There were two groups that always sold out for me. Never an unsold ticket. The Stones and the Eagles."

Joe Walsh was hired ahead of an Eagles tour of the Far East – Australia, New Zealand and Japan – which launched on January 22, 1976, at the Hordern Pavilion in Sydney. The group performed two of Walsh's songs that night, "Rocky Mountain Way" and "Turn To Stone." However, Walsh was not happy with some of the early performances: "We went to Australia. Boy, did we stink. It took awhile to get it going on stage. I had to learn Bernie's part on 30 songs and my singing part." Walsh quickly realized that performing as a member of the Eagles was a far different matter than playing with his previous groups: "The Eagles is a certain chemistry and a certain formula, and everybody has assignments and parts to play and vocal parts that need to be sung to make it work. So that's paying attention to definite pre-existing parts. We don't have as much room to improvise." Walsh eventually found his groove, and his musical contributions were beneficial to the group's overall sound.

Returning to the United States, the reconstituted Eagles made their Los Angeles debut at a three-show residency at the Forum in October 1976. While his bandmates were leisurely dressed, Walsh took the stage in a plaid flannel shirt and floppy hat. As music critic Robert Hilburn observed: "Though Walsh's guitar work, particularly on four of his own songs, gave the band a slightly harder rock focus, the Eagles' sound remains tied to the somewhat laid-back country-tinged, lyric-conscious music style that is – through the work of the Eagles, Jackson Browne and Linda Ronstadt – currently linked to this city." However, a reviewer at *Billboard* magazine declared: "In Joe Walsh, replacing Bernie Leadon, has plugged the group's only possible weak spot."

Despite touring with the Eagles, Walsh still found the time to work as a session player. During this period, he appeared on J.D. Souther's solo album, *Black Rose*, as well as on albums by Bill Wyman and Rod Stewart. While backing Stewart, Walsh was joined by a number of hard hitters such as Jeff Beck and Ronnie Wood.

▶ CHAPTER 18
HOTEL CALIFORNIA

The 1970s was the era of arena rock. A number of blockbuster albums were released during the middle of the decade, beginning with *Dark Side Of The Moon* and continuing with *Led Zeppelin IV*, *Frampton Comes Alive*, *Rumours*, *Boston*, *Bat Out Of Hell* and, of course, *Hotel California*.

Fondly recalling his contributions to *Hotel California*, Joe Walsh told *Musician* magazine, "[The] thing I'm proudest about was to be in the Eagles and have a power base to make a valid artistic statement for the generation I represent. It was a special album for a lot of people, including me, to be able to affect that many people on the planet and to feel that album was good enough to justify being rich."

Like its predecessors, the album was produced by Bill Szymczyk. Although the band wanted to record the project at the Record Plant in Los Angeles, Szymczyk wanted to work at Criteria Studios in Miami. In the end, a compromise was reached and the sessions were split between the two studios. J.D. Souther, who co-wrote a number of the album's songs, was a frequent guest in the studio. He also spent many hours at the homes of Frey or Henley, hashing out lyrics. And notably, this was the first Eagles album without Bernie Leadon and the last to include Randy Meisner.

The Eagles began recording *Hotel California* in Studio B at the Record Plant. Next door in Studio C, Lynyrd Skynyrd were working on their album, *Second Helping*. In describing the studio, Lynyrd Skynyrd's producer Al Kooper stated: "Chris Stone, a businessman, and Gary Kellegren, an engineer and idea man, had opened a studio in New York that had become very successful. They took their winnings and moved to Los Angeles, where they opened a studio like no other that had ever existed. Previously, studios were kinda antiseptic and dentist-officey. But the Record Plant's design was futuristic and rustic all at once.... Rock stars immediately flocked to a place that had a jacuzzi, three bedrooms, *and* the finest studios in Los Angeles. The personnel that staffed the place were trained to accommodate every whim of every client. It was literally like ancient Rome in its heyday."

After taking a break to compose some additional material, the Eagles moved the sessions to Florida. But there was an unusual problem at Criteria studios when the group was finishing Don Henley's touching ballad, "The Last Resort," the final track on *Hotel California*. As Tony Iommi of Black Sabbath recalled: "The Eagles were recording next door, but we were too loud for them – it kept coming through the wall into their sessions."

As the newest member, Walsh was permitted to contribute just one solo composition to the album, the ballad "Pretty Maids All In A Row," which he began writing during his Barnstorm days. Needing help to finish the song, Walsh elicited the aid of Joe Vitale. The completed song was recorded with Walsh on vocals, piano and synthesizer. It was Walsh's only lead vocal on the entire album. Years later, when Bob Dylan was asked to name his favorite Eagles songs, he told *The New York Times* that "'Pretty Maids In A Row'... could be one of the best songs ever."

Another track, "Life In The Fast Lane," was co-written by Walsh, Henley and Frey. Walsh revealed the origin of the song's memorable opening riff: "I had this lick that I played that I would warm up for a show with. And it's a coordination exercise between your right and left hand.... And I used to do that – go faster and faster." Before a band rehearsal, an excited Glenn Frey approached Walsh and demanded to know what he was playing. Frey recognized the riff's hit potential and would expand it into a full-length song. Don Henley said of the song: "This business makes it easy for you to destroy yourself.... We wrote 'Life In The Fast Lane' as a warning. We saw a lot of friends killing themselves. The sad thing is many people look at the song as an anthem. They think we're condoning people going out and screwing up their lives." The title of the song came from a conversation Frey had with a drug dealer during a high-speed ride in a Corvette.

Another track, the somber "New Kid In Town," featured Frey on lead vocals and Henley on harmony backing vocals. Walsh recalled: "I played keyboards on 'New Kid In Town' because I was the only guy who could play in [the key of] B, with all the weird fingerings and black keys."

Another track, "Victim Of Love," was essentially a live recording in the studio. Felder wanted a greater role in the band and insisted on singing the lead vocals. However, Henley and Frey were not happy with Felder's delivery. So when Felder was out for the evening, dining with manager Irving Azoff, Henley and Frey unceremoniously erased Felder's voice from the track. The final version featured Henley providing the lead vocals.

*   *   *   *   *   *

The highlight of the album was the title track "Hotel California," which became the group's iconic, signature song. Although no one in the Eagles was actually born in the Golden State, the five-transplants helped to define the Southern California lifestyle. Don Felder came up with the basis of the track in either in 1974 or '75. Under the working title, "Mexican Bolero" (later "Mexican Reggae"), the song was far different from anything the group had previously recorded. Growing up in Florida, Felder had frequently performed in the nightclubs of Miami, where he was exposed to a wide variety of Latin-style dance music.

Felder came up with the song while sitting on a couch in a rented beach house in Malibu. Glancing out the window at the sandy beach and the summer sun reflecting off the Pacific Ocean, Felder began fiddling with a unique chord progression. Playing a 12-string guitar, he recorded the melody onto a 4-track, reel-to-reel tape recorder. He then added percussion and bass, and wrote a chorus. He then composed two guitar parts for the end of the song. Felder subsequently transferred the demo onto a cassette along with more than a dozen other song ideas, and gave copies to Don Henley and Glenn Frey. It was Henley who initially recognized the song's hit potential.

The track begins with Felder playing an acoustic, 12-string Takamine guitar. Then Henley comes in on lead vocal. For the closing guitar duel between Walsh and Felder, Henley demanded that the two men play the original melody from Felder's demo tape. Not remembering how it went, Felder called home and had his wife play the cassette over the phone. Felder and Walsh would then spend two-days in the studio, painstakingly constructing the final portion of the song, note by note. Felder begins the closing solo with his '59 Les Paul and then Walsh comes in with his Fender Telecaster. Walsh recalled: "So we sat down in the control room, pretty intense, and went at it: 'OK, you do this.' 'No, no, no, I gotta do this.' Don and I were competitive, we always tried to one-up each other, and we did that in 'Hotel California,' except at the end we decided to team up, 'cause that way nobody would win. Yeah, it was a tie. Maybe everybody won." Despite his input, Walsh did not receive writing credit on the song.

Then after completing the final arrangement of the song, the Eagles recorded three distinctly different versions – the first two in Los Angeles and the last in Miami. The first version was considered too fast. The second version had a slower tempo, but Henley was forced to sing in a falsetto and sounded much like Barry Gibb of the Bee Gees. At that point, Felder decided to change the key of the song. Finally, the third and final version of "Hotel California" had a special magic.

* * * * * *

In October 1976, just as the Eagles were adding the final touches to *Hotel California*, Walsh made an unexpected musical contribution. He provided some guitarwork on two tracks by 18-year-old singer Andy Gibb. Both songs – "I Just Want To Be Your Everything" and "(Love Is) Thicker Than Water" – would reach number-one on the pop charts. Gibb was working in an adjacent studio at Criteria, where he was aided on the sessions by his older brothers in the Bee Gees.

▶ CHAPTER 19
CHECKING OUT OF THE HOTEL

Bill Szymczyk and the Eagles knew that *Hotel California* was going to be a big hit – far bigger than any of the group's previous albums. The much-revered album would sell more than 26-million copies in the U.S. alone. In fact, between the two albums, *Hotel California* and *Their Greatest Hits*, the Eagles were selling millions of records *every* month in 1977. Additionally, the Walsh/Felder guitar duel on "Hotel California" was later voted the eighth best guitar solo in rock history by the readers of *Guitar* magazine.

Critics were nearly universal in their praise of the project. A reviewer for *Melody Maker* wrote: "This album will sell by the ton, you can be sure of that. It's got the smooth refinement you always associate with the Eagles and makes it unequivocally Broad Appeal material; yet there's also a bit more aggression and raunchiness this time, so as not to alienate the hard rock fraternity too much."

To be sure, not every review was as positive. There were three "featured" album reviews in *Rolling Stone* magazine when *Hotel California* was reviewed, and the new Eagles album wasn't one of the three. A critic at the magazine wrote: "Walsh's exact effect isn't always obvious, but this record does have subtleties and edges that have sometimes eluded the group." The semi-snub by *Rolling Stone* was hardly a surprise. The previous year, the magazine was embroiled in an odd exchange of insults with the Eagles, which culminated in a much-publicized, charity softball game between the band and *Rolling Stone* staff.

The front cover of the album was designed by British art director John Kosh (known professionally as "Kosh") and featured an eerie photo of the Beverly Hills Hotel taken at sunset. A legend in his field, Kosh had designed some of the best-known covers in rock and roll including *Abbey Road* by the Beatles, *Get Yer Ya-Ya's Out!* by the Rolling Stones and *Who's Next* by the Who.

The songs on *Hotel California* became embedded in American popular culture. Henley later stated: "I was a little disappointed with how the record was taken, because I meant it in a much broader sense than a commentary about California. I was looking at American culture, and when I called that one song 'Hotel California,' I was simply using California as a microcosm for the rest of America and for the self-indulgence of our entire culture. It was, to a certain extent, about California, about the excesses out here. But in many instances, as California goes, so goes the nation. Things simply happen out here or in New York first whether it's with drugs or fashion or artistic movements or economic trends and then work their way toward the middle of America. And that's what I was trying to get at. With that record, we reached some sort of creative peak, as all bands do. You can go back and trace any band's career and find that one album that was the zenith of their productivity. That was ours, and we knew it." Walsh added: "Nobody was from California. Everybody was from Ohio or Michigan or Texas. And so, California at that time was this big hotel, this big melting pot of people with talent, trying to fit in. And that's what we meant about California at the time."

At a listening party for Warner Brothers, Don Henley announced that "Hotel California" would be the first single from the project. However, the panicked executives were uneasy about Henley's proclamation, as were a few of his own bandmates. Instead, the album's first single was the melancholy ballad, "New Kid In Town," which was released on December 7, 1976. Embraced by top-40 radio, it would become the group's third number-one single in the U.S. and the first by the group to be certified Gold by the RIAA.

On February 22, 1977, "Hotel California" was issued as the album's second single. Like its predecessor, it also reached number-one on the charts. The single's B-side was the Walsh/Vitale composition, "Pretty Maids All In A Row." Amazingly, the single spent just one-week in the top spot before being knocked out of the position by pop singer Leo Sayer.

Not a pop song in the traditional sense, "Hotel California" had eight distinct parts. And at six-and-a-half-minutes in length, it was considered too long for top-40 radio. Additionally, it was not a dance song and it featured a two-minute guitar solo at the end. Consequently, the band's label initially wanted a shorter, edited version. However, Henley stood his ground and refused to alter the song.

The album's third and final single, "Life In The Fast Lane," just barely missed reaching the top-10. And despite the heavy airplay on album-rock radio of the tracks, "Victim Of Love" and "The Last Resort," no additional singles were released from the album.

* * * * * *

The Eagles went on a lengthy tour in support of *Hotel California*. However, audiences were surprised by the group's decision to open concerts with the album's massively popular title track. The tour began in March 1977 with a pair of shows at the Richfield Coliseum near Cleveland. Bill Szymczyk observed that whenever the Eagles performed in Northeastern Ohio, "you might as well bill it as Joe Walsh and the Eagles, because in Cleveland, he's still bigger than the Eagles." Wearing a Kent State shirt, Walsh shimmied across the stage, performing a Chuck Berry-style duck walk. A reviewer at the concert wrote: "Walsh would be worth watching if you were stone cold deaf. He's Mr. Expression. He wrinkles his forehead, squints, twists his chin and expends as much effort as you would if you tried to lift the front end of a Volkswagen." Don Henley, however, was not always a fan of Walsh's stage antics and would sometimes criticize him after the shows.

On April 17, the Eagles began a 17-date tour of Europe, stopping in five countries. For some of the shows, Dan Fogelberg was the opening act. The Eagles began the tour with a four-day stretch of sold-out concerts at Wembley's Empire Pool in London. Audiences were pleasantly surprised when a 40-piece string section was revealed at the rear of the stage at the start of "Take It To The Limit." A reviewer from *Record Mirror* said of the first London show: "[There's] neon Hotel California signs either side of the stage. The back stop rises slowly to reveal a red California sunset, palm trees in silhouette against the skyline. Roars of applause for the scene, and more so [as] the Eagles slip into the opening chords of 'Hotel California.'" The critic also referred to Walsh as "a dominant member of the band." At the final London show, special guest Elton John joined the Eagles for a cover of the Chuck Berry standard, "Carol." After the concert, the members of the Eagles were presented with both Silver and Gold awards for their albums, *Hotel California* and *Their Greatest Hits*. At a post-concert party, Walsh was met by his old friends, Pete Townshend and John Entwistle.

At a show in Glasgow, Scotland, Walsh was dressed in full Scottish regalia – including a plaid kilt. Playing the bagpipes, he performed the traditional song, "Bonnie Galloway," which had taken him two-days to learn. A reviewer wrote: "The decision to include Walsh has been totally vindicated. The former James Gang leader's solos were dazzling and the interplay with the other lead player, Don Felder, was one of the many high points of the show." The group continued onto Germany and the Netherlands. Ironically, the last time the Eagles had performed in the Netherlands was 1975, when their opening act was Joe Walsh. The group finished the European tour in Sweden, where the first show was staged at an amusement park.

Returning to the U.S. in mid-May, the Eagles began another leg of the Hotel California tour with two shows in Oakland. However, on June 28, there was a troubling incident during a concert in Knoxville. Randy Meisner told Eagles biographer Marc Eliot: "We've been out for a total of eleven months, and everybody was starting to feel the strain. My ulcer was starting to act up, and [I had] a bad case of the flu as well. Still, we all sounded great onstage, the audience loved the show, and we were being called back for another encore. 'No way,' I said. I was too sick, and generally fed up. I decided I wasn't going back out." After Meisner refused to return to the stage, he got into a brief altercation with Glenn Frey, which was quickly broken up by the backstage security staff.

On September 3, after the end of the summer leg of the Hotel California tour, Meisner departed from the Eagles. As he later explained: "When the tour ended, I left the band. Those last days on the road were the worst. Nobody was talking to me, or would hang out after shows, or do anything. I was made an outcast of the band I'd helped start." At the time of his departure, Meisner was unhappy with the strains of touring, suffered from numerous health issues and wanted to spend more time with his wife.

Meisner later revealed: "I'd been singing mostly background my whole life. And I figured I was missing something by not singing out more. Listening to Don and Glenn, I knew I could do just as well or better. That's the point when I started thinking about quitting the Eagles. I was 31 – a time in your life when you want to make a decision if you want to really go for something. I wasn't going to wait until I was 40."

Meisner was replaced by Timothy B. Schmit, who had previously replaced Meisner in Poco back in 1969. Born in Oakland, Schmit was the first California native to join the Eagles. With Meisner's departure, the Eagles retired "Take It To The Limit" from their live repertoire for a number of years.

* * * * * *

In 1977, Joe Walsh discovered a new hobby – boating. He named his craft, *The So What.* However, Walsh had no idea how to navigate the large vessel: "I had a forty-one-foot sailboat and I lived in Santa Barbara, California, and I was in the Eagles. We came off a tour and I was on my boat, wishing I knew how to sail it or how it worked.... I had heard from Jimmy Buffett that David Crosby was one of the finest sailboat captains. Humbly, I walked over to his boat, met his crew, and later that day, while I was sitting on my boat, David stopped by and introduced himself, looked at my boat, hung out, and said, 'We should go sailing sometime.' A year later, in 1978, David was in the harbor again with his boat, found me, and invited me to go sailing for about a week so he could teach me how. I said, 'Okay.' Boy, did he teach me how." Crosby took Walsh under his wing and the two men sailed to a number of destinations including the Channel Islands and a place Walsh would come to love, Catalina Island. The sparsely populated island, which was situated twenty-miles off the coast of Southern California, became one of Walsh's favorite spots to unwind.

Also that year, Walsh provided some guitarwork on Jay Ferguson's hit album *Thunder Island.* He also worked on albums by Dan Fogelberg and Emerson, Lake & Palmer. Additionally, the Eagles – minus Don Felder – backed Randy Newman on his album, *Little Criminals*, which spawned the top-10 novelty hit, "Short People."

* * * * * *

The 20th annual Grammy Awards were held on February 21, 1978. The ceremony was staged at the Shrine Auditorium in Los Angeles and was hosted by singer John Denver. The Eagles were nominated in four categories. Previously, the group had won just one Grammy, two years earlier, for the single "Lyin' Eyes."

Sensing an opportunity to promote the Eagles, manager Irving Azoff wanted to make a deal with the producer of the award show. As Henry Schipper wrote in *Broken Record*, an insider account of the Grammys, "The talent lineup for the... Grammy show was unusually bland, with Debby Boone, Ronnie Milsap, Crystal Gayle, Shaun Cassidy, Dancing Machine, and John Denver representing the pop field. [The program's executive producer] Pierre Cossette needed at least one hot group for the show. The Bee Gees, Fleetwood Mac, and the Eagles had all been nominated for major awards, but neither the Bee Gees nor Fleetwood Mac would perform. The Eagles, who lived in Malibu, a short limo ride from the Shrine, were Cossette's last hope. Eagles manager Irving Azoff told Cossette the group would be happy to perform, only on one condition: that Cosette guarantee in advance that they'd won. 'I know you, Pierre. There's no way you don't know, and you gotta tell me,' Azoff insisted, according to Cossette. 'I can't put 'em up there and have them lose.' 'Irving,' Cossette protested, 'I can't tell you, because I don't know.' 'You know what?,' Azoff returned. 'I'm gonna keep them in Malibu.'"

In the end, Azoff tried to reach a compromise – if the Eagles won an award, they would play. However, according to Schipper, Azoff later contacted Cossette and stated that the Eagles "would perform after all, without a Grammy guarantee.... But Azoff, notorious for his tough and sometimes punitive managerial style, was apparently stringing Cossette along. The Eagles never showed." In the end, the Eagles won two prizes that night – Record Of The Year for the single "Hotel California" and Best Arrangement For Voices for the track "New Kid In Town." Instead of the Eagles standing at the podium and proudly accepting their prizes, pop singer Andy Williams accepted the awards on behalf of the group.

Afterward, Azoff was livid and still doubted Cossette's claim that he was unaware that the Eagles would win two Grammys. Meanwhile, without knowing the backstory of what had conspired behind the scenes, the music press reported that the Eagles had snubbed the event. However, Don Henley offered a humble explanation for the group's absence: "We thought the competition was too tough. We didn't expect to win it."

▶ CHAPTER 20
THE LONG RUN

After the spectacular success of *Hotel California*, the Eagles were heavily pressured by Warner Brothers to record a very similar album. Walsh recalled: "It made us paranoid. People started asking us, 'What are you going to do now?' and we didn't know.... We lost perspective. We kinda sat around in a daze for three months. The only thing that we had going for us was our trust in each other."

The sessions started with a goal of recording a double-album. Initially armed with twenty unfinished songs, the group first recorded the backing musical tracks before writing any lyrics. Glenn Frey explained: "Don and I did not have any fun working on *The Long Run* together. Henley and I would sit across from each other for hours not saying a word. We would sit trying to write, but we were both afraid to suggest a lyric or chord in case it wasn't perfect – in case it wasn't great." Walsh added: "The thing that eventually became an incredible burden for the Eagles was trying to figure out what kind of intellectual statement you're gonna make about something. I was trying to get 180 degrees away from dwelling on anything, and just make music that would speak for itself."

The sessions for *The Long Run* began in March 1978 and continued, on and off, for the next eighteen-months. The group worked at multiple studios in Los Angeles before eventually heading to Bill Szymczyk's newly built Bayshore studio in Miami. By this point, Szymczyk had become an integral part of the Eagles and was a close confidant of the group's members. As Henley later stated: "He's a wonderful guy. He's sort of a father to all of us – he was a mediator, a psychiatrist, a counselor. And there's a careful quality about him. But then that's why we hired him in the first place."

Taking a break from the recording sessions, the Eagles began a short tour of the U.S. and Canada, starting with a date at the Coliseum in Edmonton in July 1978. At a stop in Cincinnati, a reviewer wrote: "As one fifth of the Eagles, Walsh is supposed to have equal billing with Glenn Frey, Don Felder, Don Henley, and the newest Eagle, former Poco bass guitarist, Timothy Schmit. This is what is supposed to be. But it was not the case Wednesday night. On the stadium's stage it wasn't *The*

Eagles. It was the Eagles starring Joe Walsh.... After only two-and-a-half years with the group, Walsh has thoroughly revitalized the Eagles." The tour ended on August 29 in Miami.

* * * * * *

The Eagles quickly finished the album's first track, "I Can't Tell You Why," a ballad that featured Timothy B. Schmit on lead vocals. But after that, the sessions dragged on for months. The band's record company constantly nagged Irving Azoff for updates on the album's expected completion date. He stated at the time: "We only hear from them about ten times a month. When they project a $116 million year [profit] because Linda Ronstadt and the Eagles are going to release albums, and then come up $40 million short from not having an Eagles album, they hurt." Similarly, Joe Walsh stated: "We couldn't even show up at each other's houses to jam or even sing old Beatles songs without the record company getting wind of it. It got to the point where we would burp, fart or pick our noses, and they'd say, 'That's fine, let's ship it, because as long as you guys have a record out, we can put new speakers in our wives' BMWs.'"

Eventually, the Eagles recorded a Christmas single in 1978 to placate their label until the much-delayed album was finished. The group released the bittersweet ballad, "Please Come Home For Christmas," which was originally recorded by blues crooner Charles Brown in 1960. The single gave the Eagles a top-20 hit and became an instant holiday classic. For the B-side, the group recorded "Funky New Year," which was an original song written by Don Henley and Glenn Frey. The two tracks were recorded in just one-week.

After a full year of struggling in the studio, the group abandoned the notion of a double-album and instead focused on recording a single disc. Several unfinished songs were simply shelved, despite their hit potential. One of the songs that didn't make it onto the album was titled, "You're Really High, Aren't You?" The title came from a conversation Walsh had with one of his bandmates.

Some of the album's songs were written as a reaction to the rise of disco during the late-1970s. One track, "The Long Run," was intended as a statement that the group's music was more timeless than the disco craze. Another track, "The Disco Strangler," was intended as a commentary on the shallow nature of the nightclub scene. But while the group's songs may have been timeless, the Eagles' tenure as a band was about to end.

Another track, "Heartache Tonight," was a mid-tempo rocker written by Henley, Frey, J.D. Souther and Bob Seger. While Frey provided the lead vocals, Walsh played the slide guitar. And the track, "Those Shoes," featured Walsh and Don Felder on dueling talk boxes. Meanwhile, the track, "The Greeks Don't Want No Freaks," was a tribute to the great garage-rock classics of the mid-1960s. The song was inspired by Henley's memories of playing at fraternity parties in Texas during his teen years.

Another track, "In The City," was originally recorded as a Joe Walsh solo track for the movie, *The Warriors*. The film's music score was supervised by Barry De Vorzon, who was best known for producing the Chicago-based pop-rock group, the Association: "Joe and I were friends and I just saw an opportunity to work with him. And plus, I thought it'd be great to have Joe Walsh sing the end title. So I said, 'Hey, Joe! Would you consider singing the end title and we'll write a song together?' And he said, 'Great!'"

At a studio in New York City, Walsh and Joe Vitale were shown clips of the unfinished film, and then sat down to write a song. Walsh recalled that the film "was made about gang-type city situations, and I related to that, having grown up in New York City. It was a positive statement to go against the desperation of miles and miles of concrete and growing up in a city." After the track was finished, De Vorzon recalled: "So I brought ['In the City'] to the studio and the producers, and of course they were very happy." However, after Henley and Frey heard the finished track, they convinced Walsh to record a new version of the song with the Eagles for inclusion on *The Long Run*.

Meanwhile, with Walsh and Felder spending so much time at Bayshore in Miami, they decided to rent a house together, about 15-miles away on the luxury island of Key Biscayne.

▶ CHAPTER 21
BUT SERIOUSLY FOLKS

Taking advantage of a two-month break, Joe Walsh found the time to record a solo album. For the project, Walsh hired bassist Willie Weeks, singer-keyboardist Jay Ferguson and drummer Joe Vitale, who had just finished backing Peter Frampton on a world tour. Before entering the studio, producer Bill Szymczyk wanted the band to first practice the songs at a cabin he owned in North Carolina. But a major snowstorm thwarted the plan.

Instead, Walsh and his band rehearsed the songs on a 72-foot yacht named *The Endless Seas*. Departing from its base in Coconut Grove, the ship sailed down to Plantation Harbor in the central Florida Keys. Szymczyk recalled: "We spent a week down in the Keys hashing those tunes out. Pretty much everything on the album we rehearsed on that boat." While Walsh and his bandmates practiced the songs in the craft's spacious 30-foot-long main room, Szymczyk sat in front of a basic four-track recorder on the boat's deck and observed the sessions through a port hole. In the evenings, the band gathered to listen to the tapes.

Not surprisingly, the other four members of the Eagles all contributed to the album. While Glenn Frey, Don Henley and Timothy B. Schmit provided backing harmony vocals on "Tomorrow," Don Felder played a pedal steel guitar on "Second Hand Store." On another track, "At The Station," Walsh and Felder traded guitar licks, much like on "Hotel California."

The album's biggest hit, "Life's Been Good," humorously chronicled the life of a rock star. However, the song almost didn't make it onto the album. As Szymczyk recalled: "We got back to my studio, which by this point was set up at Bayshore in Miami. All the way through making this record, [Walsh] was hesitant about putting this song out, because he thought the public would take it the wrong way lyrically. I was the one who was just on him constantly, saying, 'No.' At one point he wasn't even going to finish it. I told him, 'You must finish this. This is a killer record!' Finally he agreed, and the rest is history. I did change a couple of melody lines in it, so it made it easier for him to sing and gave it a more lighthearted feeling."

After the song was completed, Walsh was still unsure about how fans would react: "I never thought that would be a hit record. I had to argue with Bill Szymczyk because I didn't particularly think it was... as funny as everybody else did. I think it might have been a little *too* close to the truth, and I didn't want to overextend my sense of humor with the public." Later, Walsh explained that the song was a lampoon of stardom and "a satirical statement on the lifestyle people in my position lead. I was trying to describe the shallowness of what everybody thought was cool. Everyone missed the point, though. They said, 'Joe, do you really have a Maserati?'"

On the flip-side of the single, "Life's Been Good," was the track, "Theme From Boat Weirdos." The title was a reference to an insult – "Boat Weirdos" – that Walsh and his fellow musicians endured from other boaters while docked at Plantation Harbor. On another track, "Indian Summer," Walsh reminisced about his carefree childhood in Columbus.

The album, *But Seriously, Folks,* was released in May 1978. On the front cover, Walsh was photographed, while underwater, as a number of picnic-related items floated all around him. The photo was taken in the swimming pool at the Coconut Grove Hotel in Miami. An air tank that allowed Walsh to breathe was airbrushed out of the photo.

But Seriously, Folks became Walsh's second top-10 solo entry and his first to reach Platinum status, as many buyers pondered whether it was actually a new Eagles album. Additionally, "Life's Been Good" became Walsh's highest-charting solo single. While the album version clocked in at 8:04, the single version was edited down to 4:35.

Meanwhile, Walsh also found the time to help Joe Vitale with his second solo album, *Plantation Harbor.* It was Vitale's only album to reach the *Billboard* charts. The project also featured musical contributions by two other members of the Eagles, Don Felder and Timothy B. Schmit.

* * * * * *

In 1979, Joe Walsh announced he was running for president in open letters to *Time, Newsweek, Rolling Stone* and *Field and Stream*. Just 32-years-old at the time, Walsh was actually ineligible for the office – he needed to be at least 35. Walsh promoted his pseudo-presidential run with the platform "free gas for everyone." He also promised to make

"Life's Been Good" the new national anthem. In the process, he managed to register 100,000 new voters.

Walsh explained the origin of his campaign: "I was on stage one day and before I knew it, I had announced that I ought to be president and everybody in the audience seemed to think it was a good idea." Although intended as a gag, Walsh was surprised when fans began showing up at concerts wearing "Joe Walsh for President" shirts and hats. And ironically, Bernie Leadon, who was replaced by Walsh in the Eagles, had previously dated Patti Davis, the daughter of future president Ronald Reagan.

CHAPTER 22
RELEASING THE LONG RUN

After numerous starts and stops, the Eagles finally completed *The Long Run*. Asylum Records rush-released the album on September 24, just in time for the Christmas shopping season. *The Long Run* debuted at number-two and reached the top spot the following week, where it remained for nine-weeks. The album's debut single, "Heartache Tonight," was the group's final number-one hit and would later earn a Grammy. Two followup singles – "The Long Run" and "I Can't Tell You Why" – both reached the top-10.

However, reviews for the album were mixed. Charles M. Young, a writer for *Rolling Stone*, described his initial reaction: "Toward the end of August 1978, the Eagles told me that *The Long Run* was complete, so I flew to Miami for a listening party at the studio. Then I sat there for a week while the Eagles completed it some more. Henley, Frey and producer Bill Szymczyk hassled all night about the length of silence between songs while their friends in the lounge went mad with boredom. When they finally played the album at 5:46 a.m. the next day, I so wanted it to be a masterpiece that I couldn't hear that it wasn't. In retrospect, it was only pretty good. It wasn't inspired, and there was no amount of hard work that could make it inspired. *The Long Run* was the least of their six original albums. The Eagles were burned out."

Notable music critic Timothy White wrote: "On first listening *The Long Run* seems a modest, flawed project that's virtually devoid of the gloss, catchy hooks and flashy invention that typified earlier Eagles records. The title tune sets an unambitious tone: the group lopes along in a familiar country-rock framework, singing about youthful hopes and the virtues of tenacity.... Not a collection of hot car-radio singles, *The Long Run* is easily the band's most *un*commercial effort." Additionally, White referred to Walsh's track "In The City" as "a brittle but forceful rocker."

Robert Hilburn of *The Los Angeles Times* wrote: "*The Long Run* is a finely crafted album but it doesn't have the dramatic focus or consistency of *Hotel California*.... The Eagles have often gotten a bum rap from critics who complain that the band's music reflects too much of the leisurely pace and opulent lifestyle associated with Southern California. The truth is the Eagles weave more tension and viewpoint in their songs than almost any other major American rock group."

Meanwhile, just two-weeks later, another superstar rock act also released a followup to a smash album. But unlike the Eagles, the members of Fleetwood Mac purposely ignored calls from their label to follow *Rumours* with a similar, hook-filled, pop-friendly project. Instead, *Tusk* was considered an experimental effort and viewed as a relative failure after selling two-million copies in the U.S.

* * * * * *

The U.S. leg of the Long Run Tour began on October 8, 1979. The Eagles asked Joe Vitale to join the tour as the second drummer. Vitale recalled: "I couldn't possibly figure out how I could play in the Eagles. When they called, I said, 'What do you need me for?' I mean, Henley can hold his own. He's a fine drummer and an incredible singer and to do both, impresses the hell out of me. That's hard to do. But they said that about half the tunes needed keyboard parts and percussion stuff, and on some of the rock and roll tunes, they'd love double drums. Henley was great to play with." (Later, Joe Walsh was unsuccessful in his effort to convince Henley to make Vitale a permanent member of the band.)

The tour began with two dates at the Richfield Coliseum, located midway between Akron and Cleveland. Before the show, David Spero managed to set up a meeting between the Eagles and Cleveland Mayor Dennis Kucinich. Walsh and the other members of the Eagles received keys to the city and Kucinich was photographed holding a "Joe for President" sign.

Meanwhile, the sponsoring radio station, WMMS, encouraged concertgoers to bring "Joe for President" banners to the show. Walsh – who was wearing a vintage Kent State University t-shirt – was somewhat distracted when he saw the widespread support for his faux campaign. Nonetheless, he announced at the concert: "If I'm elected, I'll make Cleveland the capital of the universe." Bob Seger – who had co-written the Eagles' hit "Heartache Tonight" – made a surprise appearance during the show's encore, just as Walsh began playing the opening riff of "Rocky Mountain Way." At another tour stop, a *Rolling Stone* writer observed: "Walsh is the only one who moves around, jumping off the risers and doing birdman strums (which occasionally tear off his fingernails). Walsh is also the crowd favorite, generating an ecstatic response with the wonderfully absurd humor of 'Life's Been Good.'"

In March 1980, the group staged *four* concerts at the 18,000 seat Los Angeles Forum. The opening act was 1960s singer Roy Orbison. During the encore at one the shows, the Eagles were joined by the Blues Brothers – the duo of John Belushi and Dan Aykroyd.

Then on July 27, the Eagles performed the first of three shows at the 3,000 seat Santa Monica Civic Auditorium. The group was delighted to play in a small, intimate venue for a change of pace. Glenn Frey stated at the time: "When we walked into the Civic the other day, the place seemed so small. But then Joe (Walsh) reminded us how big it looked the first time we played there. That's when we were just starting out and the idea of playing the Forum... was just a dream. I mean if someone had told me in those days that we were going to play the Forum, I'd have figured I had just died and gone to heaven." The Eagles hadn't played at the Civic Auditorium since 1973, when they were touring in support of their second album, *Desperado*.

The Santa Monica concerts – along with a previous show at the Long Beach Arena – were recorded for a future live album. These were the final Eagles concerts before the notorious fundraiser a few days later for Senator Alan Cranston.

▶ CHAPTER 23
JOE AND JOHN

In the late-1970s, Joe Walsh's personal life was in a constant state of turmoil. In 1978, he divorced his second wife, Stefany. The following year, he began a relationship with Juanita Jo "Jody" Boyer. Then on April 10, 1980, Walsh married for the third time. The couple exchanged their vows at a small chapel on Santa Cruz Island, off the coast of California. The marriage would last eight years.

Although Walsh was clearly a friendly extrovert with many friends and acquaintances, he remained an enigma to those close to him. In 1979, Bill Szymczyk observed: "Joe is the hardest person I ever met to feel like you're close to.... People erect walls between themselves and the world. Then depending on how the chemistry works between them and their friends, the walls come down. Joe uses his humor to keep them in place. There's been a lot of chaos in his life that he doesn't want people to be aware of. I know him better than anyone, and I don't know him." Nonetheless, the two men eventually grew close. As Szymczyk later conceded, "I've come to think of him as the brother I never had."

At the core of Walsh's personality, he enjoyed practical jokes, making people laugh and wearing outlandish stage costumes. And as explored in the lyrics of "Life's Been Good," Walsh also earned a reputation for his destructive behavior while on the road. In 1979, *Rolling Stone* reported that Joe Walsh was "efficient at wrecking hotel rooms." However, Walsh explained at the time: "So, I'll be sitting in a hotel room wide awake, buzzin' with the energy of the concert, thinkin' 'hey, where'd everybody go?' So, I would break things and smash things, have a great time, kind of blowing off steam, so I can relax and go to sleep. And I get mad, or sometimes I just enjoy it. If I'm in a Holiday Inn or a Howard Johnson's, why not break everything? They're all cheap anyway. And it's fun – you ought to try it sometime." With Walsh leaving a trail of destruction, some hotels began demanding a large security deposit. Others simply banned him altogether.

* * * * * *

Joe Walsh became fast friends with comedy actor John Belushi during a tour stop in Chicago. The Eagles performed at Comiskey Park on August 19, 1978, along with a pair of opening acts, the Steve Miller Band and Pablo Cruise. Belushi, who was in the audience, was eager to meet the Eagles' guitarist. After the show, Belushi knocked on Walsh's door at the Astor Tower Hotel in downtown Chicago.

The two newly minted friends spent the next two-days partying. Belushi also wanted to show Walsh around town, and the two men went to Maxim, an opulent restaurant on the ground floor of the hotel. However, Walsh and Belushi were not permitted into the dining room because they were both wearing blue jeans. Despite offering a $300 bribe to the Maitre'd, they were still denied entry. Walsh recalled Belushi's reaction: "I'm not even hungry, but we're getting in this restaurant."

Jumping into Belushi's limo, the two men drove to a 24-hour convenience store and bought a can of black spray paint. Walking into an alley, they spray-painted their blues jeans. Finally allowed into the restaurant, the men ruined a pair of pricey Victorian chairs when the black paint was absorbed by the cloth fabric. Later, the two men caused extensive damage to the penthouse suite of the hotel, which the building's owner was using as his personal apartment. In the end, Walsh and Belushi had caused $28,000 in damage. However, Walsh later insisted that the destruction was not planned: "John broke a glass and I had to top that, so I picked up something and threw it and things just escalated. It ended with the whole suite trashed."

According to Walsh, hanging out with Belushi could be "scary" at times: "Belushi – you couldn't say 'no' to him. He wanted to party, you went. There was no discussing it. Keith Moon was the same way. You just shut up and nod yes and just hope for the best."

On a subsequent trip to a Japanese restaurant, Belushi decided to reprise his character from *Saturday Night Live* – Samurai Futaba. As Walsh recalled: "I went to Benihana once with John Belushi, and he decided he was going to be the cook. And he went full-on samurai. It was messy. Messy!"

Belushi later became friends with the rest of the Eagles. As Don Felder recalled: "John had a party house in inner-city Chicago, with a pool table, a bar, and a bandstand set up with guitar, drums, and a mike, and we'd just go along and jam all night, taking drugs and hanging out. He was everybody's favorite bad boy."

Meanwhile, just three-weeks after Walsh was introduced to a new party buddy, he lost the friend who had first taught him how to behave like a rock star. Keith Moon died at his London home after an accidental overdose of the drug, Heminevrin, a strong sedative he was taking to alleviate his craving for alcohol.

A month earlier, the Who had released the album, *Who Are You*. Moon's poor physical state meant that the band would not tour in support of the project. While recording the album, Moon's addictions had affected his skills as a musician. In a conversation with bandmate Roger Daltrey, Moon revealed he was desperate to clean up his act.

▶ CHAPTER 24
THE EAGLES BREAK UP

Despite an impressive amount of record sales and an unhealthy amount of fan adoration, Joe Walsh and his bandmates in the Eagles were no longer enjoying themselves. Something had to give. The group had a phenomenal run in the 1970s and achieved superstar status after the release of the album, *Hotel California*. Nonetheless, the breakup of the band at the start of a new decade came as no surprise.

Glenn Frey discussed the mindset within the band during the sessions for *The Long Run*: "Towards the end, we just wanted to get the record finished and released. It is a very polished album, as well it should be after all that, and has some excellent moments, but none of us wanted to go through that again so we figured it was the right time to call it a day. Once that decision was made, I experienced an overwhelming sense of relief."

Don Henley offered a similar explanation: "The romance had gone out of it for Glenn and me. I mean, *The Long Run* was not as good as *Hotel California*, and it was an excruciatingly painful album to make. We were having fights all the time about the songs – enormous fights about *one word* – for days on end. That record took three years and cost $800,000, and we burned out. I think we knew early on that fame was a fleeting thing. That's really what 'Desperado' was all about: that you get up just to get torn down eventually, and this is a fickle business.... We were exhausted, and we were sick and tired of each other. We needed a vacation, and we didn't get one. So we just flamed out."

The event that triggered the breakup of the band occurred on July 31, 1980. In what has been dubbed the Long Night at Wrong Beach, the Eagles infamously disbanded following a fundraising concert for Senator Alan Cranston in Long Beach, California. Several months earlier, the Eagles had appeared at a fundraiser for another California politician, Governor Jerry Brown, who was dating Linda Ronstadt at the time.

Before the start of the Cranston fundraiser, the animosity between Don Felder and his bandmates, Henley and Frey, was nearing a breaking point. Felder was not political in nature and was unhappy that the band was performing for politicians at campaign rallies. However, it was a comment Felder made under his breath to Cranston and his wife that would set the band's breakup into motion. After Felder was thanked for agreeing to perform, he reportedly replied, "You're welcome... I guess." Infuriated by Felder's response, Frey went backstage and smashed a beer bottle against a wall.

In his autobiography, *Heaven And Hell*, Felder discussed the toxic verbal battle that occurred when the Eagles went onstage. While the band was performing "The Best Of My Love," Frey walked over to Felder and reportedly stated: "I'm going to kick your ass when we get off the stage." Things went downhill from there. Felder recalled: "As the night progressed, we both grew angrier and began hissing at each other under our breaths. In the sound booth, the technicians feared the audience might actually hear our outbursts, so they lowered Glenn's microphone until he had to sing. He continued to approach me after every song to rant, rave, curse, and let me know how many songs remained before our fight. 'That's three more, pal,' Glenn said. 'Get ready.'" At the end of the main portion of the show, the band members headed backstage and waited for the planned encore. As Felder and Frey waited at opposite sides of the stage, Felder could hear Frey angrily swearing.

Felder explained what he did before returning to the stage: "I remembered something Joe [Walsh] would do to release his tension. Whenever he was pissed off, he'd go somewhere and relieve his frustration by smashing something. Before returning to the stage for the encores, I told my guitar tech, Jimmy Collins, 'Take that shitty Takamine acoustic guitar I play on 'Lyin' Eyes' and put it by the back door.' When I get offstage after the encores, I'm gonna break that [guitar]." The fundraising concert ended with Walsh singing "All Night Long." This would be the final performance by the Eagles for the next 14 years.

After the show, Felder did as he promised and smashed the guitar against a concrete pillar in full view of Frey and Cranston. As Bill Szymczyk remembered: "Everybody picked that night to freak out on each other." Frey recalled: "I just told Irving [Azoff], 'I've had it,' and left town. I told him he could tell anybody in the band anything he wanted. I didn't want to say anything I'd be sorry for." In the aftermath of the public altercation, the frazzled members of the Eagles realized it was time to go their separate ways. The Eagles were born in Southern California and perished in Southern California.

Later, at a news conference, 66-year-old Alan Cranston had an awkward exchange with the media. Cranston biographer Judith Robinson chronicled how the "'usually articulate' senior senator 'seemed baffled when asked to name his favorite song' by the group. After a few moments of silence, Cranston mentioned one of the albums, inverting the title to 'California Hotel.' 'No matter,' a reporter wrote, 'many of the young concertgoers at the Long Beach arena weren't sure who Alan Cranston was either.' Tickets, which clearly stated that all proceeds would go to the senator's campaign, had sold out in forty-five minutes several months earlier." The concert had raised $125,000 for the Cranston campaign.

* * * * * *

In the early-1980s, Irving Azoff stated: "The Eagles talked about breaking up from the day I met them. There'd be one mini-explosion followed by a replacement in the band, then another mini-explosion followed by another replacement. You just had to step back and give things time to calm down." But this time around, the Eagles were serious about disbanding.

There were a number of reasons for the band's demise, most of which involved internal power struggles and the inequity of the group's earnings. While Glenn Frey and Don Henley – the group's chief songwriters – were hauling in millions of dollars from publishing royalties, Don Felder was disheartened by his bandmates' growing wealth. However, Frey insisted: "A band is supposed to be equal, but when people emerge as having certain strengths, other people are resentful of them having those strengths. Everybody makes this big deal about Don and I being the problem with the band. But I'm here to tell you right now that Joe Walsh and Don Felder – and others – created as much turbulence for the band as anybody else did, just because *they're* frustrated quarterbacks."

Henley offered a more reasoned explanation: "We were together for almost ten years, and that is a long time in this business. We broke up for all the normal reasons – the jealousy, the envy, and people going in different directions. It was a struggle from the first week to keep that band together. Glenn and I really had our hands full. There was a certain security in the band, even with the conflict."

Meanwhile, Henley would famously proclaim that the Eagles would re-form "when hell freezes over." Frey offered a similar prediction:

"There'll never be a 'Greed and Lost Youth' tour." It would take more than a decade for a polar vortex to sweep into hell.

Over the next year or so, the Eagles limped along as they put the final touches on a live album. With Frey refusing to join his bandmates at a Miami studio, the tapes were shipped back-and-forth and decisions were made over the phone. And not surprisingly, a $2 million offer by Asylum Records for two new Eagles songs for inclusion on the album was rejected by the band.

The two-disc set, *The Eagles Live*, was released in November 1980. On one track, Walsh was humorously introduced as "the next president of the United States" before he launched into "Life's Been Good." Another track, "Seven Bridges Road," demonstrated the group's polished vocal harmonies. Released as a single, it would be their last top-40 hit for more than a decade.

Meanwhile, the Eagles remained popular throughout the 1980s, despite the fact that they were no longer together. Henley recalled: "Even when we were broken up the music was playing on the radio. It took on a life of its own and kept us in the public ear. And as the old saying goes, absence makes the heart grow fonder."

Following the band's breakup, Walsh was left in the lurch. Forever the optimist, he refused to believe that the Eagles were finished. He told *Billboard* magazine at the time: "My Eagles commitment is first on my list of priorities. Doing a solo album or tour doesn't infer that I've quit the group or that we've broken up. We're kind of on sabbatical. We're trying to think, read, write and get an overall perspective on the direction we want the band to go in." But in private, Walsh was facing a hard reality: "I didn't know what to do, and I was sad. So I pretended that we didn't stop and I kept going. And basically I ended up [an] alcoholic and dependent on substances, and those things gradually convince you that you can't do anything without them. And that's how I wound up."

Meanwhile, Walsh would attend his 15-year high school reunion in 1980. He recalled: "There were all these people I'd totally lost track of, and I was in the Eagles and I was famous and all and a bunch of them didn't even know I was in the Eagles. I was just Joe."

* * * * * *

In October 1979, when the production of the film, *The Blues Brothers*, shifted from Chicago to Los Angeles, Joe Walsh was invited to spend some time with John Belushi in his studio trailer, waiting for the next scene. Joined by the film's co-star Dan Aykroyd, the trio spent two-days horsing around. Eventually, Belushi and Aykroyd decided that Walsh should appear at the end of the film. Portraying an inmate, Walsh set off a prison riot, just as Jake and Elwood Blues began performing "Jailhouse Rock." The scene had to be shot three times.

The following year, Belushi knew he had to tackle his worsening drug habit and asked Walsh for help. Walsh suggested that the actor hire a personal bodyguard. Assigned to watch over Belushi was Richard "Smokey" Wendell – a former Secret Service agent who had once guarded President Richard Nixon but was then employed as Walsh's road manager. Walsh reportedly told Belushi: "If you're looking for someone to help you get yourself together, he'll do it. But you won't like it one bit." Agreeing to the arrangement, Belushi told Wendell: "If I don't do something now, I'm going to be dead in a year or two."

Although Wendell had a challenging assignment, he did an admirable job keeping Belushi away from drugs. Shortly after signing on, Wendell joined Belushi at a New York City recording studio where he was putting the final touches on the soundtrack album of the film, *The Blues Brothers*. As Wendell recalled: "There was a song that [Belushi] wanted Joe's help with.... The session went okay, but we were working against the clock, and there were way too many people in the studio. In my experience you can always spot the people who really have no reason to be there: straphangers, entourage people. John and Joe were working, and in the interim these 'friends' were disappearing frequently into the bathroom. When they came out of the bathroom, I'd just go in and confiscate what they'd left behind [for Belushi]. There's always a basic pattern to how they do this stuff; these guys aren't that creative." Right from the start, Wendell had successfully performed the task he was hired to do.

After eleven-months on the job, Wendell decided he didn't want to be Belushi's permanent bodyguard. Belushi's health had dramatically improved and it looked as though he had finally overcome his addictions. But despite the intervention, Belushi soon returned to his old ways. In 1982, he succumbed to an overdose inside a rented cottage at the Chateau Marmont Hotel in Los Angeles. Belushi's tragic death deeply upset Walsh, but it was not enough to convince him to get clean.

▶ CHAPTER 25
JOE GOES SOLO AGAIN

The 1980s were a difficult time for Joe Walsh. While battling his many personal demons, he continued to churn out a series of moderately successful solo albums. Walsh would have his greatest success of the decade with a song from the *Urban Cowboy* soundtrack, "All Night Long." The single gave Walsh a top-20 pop hit in 1980 – one of six top-40 hits culled from the multi-platinum album.

In the new decade, the record industry experienced a paradigm shift with a new focus on music videos. Consequently, musical acts now had to sound *and* look good. MTV debuted on August 1, 1981, and on its first day of broadcasting the cable network did not air a single music video by Walsh or any of his Eagles bandmates. Not a fan of the network, Walsh declared that MTV "is why kids can't read. It's brainless, meaningless noise with no validity whatsoever. It is not constructive for society. You're supposed to listen to music, not watch it." For whatever reason, Walsh refused to accept the fact that videos were effective forms of promotion that translated into the sales of concert tickets and records. Conversely, Walsh's soon-to-be girlfriend Stevie Nicks enjoyed plenty of airplay on the network, beginning with her duet with Tom Petty, "Stop Draggin' My Heart Around."

* * * * * *

In April 1981, Joe Walsh released *There Goes The Neighborhood*, his first post-Eagles solo album. On the front cover, he was dressed in army fatigues while sitting in a Sherman tank that was parked in the middle of a Los Angeles garbage dump. Walsh admitted at the time: "It's the first time I've been on my own in about five-years. Yeah, it was a little scary at first, but I'm starting to get into it now. It's kind of fun to be able to play more freely. With the Eagles, it's kind of a formula. When there's three guitars involved, you have to restrict yourself, discipline yourself, to play more simply. So I'm enjoying this."

Both a critical and commercial success, *There Goes The Neighborhood* reached the top-20. *Billboard* magazine praised the album for combining Walsh's "characteristic wry humor with his skill of guitar-dominated rock 'n' roll." The album's standout track was the upbeat rocker, "A Life Of Illusion." Joe Vitale, who played on the song, revealed that it was an unfinished outtake from Walsh's earlier solo album, *So What*: "It didn't make it in, but we cut the track for it. We found the masters and dug it out. We never had words – we had the track done, but never the lyrics done. So the tracks were done from '74 and Joe wrote the lyrics and added trumpets and the silly stuff and all that. It ended up being a really cool tune." Former Barnstorm member Kenny Passarelli, the song's co-writer, played the mariachi-style trumpets on the song. The album also featured the track, "Rockets," which Walsh had written in the early-1960s while still in high school. Walsh had originally written another track, "Rivers (Of The Hidden Funk)," for the Eagles album, *The Long Run*. The song featured Don Felder on guitar and talk box.

Wearing army fatigues during a subsequent tour, Walsh was backed by George "Chocolate" Perry on bass, Mike Murphy on keyboards and both Vitale and Russ Kunkel on drums. A reviewer at one of the shows wrote: "Walsh goes for a large palette of sound colorings, much as he did in Barnstorm, rather than a lot of razzle-dazzle rock 'n' roll flash." At another show, a critic wrote: "Sunday night at the Oakland Coliseum Arena I watched 10,000 Joe Walsh fans go nuts throughout his first local concert as a bandleader in six-years. He's been here a couple times since with the Eagles, but they didn't count. This was the show Walsh's real fans have been waiting for."

Also in 1981, the Who's bassist John Entwistle belatedly finished his album, *Too Late The Hero*, which was recorded as a power trio with Walsh and Vitale. The sessions for the album began in 1979 at Crystal Studio in Los Angeles, during which time Entwistle first met Lisa Pritchett, who was Walsh's girlfriend at the time. Taking two-years to record, the album was finished at Ramport Studio in London, where the sessions were fun and stress-free. While working on the album in England, Walsh and Vitale stayed at Entwistle's 55-room Victorian castle, which was packed with antiques and musical instruments.

Entwistle remarked at the time: "I'm actually pleased with the album. I think it's probably the first I've felt that way about. I still enjoy listening to it. Usually when you finish, you don't want to hear it ever again. We actually sound like a band. We played really well together right from the beginning. I sort of figured it would be that way anyway.

Joe Vitale has been playing with Joe Walsh a long time. It was like me getting together with a ready-made band. I wrote a lot of the songs with Joe Walsh's playing in mind. It all fitted together. In a way Joe Walsh and I are similar players. We play a lot of chords." A British critic described the project as "a hard rock album that's slick by British standards and probably heavy metal by West Coast standards."

* * * * * *

In 1982, Joe Walsh produced Ringo Starr's solo album, *Old Wave*. The project was started at Starr's home studio inside his Tittenhurst Park estate in England and completed at the Santa Barbara Studios in California. After the relative failure of his previous album, *Stop And Smell The Roses*, Starr had been unceremoniously dropped by his label, Boardwalk Records. The album had completely failed to chart in Britain and managed to spawn just one minor top-40 hit in the U.S., "Wrack My Brain."

Starr and Walsh co-wrote most of the songs on *Old Wave*, which featured a number of topnotch musicians including Eric Clapton and John Entwistle. Wanting to focus on the recording process with a clear mind, Starr abstained from alcohol, which left Walsh without a drinking partner.

After the project was completed, Starr faced a major problem – his record company, RCA, refused to release the album. Additionally, he was unable to secure a new recording contract with a label in either the U.S. or Britain. The head of RCA's international division in the U.K. stated that *Old Wave* was "a reasonable album," however "I don't see any large sales in the U.K. so we won't be releasing it here." Sadly, the album was initially released in just two countries – Canada and Germany. Consequently, few fans were aware of the album, and it sold poorly. Blindsided by the turn of events, Starr explained at the time: "How do you think I felt? I was furious. I go round saying it's now very big in Afghanistan or wherever, oh yeah, Canada, I keep forgetting, but I was very disappointed. I liked the album. I thought it was the best I'd done. I called it *Old Wave* as a joke, as opposed to New Wave. I suppose I am the old wave generation now."

Meanwhile, during the middle of the sessions, Walsh had a fateful meeting. He was introduced to Marjorie Bach, Starr's sister-in-law. Although Walsh and Bach traveled in very different social circles, the two would occasionally run into each other over the next decade.

Also during this period, Walsh played a guitar solo on Don Henley's solo hit, "Dirty Laundry." Arriving at the studio, Walsh was instructed to play as though he was angry. Walsh obliged Henley's request and provided a forceful solo. Also that year, all of the Eagles members, except for Glenn Frey, contributed songs to the soundtrack album of the film, *Fast Times At Ridgemont High*. Walsh submitted the lighthearted track, "Waffle Stomp."

Around this time, Walsh was convinced by his former bandmate, Don Felder, to join a proposed Eagles spinoff group. The outfit also included Timothy B. Schmit and British singer Terry Reid. (In the 1960s, Reid had famously turned down offers to join Led Zeppelin and Deep Purple.) However, Walsh and Reid spent too much time engaging in extra-curricular activities and the band soon fizzled.

Later, Felder and Schmit formed a second lineup of the group which included Paul Carrack on lead vocals. Nicknamed "Malibu Men's Choir," the band submitted nearly a dozen tracks to Irving Azoff, who passed on the project without any explanation. The group subsequently disbanded. One of the group's songs, "Love Will Keep Us Alive," would resurface as an Eagles track in 1994.

* * * * * *

In 1982, Joe Walsh went through a roller coaster of emotions as he experienced a number of life-changing events. In the spring of 1982, he lost both of his maternal grandparents, Floyd and Harriet Bowen, within two-months of each other. In December of that same year, Walsh witnessed the birth of his daughter, Lucy Marie Stanton. Joe Vitale was named her godfather.

Also that year, Walsh was arrested in Montclair, New Jersey, after attending a family wedding. Following the reception, he joined his cousin and an old friend on a midnight run to explore their old high school. After climbing through a window and briefly walking around the darkened building, the three men inadvertently set off a silent alarm.

After climbing back out of the window, Walsh and his cohorts were met by police and charged with burglary. Unfortunately, the arresting officer was not a music fan, and when Walsh revealed that he was a member of "the Eagles," he was asked, "Yeah, which position do you play?" Even after explaining he was a guitarist in a famous rock group – not a member of the Philadelphia Eagles football team – Walsh was jailed for the night. The following day, the matter was resolved and the charges were dropped.

▶ CHAPTER 26
JOE AND STEVIE

On July 25, 1976, the Eagles headlined a sell-out concert at Schaefer Stadium in Foxboro, Massachusetts. The opening acts were Fleetwood Mac and Boz Scaggs. At the time, both the Eagles and Fleetwood Mac were on the cusp of achieving superstar status. Backstage, Joe Walsh and Stevie Nicks exchanged pleasantries but were not close friends.

By the early-1980s, Walsh and Nicks were each pursuing their own solo careers. Both performers had strong, charismatic personalities and shared a penchant for recreational intoxicants. But when they toured together on the same bill in 1983, something entirely unexpected happened – they became involved in a romantic relationship. While Walsh was in the middle of his third marriage, Nicks had entered into a short, ill-fated marriage earlier in the year, but got divorced just three-months later. Before that, the diminutive five-foot-one singer had dated the producer of her first three solo albums, Jimmy Iovine. And before that, she had dated a number of notable rockers including her Fleetwood Mac bandmates, Lindsey Buckingham and Mick Fleetwood.

* * * * * *

Although Stevie Nicks was an essential part of one of the most popular rock bands of the 1970s, she was not entirely happy with the direction of her career. In the autumn of 1980, she began working on her debut solo album despite some initial hostility from her bandmates in Fleetwood Mac: “They were not supportive when I first went to do *Bella Donna*, they questioned my reasons, and once they realized that I was simply looking for an outlet for my songs – because three songs for Fleetwood Mac every two years just wasn’t enough – they understood I wasn’t trying to leave the band.” As her producer Jimmy Iovine later noted: “Believe it or not, people told me that no one could bear to listen to her on more than three songs on a record. Which sounded nuts.”

But that was not the only reason Nicks wanted to record a solo project. After completing a grueling but very successful world tour to promote the Fleetwood Mac album *Tusk*, Nicks was informed by bandmate Mick Fleetwood – who was also the group's manager at the time – that the 18-month trek had earned no profit due to high production costs, despite 112 sold-out performances.

After learning of Nicks' intention to record an album apart from the band, Warner Brothers promised to increase Fleetwood Mac's royalty rate if she remained at the label as a solo artist. Ignoring the offer, Nicks co-founded her own label, Modern Records, and entered into a five-album distribution arrangement with Atlantic Records. She also hired a new manager, Irving Azoff.

Following the success of Nicks' debut album *Bella Donna* – highlighted by the duet hit, "Stop Draggin' My Heart Around" with Tom Petty and the Heartbreakers – she followed up with *The Wild Heart*, which was propelled by the debut single, "Stand Back." Touring in support of the album in 1983, Nicks hired Joe Walsh as her opening act. For the tour, Walsh added two conga players, a horn section and Greg Droman, an unknown guitarist from Akron. Walsh also hired Droman's wife, Marilyn Martin, as a backing vocalist. (In just a few years, Martin would score a chart-topping duet hit with Phil Collins, "Separate Lives.")

A warm-up performance for the Wild Heart Tour was staged on May 27, 1983, at the Aladdin Theatre in Las Vegas, one day after Nicks' 35th birthday. However, just 5,400 of the 7,500 available tickets were sold for the show. Although ticket sales for the tour were generally strong, sell-outs became more common as the tour progressed.

A few days later, both Walsh and Nicks performed at the second US Festival, which was staged over Memorial Day weekend in San Bernardino, California. The event was organized by Steve Wozniak of Apple Computers. Walsh was originally scheduled to play on May 29, which was Hard Rock and Heavy Metal Day. However, after John Mellencamp pulled out of the festival on Rock Day, Walsh took his place. As a result, both Walsh and Nicks performed their sets on the same day.

Playing for nearly an hour in front of 200,000 concertgoers, Walsh looked healthy and energized on the wind-swept stage. Behind Walsh, a smiling Joe Vitale wore a red MTV t-shirt. Walsh began his set with "Fanfare For The Common Man" and continued with mostly non-Eagles material. The highlight of the brief show was a medley of "Rocky Mountain Way" and Bob Dylan's "Rainy Day Women #12 & 35." As the sun began setting, Walsh ended his performance with his solo track,

"All Night Long."

Meanwhile, Glenn Frey had vetoed an appearance by the Eagles at both the first and second US Festival. At a press conference staged in Los Angeles, Walsh was asked why the Eagles had decided against reuniting for the festival. While seated between David Lee Roth and Paul Simonon (of the Clash), Walsh dryly replied: "It was a very interesting offer.... The Eagles decided that money... really should not be a major part of a decision to regroup and get back together. We didn't feel that should be one of the top motivations to get back together. And secondly, it wasn't enough money." (The Eagles were reportedly offered $2 million to appear at the first US Festival, the previous year. The figure was increased to $2.5 million for the second festival in 1983.)

The Wild Heart Tour officially began on June 21 in Knoxville, Tennessee. At one early stop on the tour, a reviewer wrote: "Joe Walsh opened the show with... an hour-long set of blasting rock 'n' roll... Walsh sounded a little smoother than usual, and his guitar playing was powerful, but the band was so loud at times the sound was distorted." Tom Petty joined Nicks onstage at a show at Radio City Music Hall in New York City to perform a pair of duets.

Booking a few solo shows apart from the Wild Heart Tour, Walsh appeared at the Blossom Music Center near Cleveland for two shows in June. Walsh began one of the concerts with the theme from *The Price Is Right*. With the spotlights aimed at the pavilion section of the outdoor venue, fans shouted "Joe Walsh, come on down!" Amazingly, Walsh emerged from the crowd, ran onto the stage and then launched into "In The City."

With Walsh rejoining the Wild Heart Tour, something unanticipated occurred on September 5, during a stop in Texas. As Nicks recalled: "I fell in love with Joe at first sight from across the room, in the bar at the Mansions Hotel in Dallas. I looked at him and I walked across the room and I sat on the bar stool next to him, and two seconds later I crawled into his lap, and that was it." Nicks later told her biographer, Stephen Davis: "I remember thinking, I can never be far from this person again."

Although Nicks was informed by Walsh's stage crew that he was married at the time, the news did nothing to deter the budding romance, which would continue for nearly three-years. However, the relationship was rocky and punctuated by a series of quarrels. Nevertheless, Nicks explained: "I took really good care of him and I think that is what scared Joe the most because I was too in tune with him and he was too used to being out of tune with everyone."

On September 19, following a spirited argument after a show in Denver, Walsh took Nicks on a long drive. Renting a Jeep and heading for Boulder – about two-hours away – the pair arrived at North Boulder Park. Nicks recalled: "I guess I had been complaining about a lot of things... and he decided to make me aware of how unimportant my problems were if they were compared to worse sorrows. So he told me that he had taken his little girl to this magic park whenever he could, and the only thing she *ever* complained about was that she was too little to reach up to the drinking fountain. As we drove up to this beautiful park, (it was snowing a little bit), he came around to open my door and help me down, and when I looked up, I saw the park... his baby's park, and I burst into tears saying, 'You built a drinking fountain here for her, didn't you?' I was right, under a huge beautiful hanging tree, was a tiny silver drinking fountain." The visit inspired Nicks to compose a song for Walsh's daughter, "Has Anyone Ever Written Anything For You?"

* * * * * *

In August 1983, during a break in the tour, Joe Walsh quickly recorded a solo album. Walsh was joined at the sessions by Joe Vitale, Waddy Wachtel and George "Chocolate" Perry. The first six-tracks were recorded over a two-week period at the Casino Ballroom on Catalina Island. The band was given free use of the spacious room in exchange for agreeing to stage a fundraising concert. There were few distractions on the tranquil island, which allowed Walsh and the other musicians to concentrate on their work.

While Bill Szymczyk was inside the ballroom directing the sessions, sound engineer Jim Nipar sat in an outdoor, mobile production truck. As Szymczyk recalled: "We used an old API board, which is a good workhorse board, and an old 16-track 3M machine that had definitely seen better days.... Joe's instructions to me were, 'Once I start playing, record whatever you get – I'm not gonna sit here and listen to quarter notes on a snare drum for five hours.' It was basically a plug-in-and-go situation, which kept everyone on their toes." After returning to the mainland, Walsh and the band recorded an additional four tracks at Sound Design studio in Santa Barbara.

The album, *You Bought It, You Name It*, was released in October on a subsidiary of Warner Brothers Records. The front cover featured an image of Walsh sitting in an easy chair that was superimposed onto a photo of *The USS Yorktown* at the Battle of Midway. Despite mostly positive reviews, the album just barely broke into the top-50 on *Billboard's* sales chart.

The project was highlighted by the album-rock hit, "I Can Play That Rock & Roll." In the song's music video, Walsh destroyed a hotel room with an ax, sledge hammer and chain saw. Walsh performed the song on an episode of *Second City TV*, during a skit that featured comedian John Candy. Other notable tracks on the album included Walsh's critique of the popularity of arcade video games, "Space Age Whiz Kids," and an outtake from *The Long Run* sessions co-written by Don Felder, "Told You So." Another track, "Love Letters," was an unlikely remake of a 1945 hit by pop crooner, Dick Haymes. But the most outrageous track on the album, the bawdy and comical "I.L.B.T.s," was recorded in just three-hours. Walsh said at the time: "I'm gonna get killed for that [song], but I don't care. I couldn't find a reason to not put it on the record. It's not really dirty; I just meant it to be fun. It's a true song, after all."

* * * * * *

The Stevie Nicks and Joe Walsh tour resumed on August 27 in Biloxi, Mississippi. Before a concert in Dallas, the 35-year-old Walsh made a prediction about the future of his career: "As far as I'm concerned, I'm going to be like B.B. King. I'll probably be 50 years old and still playing somewhere as long as people still come to see me."

The Wild Heart Tour concluded on November 24 with a performance in Columbia, South Carolina. Afterward, Nicks made it clear to Walsh that she wanted to continue their relationship. However, Walsh was still married and would make little time for Nicks.

In April 1984, shortly after Nicks and Walsh had one their many squabbles, Nicks attended a Eurythmics concert in Los Angeles. Backstage, she met the band's co-leader, Dave Stewart, for the first time. There was an immediate attraction between the two musicians, and Nicks asked Stewart if he would be interested in going to a party at her home. Arriving at Nicks' estate in Beverly Hills, Stewart discovered there was no party, but he wound up staying overnight.

Stewart recalled: "I was woken up at about 9:30 AM by Stevie saying I had to leave because someone might have been coming around to collect their clothes, and things could get tricky. I didn't like the sound of 'tricky,' so I phoned my management, found out where the band was staying." However, Walsh arrived early and began pounding on the locked door. He pleaded with Nicks, who refused him entry. Recollections of the event differ as Stewart and Nicks both claimed they said to Walsh, "don't come around here no more." Either way, Stewart turned the phrase into the title of a hit song. Although Nicks was initially given the opportunity to record the track, Stewart would instead give the song to his friend and occasional collaborator, Tom Petty. Stewart also appeared in the opening scene of the song's memorable music video, which featured an Alice in Wonderland theme.

Although Walsh and Nicks would reconcile, they would later break up for good at a recording studio. Nicks was practicing some new songs with her band when Walsh made an unexpected visit. A frustrated and angry Nicks helplessly watched as Walsh interrupted the sessions and then began drinking and joking with the members of her band. Meanwhile, Walsh ignored Nicks the entire time. Eventually, she announced that she was going home and asked him to join her. That's when Walsh revealed that he was leaving the following day for the start of a tour. He failed to inform Nicks that he was flying out of the country for an undetermined period of time.

Nicks later admitted: "One day my friend Sharon came and said, 'Joe told me to tell you that he's taken a plane to Australia. He says he won't be back for several months and don't try to find him.'" Reportedly, Walsh also said: "Tell Stevie I'm going because both of us are doing so much coke that one of us is going to die." Years later, Nicks revealed that she was still troubled by how the relationship ended: "There was no closure, so I've never got over it.... Maybe some day he will tell me the truth about what happened to us."

In 1986, Nicks entered rehab and was able to beat her addiction to cocaine. She subsequently became addicted to Klonopin, which she was prescribed during her treatment. Eventually, she was forced to re-enter rehab. Nicks chronicled this period of her life in the song, "Hard Advice." She recalled that the song emerged from "a lecture Tom Petty gave me one day about something that was going on in my life. I'd asked him to write a song with me – this was about two months after I came out of rehab for [addiction to] Klonopin. I was still in a fragile state, after 48 days of hell in rehab. And Tom said, 'You don't need help to write a song. You just need to get over this experience that bummed you out so bad. The relationship you were in is over, it was over a long time ago, and you need to move on.' And I went home and wrote this song."

Reflecting on how things might have turned out differently, Nicks stated: "I don't know what my relationship with Joe would have been like sober. I remember days of misery waiting by the phone; me in my house, with him saying, 'I'm going to visit you.' I would kick everyone out because I just wanted to be with him, and not a phone call, nothing... We were doing a lot of drugs and drugs make you needy." Nonetheless, Nicks continued to state in multiple interviews that Walsh was the love of her life: "We were probably the perfect, complete, crazy pair. He was the one I would have married, and that I would probably have changed my life around for... a little bit, anyway. Not a lot."

While Nicks continued to profess deep feelings for Walsh, he repeatedly displayed a more cavalier attitude concerning their relationship. Eventually, though, he had a dramatic change of heart. In 2010, when asked about Nicks' statement about being her "great love," Walsh responded: "I was flattered when I saw those comments. We were good friends." And in another interview, he said that he loved her like a "sister" and considered her a "soulmate;" however, he also admitted: "We were seeking refuge – kind of, in each other's presence.... We were on the road, we had careers. We were both lonely.... I don't think either of us could have committed to a lasting relationship in the state that we were in."

* * * * * *

Joe Walsh received a letter from Paul Christie with a very unusual request. Christie was the former lead singer of Mondo Rock. (The group had several chart hits in Australia. One of their songs, "State Of The Heart," was later recorded by Australian-born singer Rick Springfield and became a U.S. hit in 1985.) In the letter, Christie asked Walsh to join an all-star touring group called the Party Boys. The part-time Sydney-based supergroup had been formed in 1982 by Christie and Kevin Borich. Both musicians were previously members of the Kevin Borich Express, which had toured across the U.S. in 1978 as the opening act for AC/DC.

Walsh recalled: "Out of a clear blue sky some wacko writes me and says come over and let's go play some bars. This is at a point where I can't stand all the 'Hey man, you're good – here's a million dollars.'" At the time, Walsh yearned to return to his musical roots and play in small clubs – an action he called "de-Eagleising therapy." He also wanted to get away from his problems with Stevie Nicks and considered the tour a welcome diversion.

After arriving in Sydney, Walsh rented a house and spent several weeks practicing with his new bandmates. Beginning in December, the Party Boys played a series of sold-out shows on the country's pub circuit. On New Year's Eve, the group performed at the Pier Hotel near Melbourne. During the tour, Walsh focused on his solo material rather than his Eagles hits. He also threw in an occasional rock oldie like Buddy Holly's "Not Fade Away." One of the Party Boys' crowd pleasers was "Dueling Guitars," which featured an onstage musical battle between Walsh and Borich.

In an interview with an Australian newspaper, Walsh stated that he planned to stay in the country until he was "thrown out." It was difficult to tell whether or not he was joking. And when asked why he wasn't back in the U.S. promoting his latest album, he stated: "Why should I? So people can make money? I have all the money I need. I just want to play music. I love the music scene here. It's young, it's refreshing and there's a lot of energy. And I need a recharge on that.... Every day I look in the mirror to see if I've turned Australian yet."

In 1985, the Party Boys released a live album that was recorded at Moby Dicks Surf Club in Whale Beach, *You Need Professional Help*. The project included an Eagles song co-written by Walsh, "Life In The Fast Lane," as well as a ten-minute rendition of "Rocky Mountain Way." When not playing music, Walsh enjoyed sharing stories about his personal exploits.

▶ CHAPTER 27
THE CONFESSOR

When Joe Walsh was still dating Stevie Nicks in 1984, he started working on another solo album. He experienced a great deal of writer's block during the sessions and was frequently assisted by Nicks. Lyrically, Walsh wanted to take a different direction with the album: "I decided not to be funny this time. I got a little bit concerned that I was painting myself into a corner and stereotyping myself as a silly guy." The sessions took place at Goodnight LA Studios in Los Angeles. Walsh was backed by a variety of musicians including Jim Keltner, Jeff Porcaro and Randy Newman. And at Joe Vitale's recommendation, Walsh hired bassist Rick Rosas, who would soon be known by his new nickname, Rick the Bass Player.

The Confessor was belatedly released in May 1985 and was one of Walsh's poorest-selling albums. The front cover featured Walsh's face superimposed onto a 19th century painting by German artist Caspar David Friedrich. The album was highlighted by a rendition of the Michael Stanley song, "Rosewood Bitters," which received airplay on album-rock radio. (Walsh played slide guitar on Stanley's original version in 1973.) Another track, "Slow Dancing," was written by Loz Netto, a member of Sniff 'n' the Tears.

Although *Rolling Stone* magazine gave the project just three stars, the reviewer proclaimed: "This is the best album the former James Gang and Eagles guitarist has done in a long, long time." However, another reviewer called the album "as mundane as brushing your teeth."

* * * * * *

Meanwhile, Joe Walsh decided to make a return visit to Australia. Delighted with his previous stint with the Party Boys, Walsh launched another tour, this time with a pair of American musicians – guitarist Waddy Wachtel and bassist Rick Rosas. During this period, Walsh and Rosas became close friends. Also in the group was Aussie drummer Richard Harvey from the band, the Divinyls.

Calling themselves Creatures From America, the group toured across the island nation. Playing in pubs and nightclubs, the group usually charged just $10 admission, a far cry from the cost to see the Eagles. In addition to his own material, Walsh performed covers like "Will You Love Me Tomorrow" and "Cinnamon Girl." At one gig, one of Walsh's prized guitars was stolen and never recovered. During this period, Walsh put on some weight and looked unhealthy.

Returning to the U.S., Walsh went on the road for two-months in the summer of 1985. Some of the dates were as the opening act for Foreigner. For the tour, Walsh experimented with a new format: "I do a good 40-minute acoustic set at the beginning of the show and go through a bunch of old favorites that I've done on various albums and talk to the audience and tell jokes and play the piano. Then I take a 10-minute break and we go through the whole electric show, so it really gives me the chance to play all my stuff."

In July, Walsh stopped in Cleveland for what was billed as a double-header with the Cleveland Indians. The city's beleaguered baseball team had endured a lousy season up to that point – 28 wins and 58 losses – and was attracting an average of just 8,200 paying fans to their games. Following the completion of an Indians game, Walsh performed on a temporary stage that was constructed in the middle of Cleveland Municipal Stadium. Michael Stanley made a surprise appearance during the track, "Funk 49." With Walsh able to lure 25,500 spectators to the outdoor venue, *The Cleveland Plain Dealer* sarcastically asked the question: "Can you bring Joe Walsh back every Sunday?" However, the majority of the crowd who came to see Walsh's performance didn't arrive until after the end of the baseball game.

During this period, Walsh also collaborated with Steve Winwood. The pair joined forces to write some songs. Unfortunately, they completed only one suitable track, "Split Decision," which appeared on Winwood's hit album, *Back In The High Life*. Winwood had a few other notable guests on the project including Chaka Khan, James Ingram, Nile Rogers and James Taylor. Although eager to join Winwood's backing band on a tour to promote the album, Walsh was busy with other musical ventures.

* * * * * *

In the mid-1980s, Joe Walsh attempted to make a major life change. After receiving a hefty royalty check for his work with the Eagles, he purchased an 800-acre farm in rural Vermont, about 100-miles northwest of Boston. The property included a stately New England-style home, four barns and a large lake. The home – which featured a large ballroom in the rear – had been constructed decades earlier by the CEO of General Motors.

Hoping to live off the land, Walsh – a lifelong city dweller – quickly soured on the idea of farm life. Unhappy with the fierce Vermont winters and unable to find suitable workers to help maintain the property, he abandoned the idea of making the farm his primary residence. For a few years, Walsh's stepfather spent his summers living on the estate. Several years later, Walsh sold the property.

Meanwhile, in March 1985, a fire struck the Caribou Ranch studio in Colorado, fourteen years after it first opened its doors. The blaze erupted on the third floor, which housed a game room. An overworked space heater had erupted into flames and the fire spread to a pool table, which fell through the floor and into the control room below. Also lost in the blaze were many of the Gold and Platinum awards that adorned the walls of the building. With James Guercio raising a young family at the time, he chose not to rebuild the studio due to the often-unsavory habits of visiting rock musicians. (In 2014, the Caribou property was sold to a Walmart heir for $32.5 million.)

* * * * * *

In October 1986, an unknown singer-songwriter named Richard Marx began recording his self-titled debut album. Amazingly, the album featured musical contributions by three members of the Eagles. Marx recalled that his track, "Don't Mean Nothing," felt incomplete, and his manager, Allen Kovac, suggested that it needed some additional backing vocals. First, Kovac made a call to his friend, Randy Meisner. Another call was made to Timothy B. Schmit by one of the session players. Amazingly, both men agreed to perform on the track. Several days later, Meisner and Schmit arrived at the studio and added their vocal harmonies.

Marx recalled: "As Randy was leaving the studio, he said, 'I noticed you haven't cut a guitar solo on this yet.' 'Yeah,' I said. 'We still have some more overdubs to do.' Randy said, 'I'm still buddies with Joe Walsh. I bet he'd love to play on this.' I just stared at Randy.... 'I can't promise he'll do it, but I'll ask him if you want.' 'Are you kidding? I want!' A few days later my manager called me. 'Dude. Walsh loves the song and wants to play the solo. We just need to figure out a time in his schedule.'"

A week later, Walsh was slated to appear at the sessions. As Marx recalled: "I sat anxiously inside Studio C at Capitol and waited for Joe to arrive. I invited Randy Meisner to be there, and when Joe walked in and saw him, his eyes lit up and he threw his arms around Randy. They hadn't seen each other in quite a while, and Joe's affection for Randy was obvious. Joe was warm, friendly, and immediately complimentary to me about the song. We fired up the track, and Joe spent a few minutes dialing in his sound before we started recording takes. His second attempt is what's on the record. It was inspired and perfect." Released in 1987 as Marx's debut single, "Don't Mean Nothing" was a smash hit.

* * * * * *

Homecoming football games are an annual autumn tradition on America's college campuses. In October 1986, Joe Walsh returned to Kent State as the guest of honor at the university's homecoming weekend. One of his duties was to serve as the Parade Grand Marshal. Sitting in the back of a cherry red 1975 Cadillac Eldorado convertible, Walsh waved to the thousands of students and alumni along the parade route that passed by the north side of the campus.

Later that day, Walsh played an instrumental version of "The Star Spangled Banner" at the start of a football game between the Kent State Golden Flashes and the Central Michigan Chippewas. At halftime, he dutifully crowned the homecoming queen. Later in the evening, Walsh headlined a concert at Memorial Gym. At Walsh's request, the Numbers Band opened the show. Wearing a Kent State football jersey and cap, Walsh performed for the boisterous audience. Uncharacteristically, Walsh was forced to use rented equipment, while Joe Vitale played a borrowed drum kit. Before the start of the concert, Walsh gave his reason for majoring in English at Kent State – "because I wanted to learn how to talk good."

▶ CHAPTER 28
GOT ANY GUM IN MEMPHIS?

In early-1987, Joe Walsh was in the thick of another divorce. He had given up on Vermont but was also tired of Los Angeles and decided to relocate: "I wasn't getting much done in Los Angeles at the time. And Memphis was and still is a real center of undiscovered talent and just tradition. And in the West Coast's continuing search for some kind of identity, I just decided to come to Memphis and spend time there."

Walsh had another reason for moving to Memphis – he wanted to reconnect with a woman he had dated in the late-1970s, Lisa Pritchett. "Lisa was a gorgeous-looking girl – long legs, beautiful hair and an angel's face. But she could be one of the ugliest human beings on the planet," recalled Steve Luongo, a member of John Entwistle's solo band. Conversely, rock manager Bill Curbishley had a different opinion: "Deep down, she was a nice girl – and 'nice' in the real sense of the word. But then again, a victim of her own vices."

In Memphis, Walsh also spent a great deal of time helping local businessman Gary Belz design a new recording studio. Walsh recalled: "Gary asked if I would come and help make the studio comfortable for artists. I came down for about a year and a half and helped put it together. In the meantime, I kind of interfaced with the whole musical community in Memphis." Performing in various local nightclubs, Walsh recalled: "It was a real kick in the pants playing with some of the folks downtown. It was great to get back in a club situation.... There's nothing like going back to the basics to get headed off in a new direction. It really brought me around to basic blues and stuff when I probably was trying to over-intellectualize or over-orchestrate. Sometimes less is more, y'know." And at a club inside the Peabody Skyway Hotel, Walsh performed with a band that included Ron Wood of the Rolling Stones and Donald "Duck" Dunn of Booker T. & The M.G.'s.

* * * * * *

In March 1987, Joe Walsh began working on the solo album, *Got Any Gum?* The project represented a musical departure for Walsh, who was attempting to update his sound. He told his label at the time: "I don't particularly want a hit single. I already did that. I was part of a band that made you guys very wealthy. Why don't you just leave me alone and let me make my music? And they think I'm crazy."

Walsh recorded the album at a pair of studios in Memphis, Ardent and Alpha Sound. He teamed with local engineer/producer Terry Manning – best known for his work with the Texas trio, ZZ Top. Walsh was backed by Manning on keyboards, Dave Cochran on bass and Chad Cromwell on drums. Both J.D. Souther and Jimi Jamison of Survivor provided backing vocals.

Got Any Gum? was released at the end of October 1987. The album's title came from an unlikely street encounter Walsh had in New York City: "A bum came up to me on the street. Thought he was going to hit me up for some spare change, so I got some out, and he said, 'No, I don't want money. Got any gum?' And I thought, boy, that's something everyone says at one time or another." The front cover of the album featured the neon-illuminated Memphian Theater in Memphis. In the 1960s, Elvis Presley would often rent the theater for late-night showings of films for friends and family, away from prying, public eyes.

A keyboard-heavy album, *Got Any Gum?* featured eight original compositions. The first single, "The Radio Song," was a hit on album-rock radio. The song's oddball music video was filmed in black and white and featured a cameo appearance by pioneering deejay Wolfman Jack. However, the second single, "In My Car," fared poorly. The track was co-written by Walsh and Ringo Starr, and had originally appeared on Starr's 1983 solo album, *Old Wave*.

The album failed to gain traction and sold poorly. One reviewer wrote: "There is absolutely nothing wrong with this album; it's just not a fireball. It's a good Joe Walsh LP, a creature I never really expected to hear again. Whether anybody cares remains to be seen." Later that year, Walsh was dropped by his label, Warner Brothers.

Hitting the road, Walsh was backed by Rick Rosas on bass, Chad Cromwell on drums and Ed Sanford (of the Sanford-Townsend Band) on keyboards. A reviewer in Cleveland remarked: "So, from CYO dances at St. Richard's to Water Street in Kent and on to the City of Angels, it seems Joe Walsh hasn't really changed at all. I keep wondering if he went to North Olmsted [on] Saturday afternoon and mowed his parents' lawn." Another writer commented: "Clearly, Walsh remains a fan favorite because he invariably puts the fan first, showing that loyalty should come from the stage as well as the seats."

On September 19, Walsh was a performer at Farm Aid III in Lincoln, Nebraska. Taking the stage in front of 70,000 spectators, he opened with "The Star-Spangled Banner." After finishing a second song – an extended rendition of "Rocky Mountain Way" – the revolving stage started turning around for unexplained reasons. A frustrated Walsh came out after a few minutes and shouted, "I'll be back." He didn't return until after the end of the day's scheduled performances, when he sang two more songs, "In the City" and "Life's Been Good."

On October 2, Walsh appeared on *Late Night with David Letterman*. After performing "Rocky Mountain Way," Walsh sat down for an interview. Later that same month, Walsh appeared on *Arsenio Hall* and jokingly accused the fellow Kent State alum of stealing his hubcaps in Cleveland. Hall was clearly not amused.

* * * * * *

On November 20, 1987, Joe Walsh turned 40. Revealing his state of mind at the time, he proclaimed: "I've been rich a couple times and famous a couple times and the only thing that's really left is the music for me. I'm at peace with myself and, at 40, very happy."

One day earlier he flew to Cleveland, where he took over the microphone as the guest host on Cleveland rock powerhouse WMMS. Joined by Rick Rosas, Walsh spent six-hours playing his favorite classic rock hits, chatting with listeners, talking about his musician friends around Northeastern Ohio and unleashing a string of comedic one-liners. Walsh also celebrated as he always did and sounded tipsy on the air. But on this day, he also celebrated with a large birthday cake, which featured an image of an electric guitar.

Meanwhile, Walsh was finally acknowledging that the Eagles would not be reuniting. He told a reporter: "I don't see it ever happening. I don't see the Eagles ever getting back together. But if I get a late night phone call asking me to do it, I'll be on the bus, pal." Walsh based his assessment on the fact that most of his former bandmates had moved on and were enjoying successful solo careers.

* * * * * *

In 1988, Joe Walsh was deeply angered by the actions of his close friend, Pete Townshend. Writing in his autobiography, the legendary guitarist for the Who admitted: "Never much interested in cars apart from their ability to transport me quickly and safely, I turned to boats...

I bought *Blue Merlin*, a 46-foot motor-sailer with roll-away sails and a powerful bow-thruster, so it could be sailed and maneuvered singlehandedly. I sold a lot of precious guitars to make the deal: two De Angelicos, the Gibson Flying V that Joe Walsh had given me (boy, was he pissed off when he found out), the Guild Merle Travis, a double-neck white Gibson and a few lesser ones. That gave me the deposit, and *Blue Merlin* became the yacht that would finally allow me to become a real sailor."

* * * * * *

Before leaving Memphis in 1988, Joe Walsh broke up with Lisa Pritchett. Soon after, she began a long-term relationship with John Entwistle of the Who, who was married at the time. That same year, Walsh started dating a 20-year-old adult dancer, Kristin Casey. They met on a blind date in her hometown of Austin, Texas.

In 2020, Casey would publish a tell-all memoir that chronicled her relationship with Walsh. In the book, *Rock Monster*, she described her first impressions of her soon-to-be boyfriend: "He was definitely cute – nice-looking in an offbeat way – with a bouncy kind of energy not entirely contained. He had a way of speaking that was boozy and hyper, like Jerry Lewis mixed with Dean Martin and channeled by Jeff Spicoli (of *Fast Times At Ridgemont High*). After we'd exchanged hellos, Joe cocked his head and smiled at me for no apparent reason, swaying gently side to side, like a boat on the ocean. He wasn't doing anything out of the ordinary and yet he was.... I was transfixed by a mass of man-boy contradictions: sinewy biceps, boyish mop, and tender green eyes that were simultaneously curious and world-weary. He had large, strong hands with smooth, nimble fingers and a big nose, nicely offset by a wide grin and animated lips." Casey also discussed the couple's encounters with celebrities such as Jack Nicholson, Wolfman Jack, Lita Ford, Harry Nilsson and Bonnie Raitt.

In the book, Casey also addressed her engagement to Walsh and the reasons they never married. Their unstable and toxic relationship would endure for six-years, with the couple finally breaking up in 1994. And just like Walsh, Casey eventually hit rock bottom and later joined Alcoholics Anonymous. As for the often-controversial content in the book, Walsh took the high road and chose not to make any public statements.

⧐ CHAPTER 29
THE ALL-STARR TOUR

Ringo Starr had spent much of the 1970s and '80s drinking and using drugs. At his lowest point, he admitted to downing a whopping sixteen-bottles of wine per day. Then one day in the late-1980s, Starr realized that his life had spiraled out of control: "One Friday afternoon [I] was told by the staff that I'd trashed the house so badly they thought there had been burglars, and I'd trashed Barbara so badly they thought she was dead." In the aftermath, Starr recalled: "I had a second, maybe half-a-second, of clarity and I was in so much pain and I knew that Barbara... had mentioned a sort of rehab situation. She had a problem, too. She found this place in Arizona."

In October 1988, Ringo Starr and his wife – actress Barbara Bach – flew from England to the U.S. for treatment at a rehab clinic near Tucson. It was the only facility that would permit the couple to stay in the same room. Starr recalled: "I landed drunk as a skunk at the clinic. I drank all the way and got off the plane completely demented. I thought I was going to a lunatic asylum. Eight days in, I decided, 'I'm here to get help because I know I'm sick.'"

The couple spent five-weeks at the facility. Starr recalled at the time: "At some point, you realize that you've been brainless for a long time, and you're not having fun. And somehow a light goes off in your brain, telling you that you need to get help. That's what I did. I went to the clinic, and it was great for me. You're never cured, but they start the process." Ironically, Starr had previously scored a top-10 hit in 1975 with an anti-drug and anti-alcohol single, "No No Song."

Meanwhile, in 1989, concert promoter David Fishof had written to Starr, offering him $1 million to headline a musical revue. This wasn't the first time Fishof had approached Starr. Two-years earlier, Starr had flatly refused the promoter's offer to go back on the road. However, this time Starr had a change of heart: "David did a very smart thing. He *asked*. No one had for so long, and thank God, for once I felt up to the effort." After a successful stint in rehab, Starr possessed the mental acuity and physical stamina to perform on a stage.

However, Starr hadn't toured since his days with the Beatles, and that was more than two-decades earlier. Fishof had previously organized the successful Monkees reunion tour in 1986 as well as an oldies package tour featuring the Turtles, the Association, Gary Puckett and Spanky & Our Gang. A *Rolling Stone* writer observed at the time: "In the mathematics of the mainstream rock industry, one Beatle is still more impressive than three Monkees, and Fishof knows that this tour could be his great leap."

A few months passed before Starr decided to respond to Fishof. Starr was contemplating his return to the concert road, and having someone with experience in the field appealed to him. The staging of rock concerts had changed dramatically since the 1960s, when the Beatles were hampered by primitive, underperforming sound systems.

After assembling a list of who he'd like on the tour, Starr made a series of telephone calls. Amazingly, everyone he contacted agreed to join the tour. Starr initially reached out to Joe Walsh, who was in New Zealand at the time. Walsh had been considering an offer to tour as the opening act for Roger Daltrey and, later, the Who. But playing with a Beatle was a far more enticing choice. Starr recalled: "After Joe told me yes, I told him we'd been offered 30 gigs and in my naivety I said, 'Well, we can do six a week you know, and get it over with.' Anyway, Joe asked me how long it was since I'd been on tour and explained that three shows a week is great, four is OK and five is stretching it."

Staging a news conference in New York City, Starr announced the specifics of the tour, which started in Dallas and closed in Los Angeles. The band briefly rehearsed before going on the road. As Starr recalled: "The first three days of rehearsals, we just jammed the numbers. We would name the song, and go for it any way we could. We had to get to know each other. Then the next two weeks, we worked out the parts, got down to it, and pulled together the best show we could. We're not trying to break anybody's brains. We're just giving them songs they know and love."

*　　*　　*　　*　　*　　*

In January 1989, Joe Walsh returned to Australia for another run with the Party Boys. The new lineup included a second American, bassist Calvin Welch. This version of the group recorded the single, "Follow Your Heart." Eventually, Walsh invited his girlfriend, Kristin Casey, to join him. After Walsh's departure from the Party Boys, the group added notable British Invasion singer, Eric Burdon.

After the end of his stint with the Party Boys, Walsh flew to New Zealand, where he joined the country's first-ever reggae band, the Herbs. In an unlikely union, Walsh provided guitar and vocals on their album, *Homegrown*. The project, which Walsh also produced, was an interesting mix of original and cover songs, including a remake of the oldie, "Walk Away Renee," and the traditional spiritual, "Amazing Grace." Walsh provided the lead vocals on two of the album's tracks, "Up All Night" and "It's Alright." However, the most notable track on the album was the Walsh composition, "Ordinary Average Guys," which featured the lead vocals of the group's bassist, Charlie Tumahai. (A few years later, Walsh would re-record the song as "Ordinary Average Guy.") Walsh and the Herbs subsequently staged a few shows, including a performance at the New Zealand Parliament. While in the country, Walsh ran into his former bass player, Rick Rosas, who at the time was touring in Neil Young's band.

While in New Zealand, Walsh experienced an epiphany. It was late winter when he was taken by the members of the Herbs to the ancient ruins at Otataraat in Hawke's Bay – a place held sacred by the country's native inhabitants, the Maoris. During a moment of introspection, Walsh realized he was destroying himself with booze and drugs, and that he had to make some dramatic changes in his life. But the changes didn't happen right away. In fact, his drinking was getting worse as were the consequences – he was losing friends and wasting a significant amount of money on drugs.

Walsh later admitted: "Vodka was what worked for me. I would have to say that my higher power was vodka. Vodka and cocaine and Camel Light cigarettes was a great triangle for me, because the cocaine made it so you could drink more vodka, and of course the cocaine made it such that you had to have a cigarette, and of course with cigarettes you have to have a drink... and round and round you go. You see how that works?"

Years later, Walsh would reveal what he experienced on that fateful day in Otataraat: "I had a moment of clarity standing up on top and looking out at the valley. I remember that vividly and I don't know where that came from. I got goosebumps. I had a profound spiritual awakening, and that this thing I entered was not me."

*   *   *   *   *   *

While contemplating how to break free of his addictions, Joe Walsh was also preparing to go on the road with Ringo Starr. For the tour, former Beatles associate Billy Preston served as the musical director. Also in the band were Nils Lofgren, Clarence Clemons, Rick Danko, Levon Helm, Jim Keltner and Dr. John. As for the hiring of Dr. John, Starr explained: "Joe suggested him. [Dr. John] speaks in a weird language which is half English, half Cajun and half rhyming madness and that's fine if you're face to face with him, but down the telephone it's murder. I'd get off the line thinking, Mac doesn't wanna do it, then I'd talk to this other pal in L.A. who said, 'Sure he does.'" Meanwhile, some of the musicians in the band jokingly referred to Starr's group as the Ringoburys, in tribute to George Harrison's successful supergroup, the Traveling Wilburys.

The All-Starr tour launched on July 15, 1989, in Dallas. Although alcohol and drugs were banned from the dressing rooms and stage, what happened after the shows was a different matter. As Starr recalled: "When I called them originally, I explained to the band that I'd just come out of a clinic and I'd like the hotel rooms to be left as we found them. But after the show if some of the members liked to drink, I couldn't be in charge of that. And you could always spot the ones who'd had a night out when we got up the next morning for the plane."

The concerts went better than expected. On the third stop of the tour in Indianapolis, the 49-year-old, newly sober Starr told the audience: "It's great to be here. It's great to be anywhere." However, Walsh lamented something he often witnessed: "Ringo's always been surrounded by too many yes men and it's difficult with everyone going, 'Great, Mr. Starr.'" Walsh, meanwhile, would often perform an extended version of "Rocky Mountain Way" that included a short portion of the spiritual, "Amazing Grace."

During the tour, there were a number of guest performers, including Garth Hudson, Zak Starkey, Eric Carmen, Paul Shaffer, Max Weinberg and comedian John Candy; and at one show, Bruce Springsteen played guitar on four songs, including Little Richard's "Long Tall Sally." All of the shows closed with the entire band taking the stage for a raucous rendition of "With A Little Help From My Friends."

Meanwhile, there were reports in the press that Don Henley was unhappy about Walsh performing "Desperado," an Eagles song that was recorded before Walsh had joined the band. Walsh explained at the time: "I played 'Desperado' in rehearsal and Ringo and Barbara liked it so much that they requested that I do it." Henley was also unhappy that Walsh was performing another Eagles song, "Life In The Fast Lane." Henley stated at the time: "That's not his song to do. Glenn Frey and I wrote 90-percent of that song, and I sang it on the record. Joe wrote the opening guitar riff. Joe had his own solo career before he joined the Eagles, so I don't understand why he doesn't do a song that's more his, instead of doing that one. Besides, he sounds like he's got a clothespin on his nose."

Additionally, Henley chose this time to open up about Walsh's role in the dissolution of the Eagles: "I didn't want to talk about it before, but the hell with that. I don't mind telling you, Joe Walsh was one of the reasons the Eagles broke up. He was instrumental in the disintegration of that group. He was an insidious troublemaker. He would split the band into factions. He was a very divisive presence and very covert about it. He was very hypocritical. Glenn and I used to laugh and say, 'Yeah, Joe's a very interesting bunch of guys.' You can print that, too. I'm tired of being Mr. Nice Guy."

* * * * * *

In December 1989, Joe Walsh recorded an *Unplugged* segment for broadcast on MTV. The episode was billed as "Joe Walsh and Friends," and there were some expectations that the performance would be some sort of Eagles reunion. That didn't happen. As the show's producers explained: "Walsh arrived at the studio with only bass player Rick Rosas. We explained that 'friends' is actually a plural word and that, notwithstanding Rick's musical proficiency, we had been expecting the 'friends' to be somewhat recognizable to our television audience. Then we discovered that Dr. John was taping a show in the same building. So we cornered the good doctor in the men's bathroom and 'Joe Walsh and Friends' became Joe Walsh and Dr. John. All went smoothly. Joe is a consummate showman, who's certainly unafraid to delve into the deepest realms of shtick."

Taking the stage with an acoustic guitar, Walsh wore a vintage lime-green mohair jacket and slim black jeans. Also on the stage was the program's host, Jules Shear, on guitar and backing vocals. Filmed at the National Video Center in New York City, the band performed just six songs including "Rosewood Bitters," "Life's Been Good" and Neil Young's "Cinnamon Girl." Walsh also performed the Eagles hit,

"Desperado." Although Henley was unable to stop Walsh from playing the song, Henley's protests were enough to convince MTV not to air the performance of the song. The segment ended with Dr. John singing his original composition, "Let The Good Times Roll." Walsh's *Unplugged* performance aired on the network the following February.

While Henley was complaining to MTV about Walsh's selection of material, the network's vice-president, Joel Gallen, managed to convince the former Eagles co-leader to stage his own *Unplugged* episode. Henley had just won a Grammy for his solo hit, "The End Of The Innocence," and the program was the perfect outlet to celebrate the award. However, Henley's appearance didn't go smoothly. As Bob Small, the co-founder of *Unplugged*, recalled: "Don Henley kept an audience waiting outside in the sun in L.A. for four hours while they tuned a piano to his liking."

* * * * * *

The MTV decade was a prolific time for some members of the Eagles. As expected, Don Henley and Glenn Frey had the greatest amount of solo success. In 1987, Timothy B. Schmit became the fifth member of the Eagles to score a solo hit when his single, "Boys Night Out," landed on top-40 radio. Joe Walsh, on the other hand, managed to place two solo hits on the pop charts during the decade, his last entry coming in 1981 with "A Life Of Illusion." While pop music – typified by hair metal and new wave acts – didn't embrace Walsh's traditional classic-rock sound, he continued to garner strong airplay on album-rock radio. More significantly, he remained a popular concert draw and toured heavily throughout the 1980s.

However, two classic members of the Eagles failed to score any solo pop hits during the decade. Don Felder's highest-charting solo single, "Heavy Metal," was a hit on album-rock radio but just missed hitting the top-40, peaking at #43. (The song featured musical contributions by Henley and Schmit.) Lastly, Bernie Leadon was never able to place a solo single on the *Billboard* charts. With the decade ending and a new one about to start, there were hints that the various members of the Eagles might finally set aside their personal hostilities for the sake of the group.

⧐ CHAPTER 30
EAGLE RUMBLINGS

In the early-1990s, there were multiple rumors of an Eagles reunion. On one occasion in 1990, it looked as though Don Henley and Glenn Frey were finally reconciling. Henley stated at the time: "Glenn showed up at a couple of my shows in L.A. I invited him onstage, and the applause was deafening, so I think it gave him the fever. So the first day of February, he and I are going to get together to write two songs." The press speculated that Frey and Henley were collaborating on new music with the ultimate goal of reforming the group. The pair did in fact meet in March and attempted to write some material for a planned Eagles greatest hits package.

Then in late-April, three members of the Eagles got together for two performances at Henley's request. Henley was joined by Frey and Timothy B. Schmit at a pair of all-star concerts at the Centrum in Worcester, Massachusetts. Henley had organized the shows to raise funds for his charity, the Walden Woods Project. Also on the bill were Bonnie Raitt, Arlo Guthrie, Bob Seger and Jimmy Buffett. Playing for 11,500 paying customers each night, the Eagles-lite trio focused on the group's 1970s classics. After one of the shows, Henley remarked: "I wouldn't call what you saw exactly an Eagles reunion, but it was three singers. And it didn't feel like 10 years since we sang these songs. Maybe one or two." The trio had spent just three-days practicing for the shows.

* * * * * *

In February 1990, Joe Walsh appeared on the same stage as Don Henley for an unplanned, 45-minute performance at a nightclub in Los Angeles. Walsh and Henley were joined by Sting, Herbie Hancock, Branford Marsalis and Bruce Springsteen. The impromptu jam session took place at a charity event.

Continuing to tour as a solo act, Walsh was not at the top of his game during this period. In March, a concert reviewer in Pittsburgh wrote: "Walsh's manner was odd – his speech sounded slurred and listless, his movements seemed a little shaky.... He played well. But his singing? His voice broke in the middle of set-opening 'Meadows.'"

Also that year, Walsh played guitar on the self-titled debut album by the pop trio, Wilson Phillips. Walsh appeared on three tracks, two of which became top-5 hits – "Hold On" and "A Reason To Believe." The smash album, *Wilson Phillips*, would sell ten-million copies worldwide.

* * * * * *

Emboldened by the success of Ringo's All-Starr tour, Joe Walsh joined another supergroup – the Best. The six-man band also included John Entwistle, Simon Phillips (of Toto), Keith Emerson (of Emerson, Lake & Palmer) and Jeff "Skunk" Baxter (of Steely Dan and the Doobie Brothers). Fronting the Best was singer Rick Livingstone of the little-known Canadian group, Agent. The Best had initially wanted Terry Reid as their vocalist, but he was not interested.

The group was formed at the China Club in Hollywood. The popular venue hosted a weekly Pro-Jams night, which attracted a series of notable rock musicians who would sit in with the band that was playing onstage. On one occasion, a Japanese promoter asked the cast of the musicians who were performing at the time if they would be interested in touring across Japan. Just like that, a supergroup was born.

The Best performed songs from each of the members' individual groups, much like in Ringo's All-Starr Band. After an initial performance in Hawaii in late-September 1990, the group headed to Asia. Although the group's first gig in Japan was a near fiasco due to inclement weather, the remaining shows attracted large, enthusiastic audiences. At a stop in the city of Yokahama, the group performed three Walsh/Eagles songs – "Seven Bridges Road," "Life In The Fast Lane" and "Rocky Mountain Way."

Sadly, the Best existed for only two-weeks and played just five shows. Later, Entwistle and Baxter tried to resurrect the Best with a new lead singer, Mickey Thomas, who was previously a member of both the Elvin Bishop Group and Starship. The new lineup managed to perform just a few shows. Then after Entwistle rejoined the Who for a lengthy reunion tour, the Best disbanded for good.

Meanwhile, in late-1990, Walsh rehired Richard "Smokey" Wendell as his personal manager. Soon after, Wendell convinced Walsh to give rehab a try. Enrolling in a program at a facility in Los Angeles, Walsh managed to achieve sobriety. However, he soon reverted to his old ways.

▶ CHAPTER 31
ORDINARY AVERAGE JOE

In late-1990, Joe Walsh summoned his old friend David Spero to California. Spero was unemployed at the time after a ten-year stint as the head of a regional office for Columbia Pictures. For the previous year, he had been selling off portions of his extensive record collection in order to survive.

Spero was a well-liked, widely recognized figure around Northeastern Ohio. His first claim to fame came at age thirteen when he began working on *Upbeat!* – a syndicated music variety show filmed in Cleveland. Airing on more than 100 television stations around the country, the program was produced by Spero's father, Herman, and was hosted by an affable Dick Clark look-alike from Canada named Don Webster.

The weekly show was filmed every Saturday afternoon at the studios of WEWS-TV and featured lip-synced performances by rock and R&B stars as well as by emerging local acts. Spero explained how the show was able to present top talent: "We were lucky with good clubs here. We'd get Lou Reed and the Velvet Underground and Canned Heat over from La Cave appearances in University Circle. The Fifth Dimension and Aretha Franklin came over from Leo's Casino at E. 75th St., and the Grande Cleveland at WHK Auditorium would have Deep Purple, the Moody Blues and Procol Harum." The local acts on the show included the Baskerville Hounds, E.T. Hooley, Jack Rabbit (which featured a young Chrissie Hynde), the Chylds and, of course, the James Gang. The Grasshoppers, who were the program's house band for a few seasons, featured future Cars co-founder Benjamin Orr.

Walsh and Spero first met in the late-1960s during the taping of a free, outdoor concert that was sponsored by a local radio station. A few years later, Spero worked as a deejay at a pair of pioneering FM rock stations in Cleveland. By the early-1970s, he had left radio and turned to artist management.

When Walsh contacted Spero in 1990, he had left the music industry altogether. Spero recalled their conversation: "[Walsh called] me up and said, 'Listen, I got a new record, I want to do a couple of dates. And I wonder if you could help me put a few things together.' He was looking for a manager, and asked, 'Do you know anybody who's interested?' I sat there and thought, 'Wow, maybe I'm interested! I'll come out and talk to you about it.' Joe left me a first-class plane ticket, and a limousine picks me up at the airport. It took me right to his house, and the driver said, 'Just go right in. Door's unlocked.' It was like 11 A.M."

However, Spero was in for a surprise when he arrived at Walsh's home. According to *The Cleveland Plain Dealer*: "Spero was shocked. While Walsh was known for being a party animal supreme in the tradition of room-wrecking rockers, this scene was weird beyond belief. The mansion was empty. Save for the backseat from an Econoline van and a piano, there was no furniture. 'Hellooo, Joe? Hellooo?' Spero called.... Spero walked slowly from room to room, looking for Walsh. He was hoping he wouldn't come across anything horrific. Spero finally found Walsh in a downstairs room, asleep, wrapped in an old comforter on the floor. There was one problem. Spero says when he walked in, he saw a handgun on the floor near the guitarist. Spero wasn't about to startle him. He quietly backed out of the room."

Spero noticed something else: "Meanwhile the answering machine is going crazy. It's like: 'Hello. This is Ringo. Joe, give me a call when you get a chance.' And, 'Hello. Pete Townshend here. Joe, I've got a question for you.' So, now I'm getting psyched, but I still don't know what's going on." At that point, Spero decided to leave. Later in the day, Spero and Walsh spoke on the phone and then had a formal meeting that was attended by Walsh's business manager and personal attorney.

As for why the house was unfurnished, Spero learned that Walsh had just purchased the property. The gated, 5,100-square-foot, split-level home was situated in the exclusive Studio City enclave of Los Angeles and boasted spectacular views of the nearby mountains.

* * * * * *

After hiring a manager that he trusted and knew well, Joe Walsh signed with a new label, Pyramid Records, which was distributed by Epic. Walsh had recorded a new album in August 1990, but its release was delayed for several months until he finished sorting out a number of issues in his personal and professional life.

The album, *Ordinary Average Guy*, was mostly recorded at Pyramid Studios near Chattanooga, Tennessee, and featured dozens of musical guests including Ringo Starr and Jimi Jamison. During the sessions, Walsh and a number of his fellow musicians engaged in some hard partying at the studio as well as at their hotel, the historic Chattanooga Choo Choo. On the album's cover, Walsh struck a classic rock star pose inspired by his friend, Pete Townshend. The album spawned two radio hits, "All Of A Sudden" and the quirky, "Ordinary Average Guy." Additionally, Joe Vitale provided the lead vocals on the track, "School Days." The album received mostly positive reviews, with one critic writing: "Since the break-up of the Eagles, Walsh has run hot-and-cold with his solo records. This album's one of the warmer ones." However, with grunge, alternative-rock and rap dominating popular music in the early-1990s, Walsh's classic rock album was not widely embraced by radio.

* * * * * *

In 1991, David Spero arranged for Joe Walsh to go on the road with the Doobie Brothers. Walsh was happy to sign on as the opening act, which meant less responsibility. For the tour, he hired keyboard virtuoso, Al Kooper, who was best known for playing the electric organ intro on Bob Dylan's seminal classic, "Like A Rolling Stone." However, Kooper hadn't toured for ten-years since backing Dylan in 1981 and was hesitant about returning to the road. Walsh and Kooper had been friends since 1975, when Walsh worked on Kooper's hit album, *Act Like Nothing's Wrong*. Also in Walsh's band were bassist Rick Rosas, Joe Vitale and a second drummer, Chad Cromwell.

The tour began in June, and most of the dates were at large, outdoor venues. However, trouble started when the Doobie Brothers began playing practical jokes on Walsh and his band. Never one to back down, Walsh reciprocated in a big way. As Joe Vitale, Jr. recalled: "During the tour, the Doobie Brothers thought it would be a funny practical joke to serve the Joe Walsh Band drinks, like waiters, during their set. This triggered a full scale thermal nuclear practical joke war for the rest of the tour. Every night, there was something hysterical happening at some point in both band's sets. It culminated in Cincinnati.... During the Doobie Brothers set, Joe Walsh had something up his sleeve to win this war. Earlier, he had gone to the Cincinnati Zoo and had them bring a *lot* of animals to the show to parade across the stage during the Doobie Brothers' song 'Jesus Is Just Alright' complete with Walsh dressed as

Noah. To use the phrase, it was truly epic."

On July 20, at the Nautica Pavilion in Cleveland, Walsh reunited onstage with Jimmy Fox and Dale Peters of the James Gang. Joe Vitale recalled: "It was funny the way it went down. Joe says to the audience, 'Hey – how about a James Gang song?' The crowd goes yeah, yeah, yeah, and he says, 'Well how about the James Gang!'" Greeted by thunderous applause, the trio performed three songs beginning with a bluesy rendition of "Funk #49." In the end, the tour with the Doobie Brothers had gone well and Spero had proven his worth as a manager. Meanwhile, while Kooper was out on the road, he learned that his wife was leaving him.

During this period, Walsh's drinking was getting worse and his performances were suffering. One reviewer wrote: "His guitar licks are hotter than ever, but like most aging rockers, his voice has begun to show some wear. On several songs, Walsh had to forego the high notes, giving those songs a new sound." Another critic noted Walsh's declining physical condition: "At 43, the wizened musician is thin and frail-looking; his hair is graying; he moves slowly across the room, peering through thick glasses."

* * * * * *

In October 1990, Joe Walsh was hired as a guest deejay by Seattle classic rock station, KISW. He was paid $10,000 for a one-week stint behind the microphone. Walsh was accompanied on the assignment by his personal manager, Richard Wendell, whose job was to keep his boss out of trouble. Walsh and Wendell stayed at a Sheraton Hotel, where they were given star treatment.

At the radio station, Walsh was given free rein to play what he pleased. However, one day, he went off-script. Beau Phillips, the station's general manager, recalled: "Joe had been on the air for a short time when our music director buzzed me on the intercom. He asked 'Do you recognize this song that Joe is playing?' I turned up the radio in my office and had no clue what the song was. We'd agree that Joe would stick reasonably close to KISW's playlist. But he was already going rogue. So I strolled down the hallway toward the studio and opened the control room door, 'Hey Joe, how's it going so far?' 'Great, how ya doin'? Does my show sound good?' I said, 'Yeah, we love having you here, Joe. By the way, what is this song called?' Joe replied, 'Uh, it's the

Michael Stanley Band. They're from my hometown, Cleveland.'"

Later in the week, Walsh received an unexpected telephone call from Irving Azoff. Don Henley was attempting to reform the Eagles, and Azoff wanted to know if Walsh would be interested in rejoining the group. An ecstatic Walsh agreed to reunite with his former bandmates.

Walsh finished his week in Seattle with an intimate nightclub concert for 500 of the radio station's listeners. However, a few days after Walsh's departure, the station received a telephone call from the Sheraton, asking who would be paying for the $1,500 liquor bill and the $8,500 worth of damage to the hotel room. Phillips telephoned Wendell, who agreed to take care of the matter.

Soon after, Walsh and some of his Eagles bandmates gathered in a recording studio and worked on some new songs while waiting for Glenn Frey to arrive. However, Frey had a last-minute change of heart and the sessions were cancelled. At the time, he was recuperating from an operation on his colon. Additionally, Frey was newly married and had a young wife who was expecting their first child. As such, his priorities were not with his former group. There would be no Eagles reunion at that point.

▶ CHAPTER 32
JOE AND GLENN

In the spring of 1992, George Harrison made a surprise announcement. He was staging his first full-length concert in Britain since the Beatles' historic rooftop performance in 1969. Harrison organized a fundraising show for the Natural Law Party of Britain on April 6, a few days before the national elections. The concert was headlined by Harrison and featured a pair of opening acts, Joe Walsh and Gary Moore.

Taking the stage at the Royal Albert Hall in London, Walsh played a tight, five-song, 30-minute set that began with "Pretty Maids All In A Row." And in the middle of "Funk #49," Walsh inserted a few riffs from the Kenny Loggins hit, "Footloose." Walsh's drummer for the show was Zak Starkey.

Harrison began his 16-song set with a Beatles track from *Revolver*, "I Want To Tell You," and closed with the Chuck Berry classic, "Roll Over Beethoven." Backstage after the concert, Harrison revealed that he was considering going on a solo tour later that year and asked Walsh if he would be interested in joining the backing band. An excited Walsh quickly accepted the offer. However, the tour would never come to fruition. Instead, Harrison's 12-date jaunt across Japan with Eric Clapton the previous year would mark the former Beatles' last-ever tour.

* * * * * *

Also in 1992, Joe Walsh released the solo album, *Songs For A Dying Planet*. It would be his last solo album for the next twenty-years. Reuniting with Bill Szymczyk – who shared production duties with Joe Vitale – Walsh worked on the project over a three-month period at studios in Los Angeles and Charlotte, North Carolina.

The album opened with the track, "Shut Up," which humorously targeted his former Eagles bandmates, Don Henley and Glenn Frey. A surprise on the album was a cover of the oldie, "Will You Love Me Tomorrow," which was originally recorded in 1960 by the Shirelles. The album spawned just one hit on album-rock radio, "Vote For Me."

A very poor seller, this was Walsh's first studio album that failed to chart, either in the U.S. or U.K. However, that same year Walsh made a surprise appearance on the country charts. Teaming with Kix Brooks – of the duo Brooks & Dunn – Walsh scored a hit with the single, "New To This Town." Also during this period, Walsh recorded a notable duet with Steve Earle. Their remake of the Carl Perkins classic, "Honey Don't," was featured on the soundtrack of the film, *The Beverly Hillbillies*.

Also that year, Walsh decided to run for vice-president. Hitting the road for his Vote For Me Tour, he would take the stage dressed as Uncle Sam. For the tour, Walsh was backed by two drummers, Joe Vitale and Zak Starkey. The opening act, Brother, consisted of a trio of real-life brothers from Australia who played the bagpipes.

* * * * * *

Three-years after the first All-Starr tour, Ringo Starr took another revue on the road in 1992. Both Joe Walsh and Nils Lofgren signed up for a second time. The revised lineup also included Burton Cummings, Dave Edmunds, Tim Cappello, Todd Rundgren, Timothy B. Schmit and Zak Starkey. Starr – who cut off his signature pony tail before the tour – said at the time: "This band has a different feeling. It's more rock 'n' roll, more of a guitar lineup. It's what I was looking for, and that's the beauty of the All-Starr Band concept: It can change into whatever I'd like." Starr decided to schedule the tour to coincide with the release of his tenth solo album, *Time Takes Time*. And this time around, he didn't have any trouble finding a record label to release the project.

The U.S. leg of the tour began on June 2 at Fort Pierce, Florida, and continued until June 28 with a stop at Bonner Springs, Kansas. Starr told a reporter in Ohio: "Joe's brilliant. A lovely man. Everywhere we go he's really loved." Although Walsh and Starr were becoming closer friends as the tour progressed, a star-struck Walsh said of Starr: "From time to time I still am in awe of him, but getting to know him as a friend, he's so nice.... Sometimes I look over and see him and say, 'Holy smoke, I'm on stage with Ringo.'"

When the tour hit Cleveland, Walsh and Starr were stopped by police. As Walsh's manager David Spero recalled: "We're leaving the airport and the light wouldn't change. It's 1 in the morning and we're sitting there. Joe and Ringo are egging me on, saying, 'Come on. Just go, just go.' So I went. Within seconds, of course, a police car comes up behind us and pulls us over. The policeman comes up to the car and says, 'You know, you went through that light.' And I start to say, 'Well, I waited for...' And he doesn't want to hear about it. Then he shines his flashlight inside the car and says... 'It's Joe Walsh. And Ringo Starr!' I say, 'They made me do it,' and he let us go."

The European leg of the tour began on July 2 at the Göteborg Festival in Sweden and ended on July 24 in Rome. A performance at the prestigious Montreux Jazz Festival in Switzerland was recorded for release on CD and video. Returning to the U.S., the third leg of the tour began on August 1 in Seattle and ended with three dates in early September at Caesar's Palace in Las Vegas. Walsh had left the tour before it landed in Las Vegas. At one of the final shows, legendary singer-songwriter Harry Nilsson made a surprise appearance and sang his hit, "Without You."

Just three-weeks after the end of the All-Starr tour, Joe Walsh headed back on the road, beginning with a September 26 show in Atlanta. His stripped-down band consisted of Rick Rosas and two drummers – Joe Vitale and Zak Starkey.

When the tour stopped in Cleveland on Halloween, Walsh wore a patriotic costume. A local reviewer wrote: "It wasn't just a concert Saturday night. It was a 'Walshapalooza.' The zaniest and most colorful one that former Kent Stater Joe Walsh has done here. Not only did home boy Michael Stanley pop up at the Palace [Theater] to do a song he and Walsh had recorded 19 years ago, but the 1970s group, the James Gang, reunited in the middle of the show." And during the performance of "Ordinary Average Guy," a ping-pong game erupted at the front of the stage. At another point in the show, Vitale's son – 15-year-old Joe Vitale, Jr. – took over on drums. The solo tour ended on November 15 in Fort Myers, Florida.

*　*　*　*　*　*

In June 1992, when Glenn Frey was asked about reforming the Eagles and touring with Joe Walsh, he responded: "I don't want to get into the case of Joe Walsh. Just try to imagine yourself addled at the hip for over a year and a half with that guy!" Meanwhile, in September, Frey was scheduled to perform at the Agora in Cleveland. Two days before the show, Walsh's manager, David Spero, invited Frey and his band to dinner. According to *The Cleveland Plain Dealer,* at the restaurant, "Frey complained that he had been reaching out to Walsh, but that his former bandmate hadn't returned his calls. Spero told Frey that he and Walsh also had been trying to call him, but Frey had not called them back either. Both had gone through Eagles manager Azoff's office, Spero says."

Consequently, Spero decided to stage a prank in order to get Walsh and Frey talking again. The next day, Spero convinced Frey to make an appearance on the Cleveland classic rock station, WNCX, to promote his upcoming concert. Frey was interviewed by local rocker Michael Stanley, who was the station's afternoon deejay. While Frey was on the air, Spero contacted Walsh and convinced him to call Stanley's show to promote his own upcoming concert.

Stanley – who was told about Spero's plan – took Walsh's phone call and put him on the air with Frey. A bewildered Frey was caught off guard and quickly realized that Spero was behind the stunt. Amazingly, Walsh and Frey had a pleasant conversation over the next several minutes. However, Spero later recalled: "Glenn was giving me the finger through the glass in the radio booth the whole time." During his conversation with Walsh, Frey made a conciliatory move and pledged to close his Cleveland show with the Walsh classic, "Rocky Mountain Way."

More significantly, Walsh and Frey agreed to a meeting in Los Angeles, where both men lived at the time. Then in November 1992, Frey invited Walsh to appear as a musical guest at a concert in Los Angeles. Frey recalled: "I said, 'Would you do four or five songs? I've got a big band. They can play anything and they already know 'Rocky Mountain Way.'' So Joe came down and we had a really great time." A few months later at another Frey concert in Florida, Walsh again took the stage as a surprise guest. At that point, the two former bandmates recognized they had stumbled upon a winning formula and decided to team up for a co-headlining tour. However, Frey brushed aside the possibility of reuniting with his former group: "The Eagles are like a great white shark that devours everything."

In the summer of 1993, Frey and Walsh went on the road for the Party of Two tour. Unofficially, Frey dubbed it the NBA tour – "That stood for No Blow Allowed," Spero later admitted. Frey and Walsh assembled a 14-piece band, which included backup singers. Frey said at the time: "Joe and I individually are not as strong as we are collectively in the concert market. So we're sort of helping each other out by touring this summer." Walsh explained: "Glenn plays a couple and then I come out and we play a couple of mine and the rest of the show is together.... We have an intermission and after that we come out and do an Eagles segment." Some of the Eagles songs on the setlist included "New Kid In Town," "Peaceful Easy Feeling," "Life In The Fast Lane" and "Desperado." However, the duo surprised audiences by playing unlikely rock oldies like "My Girl" by the Temptations and "I Saw Her Standing There" by the Beatles.

At a sold-out show in Cleveland, Frey participated in some uncharacteristic onstage antics. A reviewer wrote: "It was Frey who wound up on a kooky note. He wore a colorful dinosaur head during the finale, Walsh's 1973 'Rocky Mountain Way.' It was the first time and the last time he'd do that, he said later. It was hot under there."

However, during this period, it was very apparent that Walsh was not taking care of himself. One concert reviewer noted: "Walsh looked like he should have been working the crowd for loose change, and his class-clown stage persona didn't do much to alter that image."

⏵ CHAPTER 33
HELL DOES FREEZE OVER

In 1993, more than a dozen country music stars submitted songs to the tribute album, *Common Thread: The Songs Of The Eagles*. The project was the brainchild of Don Henley, who wanted to raise funds for his charity, the Walden Woods Project. The album featured only one song co-written by Walsh, "The Sad Cafe," which was performed by Lorrie Morgan. Amazingly, no one recorded a rendition of "Hotel California." Apparently, the song's complex guitar solos were too challenging. Additionally, only one member of the Eagles appeared on any of the tracks – Timothy B. Schmit provided harmony vocals on Vince Gill's version of "I Can't Tell You Why."

After Travis Tritt recorded his countrified rendition of "Take It Easy," he took a chance and asked all five members of the 1980 lineup of the Eagles to appear in the song's music video. Amazingly, all five men agreed to the request. They participated, in part, because the tribute album was being released by Giant Records, a new label that was launched by Irving Azoff.

The video was filmed in early-December at a bar in North Hollywood. Tritt was shocked by the lack of drama or conflict between the members of the Eagles. In fact, they got along pretty well. Henley, who was the last to arrive, recalled: "That's when we were all really in a room together for the first time. They had instruments set up and we jammed: we played 'Rocky Mountain Way' and 'Take It Easy' and some blues. And we kind of liked it. That was the beginning." Meanwhile, *Common Thread* would sell three-million copies, clearly indicating a strong demand for the group's music.

* * * * * *

In February 1994, Glenn Frey and Joe Walsh were scheduled to appear at a charity fundraiser in Aspen, Colorado. A resident of the area since 1985, Frey wanted to aid the Aspen Grassroots Experience. Irving Azoff and a number of Eagles members also owned homes around Aspen, so it wasn't a big surprise when Don Henley asked to join his former bandmates at the event.

Frey relayed his reply to David Spero, who forwarded it to Azoff. Henley received a copy of the set list and was told *exactly* when to arrive. The reply also stated that if Henley was late *or* early to the rehearsal, he would not be welcome. The strict conditions were meant to send a message to the overbearing Henley that the members of the Eagles were equals and that he was no longer in charge. Henley arrived at the correct time and the trio practiced their set. At the fundraising concert, the Eagles semi-reunion was warmly received. Afterward, the three men attended a party at Azoff's home.

On the following day, Frey contacted Spero to set up a meeting with his former bandmates. In a tense discussion, Frey proposed reforming the Eagles, but only if certain conditions were met – what Spero later referred to as "Frey's Commandments." These included: no drugs or alcohol while on tour, no verbal abuse of the road crew and no fighting within the group. Although the rules were sensible, Frey wasn't sure his bandmates could actually follow through on their promises to change their ways.

Henley, who was eager to reform the Eagles, reasoned at the time: "We all did our solo things, got our solo aspirations covered. People like to see a group; there's something magic about a band. None of us in our individual capacities was as big a deal as we are together. None of us could draw the kinds of numbers and sell the kind of tickets and inspire the kind of enthusiasm that we do together."

Similarly, Frey stated at the time: "We've all grown up a lot. When you first break up, the wounds are open.... There is going to be some anger and some hurt. But as years go by, all you remember is the good times. I said when we got back together, 'I don't live in the past. As far as I am concerned, this is Day One. Nobody has to make any reparations.'" After the members of the group had agreed to reform, Azoff sent out faxes to multiple media outlets with the short message: "Hell Freezes Over."

* * * * * *

After the Eagles agreed to reunite, Joe Walsh received an ultimatum from his bandmates – he was ordered to attend a drug rehab program as a condition of rejoining the group. Walsh was clearly in a poor mental and physical state, and he knew he had to confront his addictions. The night before entering rehab, a deeply distressed Walsh ate a meal at a restaurant with his friends, Chad Cromwell and Rick Rosas.

On the following day, February 28, 1994, Walsh entered a rehab clinic in Marina Del Rey, California. He was driven there by Irving Azoff and Don Felder, who himself had given up drinking in 1980. At the twenty-bed facility, Walsh was surprised to run into Kurt Cobain of Nirvana, who was battling a heroin addiction. Eventually, Cobain would scale a six-foot wall and escape from the clinic.

Initially, Walsh planned on staying for just ten-days. But he quickly realized that the process would take much longer, and that his recovery could be accomplished only one day at a time. Walsh made a few more changes during this period – he cut off his long hair and began gaining some weight. More noticeably, his personality changed. Without booze or drugs, he became more subdued and his behavior was less erratic. In the evenings, Walsh would leave the clinic to rehearse with the Eagles. He was driven back and forth by David Spero. In all, Walsh would spend a month at the facility. Meanwhile, Richard "Smokey" Wendell was tasked with making sure that Walsh stayed sober. Additionally, Walsh had to deal with a second crisis at the time. His home in Studio City was extensively damaged in an earthquake. He lived on a boat in Marina del Rey until the repairs were made.

After achieving sobriety, Walsh tried to make amends with a number of people, including his ex-wives. But the efforts were not always welcome. Walsh recalled: "Some people say, 'Up yours.' But the important thing is me. I'm better for it." Walsh also began attending Alcoholics Anonymous meetings where he met fellow alcoholics. Following the program's individual steps to recovery, he felt empowered and in control of his life. He prayed, found faith and accepted his own shortcomings. And during the Hell Freezes Over tour, Walsh would often search out local A.A. meetings. In interviews, he would never shy away from his past addictions and would refer to his alcoholism as a disease.

As for the ultimatum from his Eagles bandmates, Walsh later stated: "The Eagles heading out on the road was great incentive for me to put my life back together again. I thanked them for asking me, and I thanked them for giving me a reason, a focus with which to pull myself back into the real world."

▶ CHAPTER 34
THE REUNION

The 1994 Eagles lineup consisted of Don Henley, Glenn Frey, Don Felder, Timothy B. Schmit and Joe Walsh. The reunion kicked off with an appearance on *Unplugged*. The band scheduled two shows at the Warner Brothers Studios in Burbank on April 25 and 26. The best performances from the two sets were later broadcast on MTV. A *Billboard* magazine writer excitedly reported: "We were told by MTV... that we had a ticket for the April 26 taping, on one condition: 'You cannot, under any circumstances, review the show.' We accepted, deeply honored to witness the historic occasion, especially without paying the excessive ticket prices ($100-plus) that fans will shell out for the summer tour."

Just a few days before the two shows, Henley informed Felder that the band would be performing an acoustic version of "Hotel California." Felder and Walsh spent several hours practicing the band's signature hit on acoustic, nylon-stringed guitars. Just before the performance, Henley told Felder that he needed to come up with some sort of special introduction to the song. Felder obliged by improvising a flamenco-style melody.

At the first show, the Eagles performed more than twenty songs, beginning with "Peaceful Easy Feeling" and closing with "Desperado." One of the night's surprises was "Help Me Thru The Night," a solo Walsh track from his album, *So What*. The group was well-received by the boisterous audience.

During the closing portion of "Hotel California," Felder confidently played his guitar with complete ease, while a tense Walsh was uncharacteristically focused on his instrument. He was clearly having a difficult time performing music without booze or drugs in his system. Walsh, who looked a bit scraggly, explained: "It was terrifying going onstage. I had to learn how to do everything all over again, sober. My sense of humor was maybe the last thing to come back." On the second night, the Eagles played nearly all of the same songs and were accompanied on a number of tracks by the Burbank Philharmonic Orchestra.

On October 26, *Hell Freezes Over* premiered on MTV. The much-anticipated telecast was a huge hit for the network. An accompanying album was released two-weeks later. It featured just eleven-songs from the *Unplugged* sessions and four newly recorded songs – "Get Over It," "Love Will Keep Us Alive," "The Girl From Yesterday" and "Learn To Be Still." None of the new songs were written by Walsh. The album debuted in the number-one spot and spawned two moderate hits including the politically charged, "Get Over It."

* * * * * *

The Eagles planned a six-week tour as a test run to see if there was still a demand for the group's music and to determine if the five members could truly set aside their past differences and unify as a group. Don Felder proclaimed: "It's being called a resumption, not a reunion. As far as everyone can see at this point, the Eagles will continue."

Additionally, the Eagles chose not to sign with a record company and turned down all but one multi-million-dollar sponsorship offer. However, that deal fell through at the last second. As concert promoter Barry Fey recalled: "Managing the Eagles had to be a handful. Irving [Azoff] said to me once, 'You know how crazy these guys make me, Barry?' And he went on to tell the story of how he was negotiating with Budweiser to be the sponsor of the 1994 'Hell Freezes Over' tour. He said it took weeks to put a deal together, very difficult negotiations, but he finally got Bud to agree to pay $13 million. He said they were all in an attorney's conference room somewhere and everybody for Budweiser was happy with the deal and everybody with the band was happy and just before the papers were signed, Henley said, 'One more thing... you gotta let the whales go from Sea World,' which Anheuser-Busch owned. Irving said the big shots for Budweiser didn't say a word; they just packed up their briefcases, got up and left. The tour went on without a sponsor."

Before the start of the Hell Freezes Over tour, Walsh was strongly encouraged to change managers. According to *The Cleveland Plain Dealer*, David Spero said "he was told by Eagles manager Azoff that Frey and Henley wanted Walsh to be managed under the Azoff umbrella... Otherwise, he'd be paid as a sideman, as opposed to being a member of the band. Staying with Spero would mean a major reduction in Walsh's salary, Spero says. As it was the best thing for his client,

Spero agreed with Walsh to fire him." At the time, Spero had a growing stable of acts he was managing, including Dickie Betts and Richie Furay.

Meanwhile, the Eagles had to adjust to the new demands of concert production, which now meant five semi trucks of equipment and huge screens on both sides of the stage. The Hell Freezes Over tour launched on May 27, 1994, with a six-show residency at Irvine Meadows in Laguna Hills, California. A reviewer at one of the performances observed: "It was evident why the other Eagles allowed Walsh – who these days looks much like a college professor – to dominate the proceedings: he rocks. For a so-called rock 'n' roll band, the Eagles' repertoire was extremely ballad-heavy; with a set-list including 'Lying Eyes,' 'I Can't Tell You Why,' 'New Kid In Town,' 'Desperado,' Walsh's 'Funk #49' and 'Rocky Mountain Way' were guaranteed to bring a dozily nostalgic audience to its... feet." On the tour, the Eagles also performed a number of solo hits by the group's individual members. Walsh stated at the time: "I love playing Don's 'Dirty Laundry' song. It has some challenging guitar parts. And I enjoy Glenn's 'You Belong To The City.'"

At the start of the tour, the members of the Eagles were on their best behavior. However, as the tour progressed, the old animosities returned. According to Spero, tensions within the band began to simmer: "You had five guys with five different assistants. They arrived at the hotel from the airport in five different vans. In the hotel, they had rooms on five different floors. At the show, they stayed in five different dressing rooms. Nobody hung out. No cameras were allowed anywhere. Everyone was guarded and tense. Things began to sour between Glenn, the leader, and guitarist Don Felder." Similarly, Walsh's girlfriend, Kristen Casey, observed: "The tour seemed so spiritless.... There were no group dinners or socializing. From what I could tell, the guys barely spoke to each other. Once, three band members ended up in the same elevator, then proceeded to pretend the others weren't there. They ignored each other through the lobby.... It was the antithesis of the Ringo tour."

Eventually, the five men learned to work with each other, realizing they all had the same, common goal. Walsh put it succinctly when he stated: "When we coexist and stay out of each other's business and when we just really all show up on stage and focus, we do love to play together. When we give each other lots of room so we don't get on each other's nerves and when we stop arguing about everything, that's the secret of longevity." Henley also made an effort to change his ways: "We made a deal with one another. To be less tumultuous and emotional. It took us a few months to work it out, but once we got comfortable it was like a shoe that fits. And I think we were flabbergasted at the warmth of the reception that we got after being away for fourteen years."

Meanwhile, Walsh had been sober for several months. Adapting to a new lifestyle, he distanced himself from his former drinking buddies. Instead of asking for alcohol in his contract rider, he now requested fresh carrots and a bottle of Listerine. And instead of spending his off hours partying, he now stayed in his hotel room and operated his ham radio. Walsh revealed another difference between touring in the 1970s and the 1990s: "We discovered sleep. That's a big difference right there." The first leg of the tour ended on September 15 at the Spectrum in Philadelphia. The reunion was a major success, and all but one of the first 45 shows were sellouts.

* * * * * *

In 1994, the Eagles were criticized in the press for charging $100 per ticket for their Hell Freezes Over reunion tour. Just one year earlier, top-level acts such as Paul McCartney, Bruce Springsteen and the Grateful Dead were charging between $26 and $32.50 per seat, with little in the way of any tacked-on service charges. However, David Crosby, who was touring at the time as a part of Crosby, Stills & Nash, would ignite a storm of controversy when he told a reporter: "What they do in terms of the gigs and the pricing and the rest of it is completely out of our hands. Anybody who thinks it's too much money shouldn't come."

Responding to the band's critics, Don Henley argued: "I'm not going to name any names, but several artists went above $100 before we did. Unfortunately, some DJ in Boston – a self-appointed crusader with questionable motives – decided that he would make us the villains in the debate about this issue. I've always found it interesting that the norm in any other business, be it corporations, sports teams, movies, etc., is that the people who excel, the ones who stick around the longest and accomplish something good, the ones who have a track record, are paid more for their services. Call it rank, tenure, seniority, or whatever you want – that's the way the world works. So, why should the music business be any different?" Irving Azoff reportedly selected the $100 price point to thwart scalpers who were making a hefty profit by reselling Eagles tickets. Don Felder, meanwhile, offered a more conciliatory tone before a 1994 concert at the 70,000-seat Citrus Bowl in Orlando, where the ticket prices topped off at $85: "If people can't afford to come to the show, they'll be able to see it on HBO, live from somewhere, in October."

*　　*　　*　　*　　*　　*

With the Cleveland Indians earning their way into the 1995 World Series, a pair of Northeastern Ohio rockers were selected to sing the national anthem before the start of the games against the Atlanta Braves. While Chrissie Hynde performed "The Star Spangled Banner" for Game 1, Joe Walsh sang the anthem at Game 5 on October 26. Wearing a formal dress shirt under a baggy World Series jacket, a noticeably nervous Walsh waved to the crowd and then launched into an acapella version of the song. Walsh explained that it was a difficult song to perform as a soloist: "You can't be more naked than when you're singing that. I wouldn't do it anywhere else but in Cleveland." Walsh had a genuine love for Cleveland sports teams and joined the public protests after the Browns left for Baltimore, following the completion of the 1995 season

*　　*　　*　　*　　*　　*

The Eagles began the North American leg of their Hell Freezes Over tour on January 1, 1995, in Tacoma, Washington, and finished on May 14 at the Cajun Dome in Lafayette, Louisiana. In all, the group performed nearly sixty-shows. After a six-month break, the Eagles headed for Asia in November 1995. Enroute, they performed a stopover gig in Hawaii at Aloha Stadium in Honolulu. After seven shows in Japan, the band then headed to New Zealand and Australia, closing the leg of the tour with a performance on December 9 at the Cricket Ground in Sydney.

Amazingly, the Eagles had not fallen of out of favor, even with the constantly changing face of popular music. Commanding a guaranteed minimum of $1 million per performance, the group realized they could sell out large venues without releasing any new material. Consequently, in 1995, the Eagles had the highest-grossing tour of the year.

That same year, Walsh announced that he would be spending part of the year in his hometown of Wichita: "I like the way life flows here, which is in contrast to the craziness of what I do... I like the pace here, and the people. I feel safe. There's a lot of general friendship here, and the people are nice. I'd rather be surrounded by that."

Walsh purchased the house where his birth father was born and raised. Built in 1890, the stately Victorian-style dwelling had 12-rooms and a large front porch. However, the structure had been neglected for a number of years and was in serious disrepair. Nevertheless, Walsh had the financial means and desire to rehabilitate the home. But despite his best intentions and emotional attachment to the city, he never got around to finishing the project. Eventually, in 2003, Walsh donated the property to a local women's charity. Unfortunately, the group was unable to raise the necessary funds to complete the restoration.

* * * * * *

In May 1995, Walsh released a two-disc retrospective of his lengthy career, *Look What I Did!: The Joe Walsh Anthology*. The project featured 34-songs, spanning from 1968 to 1993. One track – the previously-unreleased full version of "Decades" – featured a snippet of the Beatles' classic, "A Day In The Life." Surprisingly, the set contained no songs from Walsh's tenure with the Eagles.

Walsh's former manager David Spero, who worked on the project for two-years, explained: "It's the coolest thing I've ever done. It was great. I got to go back and listen to everything. Joe wasn't too keen on doing it at first. But he got into it after awhile. He's an important artist in rock history and he deserves this legacy." Also that year, Walsh contributed three songs to the soundtrack of the television series, *A Future To This Life: Robocop*. One of the tracks, "A Future To This Life," was a duet with Lita Ford.

Meanwhile, in 1996, the Eagles launched a 27-date trek across North America and Europe, which earned $30 million. Afterward, the band took a lengthy break. Overall, the two-year Hell Freezes Over world tour had racked up a staggering 3.4 million ticket buyers.

* * * * * *

Joe Walsh made several guest appearances on *The Drew Carey Show*. On a Cleveland-themed episode titled *Drewstock*, Carey and his friends were closing down their Buzz Beer brewery and threw a party to dispose of the leftover stock. In addition to Walsh, dozens of Cleveland luminaries made cameo appearances including Mayor Michael White, Browns quarterback Bernie Kosar and actor Martin Mull. But when Cleveland Indians slugger Albert Belle was unable to attend the taping, the show's producers brought in Dave Winfield.

At the end of the episode, Walsh was joined by the legendary Little Richard (who was *not* from Cleveland) for a brief performance. Actress Pam Stone recalled: "I was at that final scene, as were the rest of the cast, crowded around the musicians. I seem to remember being positioned directly behind Joe Walsh's left buttock as he stood atop a table playing and singing 'Rocky Mountain Way.' Richard accompanied him on piano, performing with gusto, complete with his trademark, 'woo!' and reading the lyrics of the song from a Teleprompter. It was magic."

Carey returned the favor later that year at a Walsh concert in Cleveland by taking the stage as the guest emcee. A reviewer at the show wrote: "Walsh sang and played hard, switching from guitar to guitar, donning silly hats and entertaining the crowd between songs with his usual goofball remarks. He showed off his versatile chops, seldom descending to the level of mere flash."

The concert was part of Walsh's Anthology Tour '97, which celebrated the release of his greatest hits set. Walsh selected a number of notable classic rock acts to open the shows including Alice Cooper, Eddie Money and REO Speedwagon. However, one of the opening acts – Leslie West of the group Mountain – insisted he was promised an opening slot at all of the shows on the tour and later sued Walsh.

Meanwhile, after achieving sobriety, Walsh still wasn't comfortable writing and recording new music. He admitted at the time: "I was going into the studio, but I chickened out. I just felt I wasn't ready. I'm looking forward to pairing up with some of the guys in the Eagles to do some writing, but there are no serious plans. Maybe I should get in the studio with these guys I'm working with now because it's a really good band."

* * * * * *

Joe Walsh suffered a pair of personal tragedies during this period. His sister-in-law, 36-year-old Susan Walsh, disappeared in July 1996. The case was later the subject of both *Unsolved Mysteries* and *Disappeared*. A former writer for *The Village Voice*, she was married to

Joe's half-brother, Mark Walsh. And on March 31, 1997, Joe Walsh lost his mother at the age of 69.

▶ CHAPTER 35
THE INDUCTION

In January 1998, the Eagles were inducted into the Rock and Roll Hall of Fame during their first year of eligibility. The ceremony was staged at the elegant Waldorf Astoria in New York City. Also inducted that year were Fleetwood Mac, Santana, the Mamas & the Papas, Lloyd Price and Gene Vincent.

Decked out in a tuxedo, a smiling Jimmy Buffett inducted the Eagles with a short speech: "The Eagles created their own style, blending banjos and electric guitars, harmonies from the heartland and cutting-edge lyrics from the fault line, and God knows what they did for the chamber of commerce of Winslow, Arizona.... [They] are as popular today as they were in that incredible summer back in 1972."

Don Henley was the first member of the group to take the podium. Opening his remarks, he joked: "We are all grateful, all grateful and honored for the opportunity and for the good fortune that had brought us all together on this *suspicious* occasion." He thanked, in order, Irving Azoff, Bill Szymczyk and Glyn Johns before closing, "hell, I'll even thank David Geffen."

While the other members of the group wore finely tailored, conservative, dark suits, Joe Walsh – always the jokester – wore dark sunglasses and a burnt-orange, brick-patterned jacket and pants. Eliciting a boisterous reaction from the audience, Walsh leaned into the podium with his trademark greeting, "Hey, how ya doin'?" He continued with a very short speech: "I would like to thank the people from Kent, Ohio; Akron, Ohio; and Cleveland, Ohio, for believing in me. I'd like to thank Bill Szymczyk for finding me in the middle of nowhere. I'd like to thank Don and Glenn for writing those songs." Glenn Frey, who was the last to speak, said: "A lot has been talked about and speculated about over the last 27-years about whether or not we got along. We got along fine. We just disagreed a lot. Tell me one worthwhile relationship that has not had peaks and valleys."

Old disputes were set aside for the occasion, and all of the past and present members of the group – including Bernie Leadon and Randy Meisner – took the stage to perform a pair of Eagles classics, "Take It

Easy" and "Hotel California." It was the first and only time that all seven members performed together on the same stage.

Then in early-April, Walsh attended the opening of a new wing at the Rock and Roll Hall of Fame in Cleveland. Also present were fellow inductees Little Richard, Bo Diddley, George Clinton, Michelle Phillips and Ruth Brown. At the ribbon-cutting ceremony, Walsh wore a bright red suit and held a chain saw instead of a customary pair of oversized scissors. As part of the festivities that weekend, Walsh was interviewed in front of an audience. He talked about his career as well as his sobriety and performed a few songs.

While in Cleveland, Walsh had another duty to perform. He headed down to Hoopples, a weathered sports bar along the Cuyahoga River where a nearly forgotten Glenn Schwartz would perform for an audience of fifty or sixty every Thursday night. Owing Schwartz a great deal of gratitude, Walsh would have never joined the James Gang if not for Schwartz's decision to leave the group. Instead, Walsh would have been forced to take another career path, which may or may not have led to the success and stardom he eventually attained.

During this period, Schwartz – who was in his late-50s and lived out of his car – would perform a mixture of blues and gospel-inspired songs. And much like an evangelical preacher, he would passionately debate religion with members of the audience. The first time Walsh visited Hoopples, it was simply to watch Schwartz perform. Then, a few weeks later, Walsh came back as a guest accompanist.

A local reporter who was in the audience observed: "Walsh had come to play. He was getting a little refresher course from his old teacher. Together, they took the paint off the walls. Glenn led the program all night with his gospel-infused jams and jeremiads while Walsh, demurely, with his back almost to the audience, played back-up. The two traded licks and riffs while the crowd, not more than 75 people, poured on the applause." Also in the audience that night were Jonah Koslen of the Michael Stanley Band, Dale Peters of the James Gang and Joe Vitale.

On May 1, Walsh headed to New York City for a taping of the VH1 series, *Story Tellers*. The episode featured Ringo Starr, who at the time was promoting his solo album, *Vertical Man*. On the program, Starr performed his solo hits as well as some Beatles classics including a surprise choice, "Love Me Do." Earlier that year, Walsh was scheduled to join the 10th Anniversary All-Starr tour, but he cancelled a few weeks before the first date due to a prior commitment in the studio with Don

Henley.

In August, Walsh reunited with his former James Gang bandmates – Jimmy Fox and Dale Peters – for a taping of *The Drew Carey Show.* Walsh joked at the time: "I think it's going to be a great chemistry. I think Jim and Dale and me, we can handle Drew." The trio appeared in a three-episode storyline – titled *In Ramada Da Vida* – in which Carey's band was offered the opportunity to perform at every Ramada Inn across Ohio. When Carey held tryouts for a new guitarist, a who's who of rock royalty auditioned for the spot, including Lisa Loeb, Joey Ramone, Jonny Lang, Slash of Guns N' Roses, Dusty Hill of ZZ Top and Rick Nielsen of Cheap Trick. However, Michael Stanley had to bow out, telling Carey, "I gotta be in bed, like at 5 o'clock every day." In the end Carey selected Walsh, who portrayed a stoner named Ed.

Two episodes later, Walsh and his James Gang bandmates made a return appearance. However, Carey quit the group and was replaced by "Weird Al" Yankovic. Before the show aired, Walsh joked: "I guess I'm going to see myself on television. I'm going to turn the sound down and pretend it's the Joe Walsh show with special guest Drew Carey."

Also that month, Walsh appeared as a contestant on an episode of the VH1 game show, *Rock & Roll Jeopardy!* Walsh faced off against musicians Graham Nash and Mark McGrath (of Sugar Ray). Despite his strong knowledge of rock and roll history, Walsh answered only three questions during the entire program – one incorrectly. McGrath later commented: "I was sitting next to Graham Nash and Joe Walsh, and literally one of the questions was, 'Joe Walsh, who was your first wife?' Out of respect, I was like, 'All right, I'll let him answer that.' And I look over at him, and he's swatting flies. I'm like, 'All right, I'll buzz in.' They're two icons of rock who did the '70s right, if you know what I mean. They should have forgotten more than they learned."

* * * * * *

On May 15, 1999, Walsh married for the fourth time. His Italian-American wife, Denise A. Driscoll, was a well-known attorney who worked in both the public and private sectors. At the time she was employed by the San Diego County public defender office. Introduced by mutual friends in Los Angeles, the couple would later have two sons. During this period, Walsh divided his time between his homes in Los Angeles and the suburban San Diego community of Encinitas.

▶ CHAPTER 36
FELDER DEPARTS THE EAGLES

Several years after the Eagles reunited, the strife within the band continued to fester. At the end of December 1999, the Eagles recorded two of their concerts, from which twelve tracks would later be released as part of a boxed set, *Selected Works: 1972-1999*. These performances marked the final time Don Felder would perform with the band.

Felder frequently complained about receiving a smaller percentage of the band's earnings than some of his bandmates. He later explained: "The more successful the band became, in my opinion, the more it became focused on money, the more of a business relationship it became and the less of a friendship.... It was time for me to be David and face Goliath. I had my one little rock to hurl, to try to do what was fair for everyone." With hostilities building, Felder was eventually fired from the band by Don Henley and Glenn Frey in February 2001. Following his forced departure, Felder sued Henley and Frey for a reported $50 million.

Henley and Frey countersued and also attempted to block the publication of Felder's tell-all autobiography, *Heaven And Hell: My Life In The Eagles*. Joe Walsh later said of Felder's firing and his book: "To be honest, I've tried not to worry about it too much. We couldn't say anything for a long time because we were in a lawsuit with him. Down deep, I like him. He was fun to stand next to and play with. A bunch of that (what Felder wrote) didn't concern me because some of the tension came from events before I joined the band." The multiple lawsuits were settled out of court in 2007. However, Felder's departure from the Eagles meant that one of the finest guitar duos of rock and roll was dissolved. Walsh and Felder had a special onstage chemistry that would never be replicated in the Eagles.

In 2001, the Eagles went back on the road for their first tour in five-years. The seven-week overseas trek – dubbed Evening with the Eagles – began with a show on May 29 at Olympic Stadium in Moscow, Russia. The group's lineup featured the core members – Walsh, Frey, Henley and Schmit – along with a host of session players. Multi-instrumentalist Steuart Smith was Felder's replacement in the touring version of the group. A native of Baltimore, Smith had worked with a series of rock bands in Washington, D.C. during the 1980s. Discovered by Rodney Crowell, Smith played on Crowell's 1988 album, *Diamonds And Dirt,* which spawned five number-one country hits. Afterward, Smith performed with a series of pop and country acts, including Rosanne Cash, Dolly Parton, Wynonna Judd and Shawn Colvin. In 1994, Smith worked with country star and future bandmate, Vince Gill.

* * * * * *

In January 2001, Joe Walsh made a guest appearance on *Drew Carey's Improv All-Stars.* The program was filmed at the MGM Grand in Las Vegas. Walsh demonstrated his natural comedic talent as he managed to outshine several professional comics. Then in April, Walsh appeared on *The Chris Isaak Show.* On the episode, Walsh and Isaak were both bidders at an auction of Scotty Moore's prized Gibson guitar from the 1950s, which was used on a number of early Elvis Presley sessions at Sun Records.

Meanwhile, Joe Walsh's wife, Denise, contacted Kent State University about securing an honorary degree for her husband. A number of letters of support were submitted by Walsh's friends and colleagues.

In October, the Board of Trustees at the university unanimously voted to grant Walsh an honorary degree – a doctorate of music. Kent State bestowed such degrees to "persons of acknowledged eminence in the arts, letters, sciences, the professions or public service." According to Ginny Carroll, the chair of the committee: "Some people have teased me about giving this, but it's honoring someone in a field that he probably wouldn't get a degree from in such a competitive field."

In December, Walsh arrived in Kent for the formal ceremony. Dressed in a dark cap and gown, Walsh was presented with a diploma by the university's president, Carol Cartwright. Afterward, Walsh stated: "I've been a junior for 27 years, in good standing, I might add. It kind of puts closure on my school days." Afterward, Walsh established a scholarship at the university's music department.

In November of that year, *The Cleveland Plain Dealer* reported that Walsh might be on his way to becoming a television actor: "Rocker Joe Walsh is in final negotiations to star in a pilot of a comedy series that is being co-written by Drew Carey.... The pilot is being produced by Warner Brothers TV for NBC and involves an accountant who goes to work for a rock star. Walsh, a guitarist who played in the Eagles and the James Gang and went to Kent State University, will play the rock star."

Walsh explained at the time: "[I] have a healthy friendship with Drew Carey. We've been talking about developing a pilot loosely based around 'Life's Been Good'... for a sitcom. But nothing is definite.... I've learned not to count on anything in this business." Ultimately, the project did not come to fruition.

* * * * * *

In 2002, Joe Walsh would lose yet another of his longtime musician friends – John Entwistle of the Who. Walsh recalled his final meeting with Entwistle at the NAMM music convention in Los Angeles, five months before his death: "I spent a while with John in his dressing room and then we went out to eat... I noticed that he was having trouble hearing. Also, he was not making sense like the John that I had known. I didn't know if he was just too drunk, or whatever. At one time, that's how all of us rockers would get to be late, late at night.... Once I had got sober, John and I were living in totally different worlds. I went to see him a couple of times, but I didn't hang out all night and into the next morning like I used to – and as he was still doing. So, we had got to be a little distant from each other."

Also that year, the Eagles toured across North America for the first time since 1995. In July, the tour included a stop in Joe Walsh's *other* hometown of Wichita, Kansas. As he recalled: "Management asked all of us if there was a particular place we'd like to play. We played in Texas for Don Henley. We were in Grand Rapids for Glenn Frey. Timothy (B. Schmit) is from Sacramento, so we played in Reno. And I picked Wichita. Everybody kind of looked at me funny, but I don't care."

At one stop on the tour, a reviewer wrote: "The wildly enthusiastic crowd... ended up getting more than just an Eagles concert. They also got a Don Henley solo concert, a Glenn Frey solo concert and a Joe Walsh solo extravaganza, to the point where one audience member wailed, half-seriously, 'I paid $97.50 to see the Eagles, and I got a James Gang concert instead.'"

Meanwhile, Walsh's obsession with vintage electronic devices became evident during the tour. As *Rolling Stone* magazine reported: "Walsh was faced with the choice of going onstage with the rest of the band to play before 20,000 fans or staying in front of his [personal computer] to place a last-minute bid on eBay; he chose to make the band

and the crowd wait. This says less about Walsh's priorities, however, than about how his past tends to reverberate into the present."

As Walsh later explained: "This is my hobby. I'm a ham-radio operator. And I finally got all those radios I dreamed of since I was twelve, every last one of them." Walsh's prized possession was an Atwater Kent battery-operated radio from around 1921, which was originally owned by his grandfather.

Nina Blackwood, Walsh's longtime friend and former MTV veejay, revealed: "He's a little like an absent-minded professor who spends the wee hours of the night tinkering away on various inventions. His home is tiled with what can best be described as 'gizmos,' objects like lightning devices, fiber optic walls, an antique radio, paint cans suspended in mid-air, various guitar gadgets and most importantly, a shortwave radio."

* * * * * *

In 2003, the Eagles took a shot at their musical rivals with the announcement of a 34-date tour – which they humorously dubbed the Farewell I tour. *Billboard* magazine reported: "Known for its sparse sets on previous tours, this time the Eagles have added an elaborate LED video system provided by Nocturne that includes a 60-by-110-foot screen in the rear of the stage and four screens front-of-stage. The tour will also travel with two side projection screens." Also that year, Walsh was joined by Eagles bandmates Henley and Schmit on the final album by singer-songwriter Warren Zevon, who was battling terminal lung cancer.

In 2005, the Eagles released the two-DVD set, *Farewell 1 Tour: Live From Melbourne*. The project featured two new tracks, "Hole In The World" and a Walsh composition, "One Day At A Time," which was inspired by his struggles with substance abuse. This was the first Eagles album since Don Felder's firing and the last to feature Glenn Frey. The album spawned two radio hits – on the country and adult-contemporary charts – "How Long" and "Busy Being Fabulous." The album reached number-one in the U.S. and earned two Grammy awards.

Meanwhile, Joe Walsh noticed that the makeup of his audiences had changed: "A lot of guys have beautiful women in from of 'em (at concerts). I mostly have teenage guitar players watching my left hand. And grandmothers."

▶ CHAPTER 37
JAMES GANG REUNION

In May 2005, Joe Walsh reformed the James Gang. Over the years, Walsh had remained good friends with his former bandmates, Jimmy Fox and Dale Peters. Although the trio had originally reunited to write and record some new tracks, things quickly shifted. Wanting to perform in public, the group decided to book a show at a Cleveland nightclub, the Beachland Ballroom.

With only word-of-mouth advertising, the concert sold out in a few minutes. A second show was subsequently added. At the 600-capacity club, Walsh told the audience: "We're the James Gang from Cleveland, Ohio, and we had not planned... on living this long. But you're stuck with us."

Wanting to perform again, the trio drove to another club to see if they could book a last-minute show. Fox recalled: "The three of us went downtown to House of Blues and walked in the front door. We're like, 'Who can we talk to?' They couldn't believe it was us."

The following year, the James Gang regrouped for a formal tour – their first in three-decades. The tour began at the 66th annual Black Hills Motorcycle Rally in Sturgis, South Dakota, for a capacity crowd of 60,000. Fox stated at the time: "When we finished those shows last summer [in Cleveland], we began thinking in terms of maybe we could take this on the road and do something longer. We kind of felt like this was great fun and could we possibly find the time to go out with this for a while. That's how this came about, because we were able to make time in everyone's schedule. We're definitely working 10 times harder. We're taking this much, much more seriously because it's a series of concerts and we want to be great for them, so we're practicing like mad."

At the time, Walsh discussed the freedom he felt when playing in the James Gang as opposed to what was expected of him onstage with the Eagles: "I've been in a very good band, but you have your assignment and that's what you do. You know what note to sing. And we do that just about as good as anybody. But (the club shows) reminded me how much I miss turning it up and not having anything particularly in mind to play."

On August 16, the group played a hometown show at the Blossom Music Center. Fox said at the time: "We never know what to expect when we play in Cleveland. There are all these people who used to pay 50-cents to see us whenever they wanted." At the show, Walsh announced to the audience, "We're the James Gang, from the last century... and proud of it. If you were born after our records came out, you can pretend we're really cool friends of your parents."

Meanwhile, in 2006, Walsh divorced Denise Driscoll. They were married for seven-years. It was his fourth marriage.

▶ CHAPTER 38
LONG ROAD OUT OF EDEN

Even as the Eagles were finishing their 2007 album, *Long Road Out Of Eden*, no major label expressed interest in releasing the project. The songs had been recorded over a six-year period at multiple studios. During the final sessions in Los Angeles, Joe Walsh often traveled from his San Diego home to the studio on an Amtrak passenger train.

Not surprisingly, the members of the Eagles frequently quarreled during the sessions. Don Henley admitted: "Song selection wasn't difficult, song rejection was difficult, which is why we have this double CD with 88 minutes of music on it. That's the downside of being in a band. Egos must be fed; objectivity and perspective can go right out the window; art suffers. For better or worse, survival often depends on placing egalitarianism, diplomacy and compromise above all else. That is the reality of group dynamics. It's like politics, like nations."

However, Bill Szymczyk explained: "When the record was done I thought it should have been a single album. I thought there was too much there. There are probably ten tracks that were cut but never finished, and some of them are just astounding rockers. Nobody was really getting exhausted, because we were all older, married, and had kids. We were working from 10 to 6 instead of from 2 in the afternoon 'til 3 in the morning. Everybody had to go home. One had to take his kid to basketball practice."

In the end, the Eagles decided against signing with a record company. Instead, the group dealt directly with Walmart, which was given the exclusive rights to sell *Long Road Out Of Eden* for a one-year period. The album was also available on the group's website. It was Irving Azoff who had convinced the group to negotiate a deal with the nation's largest retailer: "Do you want to make pennies [per CD] from the labels, or do you want to make dollars from Walmart?" According to reports, the Eagles earned around $4 per sale.

Walsh explained the positives of not signing with a label: "When all those record companies monopolized everything, you couldn't release a record without signing your life away to those crooks. Now the moguls are history. A whole new generation took over, and we asked ourselves,

'Should we change with the times?'"

The 20-track, two-disc set was released on October 1 and would sell an impressive 700,000 copies in its first week. The album debuted in the number-one spot in the U.S., Australia, the U.K. and many other countries, which confirmed the Eagles' continued popularity. It was the group's seventh number-one album in the U.S. The album was also nominated for four Grammys, winning just one in the category of Best Pop Instrumental Performance.

One of the two discs featured traditional-style Eagles songs that emphasized the group's trademark vocal harmonies. Two tracks – "Guilty Of The Crime" and "Last Good Time in Town" – featured Walsh on lead vocals. Walsh contributed as a songwriter to only one song on the set, "Last Good Time In Town," which he co-wrote with J.D. Souther. The track chronicled Walsh's personal transformation from a party animal to a homebody. The second disc was a stab at protest music and was highlighted by the 10-minute title track, "Long Road Out Of Eden," which examined the Second Iraq War.

On August 20, the Eagles released the first of five singles from the project, "How Long." Written by J.D. Souther, it was a Vietnam War-era protest song. The Eagles had been performing the song in concert since the mid-1970s, but as a favor to Souther, who wanted to release it on his solo album, did not record it until decades later.

Later in 2007, the Eagles performed at the Country Music Association's CMA Awards. Neatly dressed in dapper suits and ties, the group performed "Busy Being Fabulous." The Eagles had agreed to appear on the program only if they were introduced by Vince Gill.

In late-October, the Eagles flew to London for an exclusive concert to promote *Long Road Out Of Eden*. The group staged no other shows during their short visit. The Eagles introduced four new songs at the start of the performance and then launched into their classic hits. Tickets to the 2,300-seat venue, which was situated inside the massive O2 Arena, cost an astonishing £950 and were available only to selected members of the music industry.

A few months after the album's release, Henley told CNN: "I can't sit here and tell you for certain that there will never be another Eagles album... You know, we got a lot of things off our chest, so to speak."

* * * * * *

Shortly before turning sixty in November 2007, Joe Walsh told a reporter: "When I was little, everyone who was 60 was a dinosaur. Now that I'm nearly 60, I'm like a little kid in a body starting to slow down. I don't feel old. I really don't." He also acknowledged his good fortune in life: "When I'm with the band I feel safer. I'm part of a community and that's part of the fun. The Eagles are one of those bands where the sum of the whole is bigger than the guys themselves. We have such good chemistry."

Don Henley, who also turned sixty earlier that year, stated at the time: "People ask 'Why are you still doing this? You've accomplished everything. There's nothing left.' I never hear painters being asked why they still want to paint after 60 or novelists why they want to write after age 60."

Also in 2007, Walsh joined country music star Kenny Chesney on his Flip Flop summer tour. After the close of the tour, Walsh had a gift for Chesney: "He gave me a big, huge bowling trophy and it said, 'The Joe Walsh Award for Winning So Many Awards.' That's my favorite one. It's the ugliest thing you ever seen." Later that year, Walsh played guitar and his signature talk box on the track "Wild Ride," which appeared on Chesney's hit album, *Just Who I Am: Poets & Pirates*.

▶ CHAPTER 39
THE LONG ROAD GOES ON

On February 3, 2008, the New York Giants defeated the New England Patriots in the Super Bowl by a score of 17 to 14. It was quarterback Tom Brady's first Super Bowl loss. In the U.S. alone, the game drew 97.5 million viewers. Although Tom Petty and the Heartbreakers did an admirable job as the halftime entertainers, the NFL had originally asked the Eagles to perform. Reportedly, Don Henley turned down the offer. Joe Walsh, meanwhile, would spend February and March in Australia, opening for Rod Stewart.

* * * * * *

At the start of the three-year Long Road Out Of Eden tour, Joe Walsh discussed the inner workings of the Eagles: "We rarely fight or disagree on things any more. We'll talk it through. Before, we used to yell and scream it through. In the old days, the friction came from being on the road or in the studio, because that's all we did. You could burn out easily. But now we have lives and families, we've learned to pace everything." Similarly, Don Henley stated: "The core of everyone's personality is the same. What we figured out is how to accept each other for who we are and work from there. And we have a certain clarity now. Nobody's mind is muddled by drugs and alcohol. We don't internalize our disagreements anymore. We can talk. In the late-Seventies, when some outrage occurred, the tendency was to take your road manager and two best friends outside the band, go someplace and get high and talk."

For the tour, the Eagles did something quite uncharacteristic. Gone were the leisurely t-shirts, blue jeans, comfortable shoes and Western clothing. Instead, everyone in the group donned dark suits and ties. While the primary members of the band were attired in white shirts, the backing players wore black shirts. Walsh commented at the time: "I don't know exactly why we're doing it. I guess Glenn came up with it.... My problem is my tie gets stuck in my guitar strings and all of a sudden my guitar doesn't work anymore. I've got to get a tie clasp, but I never get around to it."

On March 20, 2008, the Eagles began the European leg of the tour. After four shows in London and then two more in the Netherlands, the band returned to North America. However, a number of dates had to be postponed after Timothy B. Schmidt suffered a freak surfing accident, during which the board struck his throat.

After a month-long break, the Eagles returned to the road with a date on May 2, 2008, at the Stagecoach Country Music Festival in Indio, California. Later, a reviewer at a concert in Tulsa wrote: "For much of the show, the Eagles played their cool California sound with icy cold efficiency.... But the clever fingers, wacky energy and quirky humor of Walsh transformed the show into a party. His blazing guitar and passionate wail on the James Gang favorite 'Walk Away' got the crowd to its feet, and he cleverly merged Don Williams' classic 'Tulsa Time' with 'Funk 49.'" During the tour, the group introduced a few new tracks into their repertoire such as "How Long" and "Busy Being Fabulous."

* * * * * *

In August 2008, Joe Walsh became engaged to Marjorie Bach, the sister-in-law of Ringo Starr. The couple had been dating since the previous November. The younger sister of James Bond actress Barbara Bach, Marjorie was previously married to British-born entertainment attorney, Alexander Rufus-Isaacs.

Although Walsh had repeatedly sworn off "falling in love" and pledged to never get married again, he had a dramatic change of heart. Walsh announced the engagement during an interview with Chicago deejay Steve Dahl. Walsh and Bach wed in December of that year. This was his fifth marriage. Walsh recalled at the time: "I was at the Beatles' Shea Stadium concert (in 1965). And, if you had told me – at Shea – that their drummer would one day be my brother-in-law, you know, I would've ignored you. But wonderful things happened and, well, be careful what you pray for!"

As a consequence of the marriage, Walsh and Starr became even closer friends. It also helped that both men had beaten their past addictions and were still active in the music business. Walsh revealed: "When I'm flustered by something, be it relationship, personal life or career, I'll go to [Ringo]. In fewer words than most people, he will give me his take on it. Straight-across truth. I really value that." Separated in age by seven-years, the two legendary musicians would often be seen dining together in restaurants around Los Angeles. Ringo joked: "The biggest downside of Joe Walsh being a brother-in-law is that I always have to pick up the check."

In 2009, Walsh would purchase a home in Benedict Canyon, a couple of miles away from Starr's estate. On the grounds of his property, Walsh constructed a small recording studio.

* * * * * *

After playing more than seventy-shows, the Eagles finished the second leg of the Long Road Out Of Eden tour on March 29, 2009, at the Value City Arena in Columbus. Following a two-month break, the group headed for Europe. The tour would land in 17 countries over the next two-months, beginning with a May 29 performance in Malmö, Sweden. A reviewer in Birmingham, England, wrote: "Only Joe Walsh... brought the faintest whiff of loose-cannon rock-star attitude to his bellowed vocals and feverish guitar solos. With his wild blond mane and thousand-yard stare, Walsh looks like he never quite checked out of the Hotel California."

After taking another break, the Eagles returned to the road in mid-April 2010 for what was nicknamed the Eagles 2010 Summer Tour, beginning with three shows at the Hollywood Bowl in Los Angeles. For some of the concerts, the opening acts included Keith Urban and the Dixie Chicks.

On a day off from the tour, Walsh headed to Los Angeles where his brother-in-law, Ringo Starr, was being honored with a star on the Hollywood Walk of Fame. Taking the podium, Walsh declared: "He's not just the greatest drummer in rock history – from the greatest band in rock history – he's also the greatest guy I know and the most kind and helpful friend you could ever want." Following a month-long break, the Eagles headed to Australia in early-November, where they played 12 concerts. At their first stop in Sydney, the group grossed a whopping $11.6 million for five shows. The tour ended just three-days before Christmas.

In May 2010, Don Henley made a prediction about the future of the Eagles: "I had hoped that we could go for two more years and reach the 40-year milestone. But it's looking more and more likely the end of the trail is imminent." But just like his "hell freezes over" comment thirty-years earlier, Henley would be proven wrong.

On February 20, 2011, the Eagles resumed their Long Road Out Of Eden tour. Starting with a concert in Bangkok, Thailand, the group played twelve-shows across Asia over the next four-weeks. Two of the concerts were in mainland China – at the Mercedes-Benz Arena in Shanghai and the Wukesong Arena in Beijing, which was built for the 2008 Olympic games. Before the concert, Walsh remarked that the Eagles were running out of new places to play. However, the two shows were the most poorly attended of the Asian tour with around one-third of the tickets going unsold. After a final date in Hong Kong on March 18, the group took a three-month break.

On June 9, the Eagles launched a European leg of the Long Road Out Of Eden tour with a stop in Reykjavik, Iceland. At the final show on July 1, the Eagles headlined the Hop Farm Festival in England. Later in the year, the Eagles played a pair of shows in Las Vegas, which marked the end of the tour. The incredibly successful trek had taken the group to 27 countries across four continents. Afterward, the band took a well-deserved break.

In late-2011, Walsh returned to the road for a solo tour. Later, Walsh headlined a residency at the Borgata Hotel & Casino in Atlantic City. However, Walsh was embarrassed to learn that he was the headliner, not the opening act, on a bill that included 86-year-old blues legend, B.B. King.

▶ CHAPTER 40
ANALOG JOE

After a twenty-year drought, Joe Walsh finally released a new solo album. After giving up booze and drugs in 1994, Walsh struggled to write and record new material: "I didn't particularly feel in a creative mood for those first four or five years, because when I'd get into the studio, there were still a lot of triggers for anxiety attacks. If I got frustrated about writing a song or finding words, my mind would say: 'Well, you know what worked in the past.' And that was no longer an option. I had to learn to do what I do, straight and sober. And I'm much better for it. Much better."

Walsh hired ELO frontman Jeff Lynne to produce the album. Marjorie Walsh, who was good friends with Lynne, had set up a meeting between the two veteran musicians. Walsh and Lynne had crossed paths a few times back in the 1970s, but barely knew each other. In the late-1980s, Lynne emerged as a star producer. He worked on hit solo albums by Tom Petty, George Harrison and Roy Orbison – three of his bandmates in the supergroup, the Traveling Wilburys. Later, Lynne also produced two new Beatles songs, "Free As A Bird" and "Real Love."

While working with Walsh, Lynne offered a great deal of encouragement and musical guidance. Walsh explained: "What Jeff did interfaced really well with the particular batch of music that I put together. His direction took me to a place I never would've gone, 'cause I couldn't conceive it."

Walsh had another important concern at the time. Popular music had taken a number of twists and turns since he last released an album, two-decades earlier. He explained at the time: "I was listening to what's out there now, and really wondering how I was gonna fit it. Times have changed. But as I got to work, my confidence came back, and I decided, 'Let's just do another Joe Walsh album and not worry about it.'"

Additionally, Walsh had to adapt to digital-age technology. Aided by Ringo Starr's recording engineer Bruce Sugar, Walsh was taught how to use the music-making software, Pro Tools. Walsh recalled: "The last album I made, we had tape and knobs. This album, we had a hard drive and a mouse. I don't know what happened! What happened while I was gone?" Sugar observed: "Joe is definitely an 'analog man.' So we had to learn a whole new way to record." Describing the recording process, Walsh explained: "Bruce would come over and get me set up. We'd get a basic groove, with a drum machine or some samples [many of which Walsh would program himself], then he'd set me up and go home and, over two days, I could record some basic tracks. We'd pick the best stuff from several passes; that's why it sounds like a musician playing along rather than overdubbing." Walsh was joined at the recording sessions by a number of guest musicians including Ringo Starr, David Crosby, Graham Nash, Dale Peters, Jimmy Fox and former Barnstorm bandmate Kenny Passarelli.

The album, *Analog Man*, was released in June 2012, when Walsh was 64-years-old. Describing the theme of the album, he stated: "It's an observation, not a judgment. I've always written observations [about] the world, and now there's two of them. The virtual world is a new thing, and it doesn't really exist, but people are in it a lot. People try to function in the real world – the analog world – while they're texting in the digital world, and they run into the car in front of them. It doesn't work to be in both."

The album's first single, "Analog Man," explored the growing disconnect in popular music between artistry and technology. The followup single, "Lucky That Way," was viewed as a sequel to his 1978 hit, "Life's Been Good." Another track, the introspective "One Day At A Time," recounted Walsh's battle to free himself from drugs and alcohol. A live version of the song originally appeared on the Eagles album, *Farewell 1 Tour - Live From Melbourne*. Another notable track, "Family," chronicled Walsh's marriage to Marjorie, which meant adjusting to the demands of a large, extended family.

Another song was inspired by a trip to Asia. At the end of the Eagles' jaunt across Australia in late-2010, the group had nearly two-months off until the start of the Asian leg of the tour. Instead of flying home, Joe and Marjorie Walsh decided to visit India. Stopping in the metropolis of Mumbai, the couple visited a packed nightclub, where a mesmerized Walsh watched a live band play music with only laptop computers. After returning home to Los Angeles, an inspired Walsh experimented with synthesized sounds and loops on the track, "India."

In February, Walsh previewed the album for the press at the Troubadour nightclub in Los Angeles. Afterward, he played a short set with a band that included Ringo Starr on drums and, for a few songs, Jeff

Lynne on guitar. A surprise hit, *Analog Man* was named album of the year by *Vintage Guitar* magazine. The deluxe edition of the album contained two bonus tracks, one of which was recorded decades earlier. In January 1971, the James Gang had spent nearly four-hours playing rock and blues music with Little Richard at a studio in Cleveland. The entire performance was taped. Walsh had wanted to include some of the material on the James Gang album, *Thirds*, but could not get permission at the time from Little Richard's record label.

* * * * * *

Also in 2012, Joe Walsh made a couple of notable television appearances. In February, Paul McCartney was scheduled to perform his latest single, "My Valentine," at the 54th Grammy Awards ceremony. As Walsh recounted: "He needed somebody to play the guitar part. Eric Clapton actually played on the record but he was not around. So Paul said, 'Could you help me out?' and I said yeah.... Then Paul said, 'I want to close the Grammys with the end of *Abbey Road* and there's guitar players going at it at the end there and would you like to be one of them?' and I said OK. This was like the day of the Grammys." Later that same day, McCartney asked Walsh to also invite Dave Grohl and Bruce Springsteen to play on the *Abbey Road* medley, which included "Golden Slumbers," "Carry That Weight" and "The End." During his guitar solo on "Carry That Weight," Walsh managed to sneak in the opening riff of the James Gang classic, "Funk #49."

In November, Walsh appeared on the program, *Live From Daryl's House*, and decried the state of the music industry. Walsh told the show's host, Daryl Hall: "Records, record stores, record sales – it's all gone. And it's up to the young musicians to try to figure it out. There's no money in it, there's no record companies. It's free, you can download it. No one gets paid, so they can't afford to make music."

▶ CHAPTER 41
HISTORY OF THE EAGLES

In 2012, the Eagles began working on a documentary that would chronicle their complicated and turbulent past, *History Of The Eagles: The Story Of An American Band*. Supervised by director Allison Ellwood and producer Alex Gibney, the project combined vintage clips, amateur 8mm footage, concert performances and new interviews with both current and former members of the band. Amazingly, the filmmakers were able to locate footage of Don Henley and Glenn Frey when they were backing Linda Ronstadt at the Troubadour nightclub in Los Angeles. The film also featured interviews with a number of Eagles associates including David Geffen, Jackson Browne, Bill Syzmczyk and Irving Azoff, who was the brainchild behind the project.

The three-and-a-half-hour documentary was initially broadcast over two-nights on Showtime in February 2013. In the opening scene, the Eagles performed an acapella rendition of "Seven Bridges Road," inside a locker room before a stadium concert in the late-1970s. Joe Walsh offered some of the film's more heartfelt comments and provided some insights into his past struggles with drugs and alcohol. And during an old interview from the 1970s, an obviously inebriated Walsh loses his train of thought as he is questioned by a reporter. Consequently, a critic pondered: "Some of the archival footage makes you wonder just how the former James Gang star is still alive, much less thriving."

Meanwhile, ex-Eagle Don Felder had a strong reaction to the documentary: "Most of it was about Don and Glenn. But they controlled it, owned it, and paid for it, so they could do what they wanted. But it did take me back to how angry they were." Walsh, however, saw things differently. He emphasized that for the good of the band, compromises had to be made. Additionally, he stated: "The bitter fighting that the media loved to talk about really didn't take place. We argued a lot, we discussed stuff a lot, and that tension had a lot of to do with the creative process. We didn't hate each other; we didn't have fist fights, none of that."

* * * * * *

In March 2013, Joe Walsh returned to the road for a few weeks as the opening act for his longtime friend, Bob Seger. A few months later, the Eagles went back on tour for an extended two-year trek. Before the start of the History Of The Eagles tour, the group rehired its banished guitarist, Bernie Leadon, after a 38-year absence. Although the group also considered bringing back Randy Meisner, he was suffering from a number of serious health issues at the time. Don Felder, who had previously exchanged multiple lawsuits with his former band, did not receive a similar invitation. The rift between Felder and his ex-Eagles bandmates was apparently too deep to heal. The History Of The Eagles tour kicked off on July 6 in Louisville, Kentucky, the first of eleven stadium dates. The successful tour took the Eagles to twelve-countries on three-continents over the next 25-months.

* * * * * *

In April 2015, Joe Walsh returned to the city he usually called his hometown. He was in Cleveland for Ringo Starr's induction into the Rock and Roll Hall of Fame as a solo artist. Beforehand, Walsh told the assembled media: "I don't know why [Starr] wasn't inducted before. That always bothered me. His body of work as a solo artist is as valid as anybody." Paul McCartney inducted Starr by warmly reminiscing about their time in the Beatles. Taking the stage, Starr opened his comments with: "My name is Ringo. And I play drums." After his induction, Starr took the stage and performed four songs. Before playing "It Don't Come Easy," Starr requested that "an old friend of mine, Joe Walsh, help me out on this one."

* * * * * *

In 2015, the History Of The Eagles tour landed in Auckland, New Zealand. That gave Joe Walsh the opportunity to retrace his 1989 trek to Otatara Pa in Hawke's Bay, the spot where he had experienced an epiphany about his addiction to booze and drugs. At the time, Walsh was celebrating nearly eleven-years of sobriety.

On July 29, the Eagles wrapped up their tour with a show in Shreveport, Louisiana. Taking a well-deserved break, the group was planning to go back on the road in several months. In the meantime, the various members concentrated on their own separate projects. Don

Henley promoted a new solo album, *Cass County*, which he had recorded mostly in Nashville. Walsh, however, went out on a short solo tour, mostly across the Midwest and East Coast. Instead of traveling by air, Walsh leased a tour bus. The month-long stint began on September 16 with two shows at the Packard Music Hall in Warren, Ohio. For a change of pace, Walsh performed some of his lesser-known material: "I went back and went through my catalog, and there's a bunch of songs that a lot of people know but they weren't hits and didn't have radio presence."

Meanwhile, Glenn Frey joined his family for an extended vacation in Hawaii, where he was writing a play. However, he soon fell ill and was transported back to the mainland for treatment. Over the previous several years, Frey had been in declining health and was taking medications for chronic pain. According to Henley, Frey "would have to tape his hands up like a football player. I watched his hands, his fingers, became bigger and more gnarled and stiff. I knew what those fingers used to look like."

* * * * * *

In July 2015, a mural of Joe Walsh was unveiled in his old stomping grounds of Kent, Ohio. The nine-by-thirteen-foot, black-and-white artwork was painted on the side of a brick building in the downtown entertainment district, about 1,000-feet south of J.B.'s, where decades earlier Walsh had performed hundreds of times. Artist Scot Phillips and his assistant Erin Meyer based the mural on a concert photo from the early-1970s that featured Walsh wearing a Kent State t-shirt. Meanwhile, at around the same time in nearby Akron, the city erected a mural of Devo dressed in their classic, yellow industrial suits.

In October, Walsh returned to his high school in New Jersey for a charity concert. The event marked the school's 100-year anniversary. During his visit, Walsh became the second Montclair resident – after astronaut Buzz Aldrin – to receive a Key to the City. Earlier in the day, Walsh spoke to the student body about making proper choices in life as well as his struggles with addiction. In the audience were Walsh's stepfather and half-brother.

▶ CHAPTER 42
FAREWELL TO GLENN FREY

On January 18, 2016, founding Eagles member Glenn Frey passed away at the age of 67 from complications of arthritis, ulcerative colitis, pneumonia and a negative reaction to prescription medications. Timothy B. Schmit said at the time: "None of us realized how sick he was. He had a lot of health issues, but we didn't know it was so serious. He went into the hospital and didn't come back." Joe Walsh explained: "He had a medical condition that could be managed, but not cured. He could still play, but we could see him getting frail."

Don Henley said of his close friend: "Glenn never thought of himself as a great lead player, he was sort of intimidated by Joe Walsh and Don Felder, even though he hired them. But Glenn was like the glue, he was like what Keith Richards is to the Rolling Stones." While Felder had remained friendly with Bernie Leadon and Randy Meisner, he was estranged from his other bandmates, including Frey. Felder stated at the time: "I had always hoped somewhere along the line, he and I would have dinner together, talking about old times and letting it go with a handshake and a hug."

Whether or not the Eagles would continue without Frey wasn't known at the time. Henley initially stated that the Eagles were absolutely finished – this time for good. Similarly, Schmit said: "The Eagles couldn't be the Eagles without both Don and Glenn. That's why I think this thing's over. You see a lot of oldies bands still going out and playing when there's not one person left from the original lineup. I wouldn't ever want to go there." But Walsh was more circumspect: "I don't know how to process life without Glenn yet. Don and I decided we'd go separate ways for a year and then revisit that situation."

The following month, when the Eagles reunited at the Grammy Awards to perform "Take It Easy," longtime associate Jackson Browne provided the lead vocals on the song, which he had co-written with Frey. On the following day, a private memorial service was held for Frey at the Los Angeles Forum. A grief-stricken Henley gave a 45-minute eulogy for the nearly 500 mourners in attendance. Although Henley came with prepared notes, he never once glanced at what he had written.

Afterward, there was a lengthy musical tribute. Deacon Frey, Glenn's then 23-year-old son, performed a heartfelt rendition of "Peaceful Easy Feeling." Later, a teary-eyed Walsh sat at a piano and performed a song he had written for Frey. The memorial, which was officiated by actor Ed Begley Jr., closed with many of the attendees taking the stage to perform a rendition of "Already Gone."

* * * * * *

In February 2016, former James Gang guitarist Glenn Schwartz arrived in Nashville for some recording sessions with his one-time replacement, Joe Walsh, and guitarist Dan Auerbach. As a serious student of blues music, Auerbach said of Schwartz: "He was my guitar hero growing up in Akron, and man, I just borrowed so much from him when I was starting, especially when I was starting the Black Keys.... I invited him to Nashville to record, and it was amazing." Back in 2003 when the Black Keys were considered an emerging band, Auerbach had hired Schwartz as an opening act for a number of shows.

After spending a week recording some original tracks at Auerbach's studio, the trio staged a surprise concert at Robert's Western World in downtown Nashville. Backed by Auerbach's side band, the Arcs, the three talented guitarists performed a number of blues songs during a nearly 45-minute set, which featured Schwartz on both vocals and lead guitar.

Two-months later, on April 16, the Arcs appeared at the Coachella Festival in Indio, California. Near the close of their set, Walsh and Schwartz appeared onstage as special guests. They performed two songs with the Arcs – "Fear & Doom" and "Water Street."

* * * * * *

In mid-2016, Joe Walsh co-headlined a tour with Bad Company. With the future of the Eagles remaining uncertain, Walsh had plenty of time on his hands. He recalled: "I got wind that Bad Company was going to tour. I called Paul [Rodgers] and we compared notes and we agreed that together we'd be a great package and together we would be mightier than either of us individually. And so we decided to work it out, and we decided to trade off on who plays first and who closes. So, nobody's opening for anybody."

Walsh and Rodgers were old friends. As Rodgers recalled: "We definitely crossed paths. I remember meeting Joe very early on, before he had joined the Eagles. There was a party and we were sitting together in Malibu Beach, and he was telling me that he was thinking about retiring, actually, and getting away from the business altogether. And he said, 'But there's this band. Perhaps you've heard of them. They're called the Eagles... Well, they've invited me to play with them.'"

Before the start of the One Hell Of A Night tour, Bad Company guitarist Mick Ralphs decided he wouldn't be joining his bandmates. Rodgers recalled: "We'd announced the tour and Mick looked at it and just sort of went, 'I can't do this,' which wasn't great news at all. Can you imagine; Here we are, we make this big announcement, and Mick says he can't do it. I wanted to slightly berate him – 'What the heck...' but he sounded so sad he couldn't, really wasn't up to it. It's very grinding being on the road." Although Walsh offered to fill in for the ailing Ralphs, Bad Company brought in a replacement guitarist, Rich Robinson of the Black Crowes.

The 24-date tour began with a May show in Dallas and ended in July with a stop in Nashville. For the tour, Walsh assembled an eleven-piece band and four background singers. Some of the shows began with a recorded comedy routine by Ohio-born actor Don Novello, who reprised his *SNL* role, Father Guido Sarducci. At a performance in Cleveland, a reviewer wrote: "Walsh will be 69 in November, but his guitar skills remain those of a 20-year-old, and were put on display when [he performed] 'Turn To Stone,' 'In The City,' 'Life's Been Good,' 'Life In The Fast Lane' and, of course, 'Rocky Mountain Way.'" And at the Forum in Los Angeles, Walsh brought out Ringo Starr.

After a two-week break, Walsh went back on the road – without Bad Company – for a two-month solo tour, beginning with a performance at Riverbend Music Center in Cincinnati. With Waddy Wachtel back in the band, Walsh opened the first show with the rarely heard track, "I Can Play That Rock & Roll." Walsh stated at the time: "By the end of the Bad Company tour, we really got a groove going and I didn't want to quit yet, because it's really wonderful. So I added more dates. I wouldn't say it's a jam band, but it's very loose. I don't have a lot of rules. I have a couple rules of what not to do. But, other than that, it's different every night. I enjoy seeing where it goes. It's a breath of fresh air, and the audience is always in for a rare treat."

During the tour, a reviewer wrote: "I had seen Walsh perform with the Eagles here in Fort Wayne at the Memorial Coliseum in 2003 and was surprised to find that I enjoyed this solo show as much, if not more, than the Eagles concert."

* * * * * *

In December 2015, the Eagles were selected as recipients of the annual Kennedy Center Honors. However, for reasons that were never fully explained, only four members of the group – Joe Walsh, Don Henley, Glenn Frey and Timothy B. Schmit – were recognized for the award. Due to Frey's health issues, the Eagles were forced to postpone their appearance at the event until December of the following year. Staged in Washington, D.C., the ceremony was broadcast on CBS. Walsh, Henley and Schmit spent three days at various functions in the nation's capital and were also honored with a private tour of the White House.

At the ceremony, Walsh noted: "We don't have a lot of say in it; we're just supposed to sit there and look like we're cool and we have people in the government to meet and a luncheon and the actual program.... I suppose they'll get some people to show up and do Eagles songs.... It may also serve as the true swan song for the Eagles in the wake of Frey's death, too." At the close of the event, a number of Eagles songs were performed by Vince Gill, Bob Seger, the Kings Of Leon and Juanes.

▶ CHAPTER 43
JOE AND TOM

In 2017, Tom Petty and the Heartbreakers launched their 40th anniversary tour, which began on April 20 at the Chesapeake Energy Arena in Oklahoma City. The tour included a variety of opening acts including Stevie Nicks, the Steve Miller Band, Peter Wolf, Chris Stapleton and Joe Walsh. However, some of Walsh's longtime fans questioned whether he should be opening for another artist at this stage of his career.

Few concertgoers knew that Petty began the tour with a serious injury. As *Rolling Stone* chronicled: "Petty spent the entire 53-date tour struggling with severe pain from a fracture in his left hip. He got through it with painkillers and used a golf cart to move around backstage." Headstrong and motivated, Petty wasn't going to be sidelined by physical pain.

Walsh performed at 23 of the shows and got along very well with Petty. Joe Vitale, who backed Walsh, vividly remembered the Heartbreakers tour: "We watched them every night, and every song [they] did was a hit. Every person in the audience knew every word. It's funny, we need a Teleprompter, and the audience knows every word. I did several tours in my life where there were two big bands, and that was probably the best."

During the tour, Walsh performed the Eagles hit, "Take It To The Limit," which he dedicated to Glenn Frey. On June 10, when the tour landed in Cleveland, Walsh wore a LeBron James jersey and told the crowd, "It's good to be home." Walsh's final date on the Petty tour was at the Prudential Center in Newark, New Jersey, on June 16.

The Petty tour continued for another three-months. Benmont Tench, the Heartbreakers' keyboardist, remembered: "The last night, we walked out onstage to start the show and I distinctly remember looking at Tom walking out with his hands up thinking, 'This guy is so happy. He's so proud to be standing in front of these people, standing in front of this band, proud to be who he is and proud that everything is all coming together and the dream is fulfilled.' And I was looking in his eyes thinking, 'Wow if he's that happy, then I'm happy too.'" A week later,

Petty would unexpectedly pass away after taking multiple pain medications.

*   *   *   *   *   *

Coming from a family of multiple generations of military veterans, Joe Walsh was active in his support of the armed forces. Often, while touring on the East Coast, he would stop to meet with injured soldiers at the Walter Reed National Military Medical Center. And in 2016, Walsh recorded the track, "No Man's Land," for the documentary, *Citizen Soldier*, which chronicled the struggles of a National Guard unit from Oklahoma that was sent behind enemy lines in Afghanistan.

The following year, Walsh launched VetsAid, an annual, all-star fundraising concert to help veterans and their families. He said at the time: "I looked at Willie Nelson and Farm Aid as a role model; they do it every year and it draws people together, and drawing people together where they realize they're not alone, to me, is strategic in healing." The inaugural VetsAid concert was staged in September 2016 at EagleBank Arena in Fairfax, Virginia. At the event, Walsh was joined by Keith Urban, the Zac Brown Band and Gary Clark Jr.

▶ CHAPTER 44 EAGLES RETURN

In early-2017, Irving Azoff raised the subject of the Eagles reforming and returning to the road – with veteran country singer Vince Gill filling in for Glenn Frey. Gill had first met the Eagles during their Long Run Tour in 1979. Later, Gill and Frey became good friends and were regular golfing buddies.

Gill had initially made a name for himself in the late-1970s as the lead singer of the country-rock act, Pure Prairie League. With the group, Gill scored three pop hits, including the 1980 top-10 entry, "Let Me Love You Tonight." After going solo, Gill became a major star in the country field, beginning with his 1984 single, "Victim Of Life's Circumstances." Over the next four-decades, he sold 26-million albums and placed nearly thirty top-10 hits on the country charts. And in 2013, Gill contributed a rendition of "I Can't Tell You Why" to the tribute album, *Common Thread: The Songs Of The Eagles*.

Additionally, Gill had been a huge fan of Joe Walsh for many years: "Well, I always knew how great he was. I was playing 'Rocky Mountain Way' in my bedroom when I was 15. I played it in garage bands and at sound checks. I think Joe Walsh could be the most important guitar player in American rock. You got Chuck Berry and several others, and across the pond, there's Jeff Beck, Jimmy Page, and Eric Clapton. I think Joe is every bit as important as any of those guys. He plays with great brevity and restraint; there's always so much thought he puts into each note. That's what I like about him – his patience. It's not about whittling a bunch of notes and trying to impress you. It's the way he'll bend a note, the time and care he'll put into it. I'm just in awe of him." Growing up as a fan of both country and rock music, Gill would later work with a number of rockers, including Alice Cooper, the Doobie Brothers and Aaron Lewis.

Meanwhile, Don Henley stated at the time: "After Glenn passed away, none of us could really see into the future. He was the founding member of the band and we didn't really see how we could go on without him. We didn't consider it. We didn't think the fans would embrace it. And so we just drifted. We had a year of mourning, so to speak." But after recalling Deacon Frey's impassioned performance the previous year, Henley informed Azoff that any new Eagles lineup must also include Frey's son: "Obviously a reunion was the last thing on my mind at that point. But the image of him singing so bravely stayed in my mind."

Walsh and Henley had initially planned to slowly bring Vince Gill and Deacon Frey into the Eagles with a series of small showcases that combined music and story-telling segments. Instead, it was decided that a better solution was to go on the road as the "refurbished" Eagles. The group would debut in a big way at a pair of stadium shows in Los Angeles and New York.

However, there were concerns about fan reaction to the revamped lineup. As Henley conceded: "No, we didn't know if they would accept Vince and Deacon or not. That was soon put to rest. The crowd at the Dodger Stadium just embraced Deacon, and Vince too. I think it surprised them. It surprised all of us. That's when we knew we might be able to do this, we might be able to continue." Walsh agreed with Henley's assessment: "We rehearsed and I was really nervous about it, but we played a couple shows and got great reviews and it just felt right onstage. It felt great. So we took a deep breath and recommitted and yes, next year we're going to play between 40 and 50 shows. It sure feels good to play our music for people again."

Walsh, who had watched Deacon Frey grow up, was given the responsibility of providing him with some musical coaching: "He could play the songs, he could sing the songs, but not at the same time. At the Dodger Stadium I told him: 'Look, breathe. If you panic, you're gonna think everyone's looking at you. They're not.'" Henley agreed: "It was difficult for Deacon in the beginning. It was emotional for him."

Meanwhile, Vince Gill and Deacon Frey divided the lead vocal duties on Glenn Frey's various songs: while Gill provided the lead on songs like "New Kid In Town" and "Lyin' Eyes," Deacon sang "Take It Easy," "Peaceful Easy Feeling" and "Already Gone." One concert reviewer wrote: "Young Frey was featured early in the set on a song his dad sang, 'Take It Easy,' and it was a Zen-Glenn moment. He doesn't yet have the range or the confidence that his father had... but the all-star talent is there."

Additionally, Gill realized that he had to adjust his guitar-playing style: "There's not a lot of improvising. It's all about part-playing, which is really why those Eagles records are so good; it's because guys aren't out there on the end of the stage showing off. And people know those solos; they know the fills. Nothing is taken for granted. Nothing is out of step." Amazingly, nearly five-decades after forming, the Eagles were still able to draw sell-out crowds all over the globe. The extended tour by the new lineup of the Eagles continued until June 2019.

*   *   *   *   *   *

On August 13, 2017, Joe Walsh and the members of Barnstorm were inducted into the Colorado Music Hall of Fame. The event was staged at Fiddler's Green Amphitheater in Denver. Also inducted were Dan Fogelberg and the Caribou Ranch recording studio. Vitale said at the time: "It was really fun and I thought the band played amazing. This isn't Cleveland, but the Colorado Hall of Fame is a big deal here. They embraced us and the song ('Rocky Mountain Way'). It was quite an evening."

Meanwhile, a 40th anniversary deluxe edition of the blockbuster album, *Hotel California*, was released in November 2017. The box set also included a DVD of a concert from the late-1970s. Joe Walsh stated at the time: "It's great to watch. I can't believe how young we are – I don't even remember being that young. But we played our asses off."

Also that month, Joe Walsh celebrated his 70th birthday at a private club in Los Angeles. Walsh was joined onstage at the celebration by a number of his rocker friends, including Ringo Starr, Joe Vitale and Kenny Passarelli. Amazingly, four of Walsh's current and past Eagles bandmates also turned 70 that same year – Don Henley, Timothy B. Schmit, Bernie Leadon and Don Felder. Henley, meanwhile, celebrated his birthday with a concert in Dallas, where he was joined onstage by Walsh, Schmit, Stevie Nicks and Patty Smyth.

*   *   *   *   *   *

In the 1980s, before an appearance at the Blossom Music Center in Ohio, Joe Walsh was asked by a radio deejay, "So where do you call home these days?" Walsh laughed as he replied, "Wherever I wake up." As with most successful rockers, Walsh would acquire multiple homes throughout his career.

In the late-2010s, Joe Walsh began to unload some of his homes. In 2018, he would sell his home in Studio City for $1.9 million. The following year, Walsh placed another Los Angeles-area home, this one near Beverly Hills, on the market for more than $5 million. He had purchased the home six-years earlier. Also in 2019, a four-acre horse ranch in Encinitas purchased by Walsh and his then-wife went on the market for nearly $3 million. And in 2017, Walsh's old house in Montecito burned down in the massive Thomas Fire, which consumed nearly 1,100 structures. However, the guest house, where Walsh had written and recorded a number of songs, was saved by firefighters.

And in 2019, Walsh continued to make a number of guest musical appearances. In November, he joined the Black Keys at the Forum in Los Angeles to perform "She's Long Gone," from the Akron duo's breakthrough album *Brothers*, and the Glenn Schwartz track, "Water Street." Also during this period, Walsh co-wrote a song with Sheryl Crow on her album, *Threads*. Walsh joined Crow for a performance of the song on the program, *CMT Crossroads*. Additionally, Walsh teamed with his old friend Chrissie Hynde on the track, "Get The Money," by the Coattail Riders, a band formed by Taylor Hawkins of the Foo Fighters. Walsh had first met the Foo Fighters in 2014, when they asked him to appear on an episode of the mini-series, *Sonic Highways*.

▶ CHAPTER 45
A PANDEMIC BREAK

In late-2019, the Eagles announced a stadium tour to celebrate their seminal 1976 album, *Hotel California*. At the shows, the group played the album in its entirety, followed by a two-hour set of various other songs. In preparation, the Eagles played three shows at the MGM Grand Garden Arena in Las Vegas. A reviewer at one of the performances wrote: "By sheer force of personality, the second half of the show belonged to Joe Walsh, who's been lighting a fire under this band since 1975, give or take a few decades of downtime. A guitar genius, a hall-of-fame goofball and enthusiastic maker of fast-lane life choices, Walsh is still breathing today because Felder and Eagles manager Irving Azoff drove him to rehab.... On Saturday, he was a show unto himself, contorting his face like a man fumbling for ecstasy and his locker combination at the same time, strafing 'In The City' with swampy wah-wah effects and riding the talk box solo on 'Those Shoes' straight into psychedelic space."

The Hotel California Tour officially kicked off on February 7, 2020, in Atlanta, and featured a 22-voice choir and 46-piece orchestra. Don Henley described the show's elaborate introduction: "While people are coming into the auditorium, we're singing [a portion of 'Hotel California'] in a spooky, drawn-out fashion. We have thunder and the sound of wind bouncing around all over the auditorium. Lights are flashing, as if they were lightning bolts. Then just as things come to a peak, a tall fellow, dressed in a black, antique European bellman's costume and a cape, walks across the stage, holding the vinyl album *Hotel California*. He takes it out of the jacket, blows off the dust – a symbolic gesture – places it carefully on the turntable and puts the stylus down." With the curtain rising, the band then launched into their nearly seven-minute-long anthem, "Hotel California."

In March 2020, the Eagles were forced to postpone the rest of the Hotel California Tour due to the worsening Covid-19 crisis. The tour was originally scheduled to continue until late-April and then resume in the summer. However, the pandemic would decimate the entire music industry as artists stopped touring, nightclubs were shuttered and countless musical acts were put out of work.

Meanwhile, Walsh was also planning to perform with his former group, Barnstorm, at the fifty-year commemoration of the 1970 Kent State shootings on May 4, 2020. Both David Crosby and Chrissie Hynde were also scheduled to perform. However, like nearly every other public event, the memorial concert was cancelled.

With a great deal of time on his hands, Walsh approached SiriusXM to inquire about hosting his own channel. After getting the runaround, he explored other options. He subsequently reached out to a local, non-commercial radio station in the Los Angeles area. At KCSN, an FM station licensed to California State University in Northridge, Walsh hosted a weekly, Saturday afternoon program, *Joe Walsh's Old-Fashioned Rock 'n' Roll Radio Show*.

Walsh was given free range to play whatever he liked. Speaking in his recognizable drawl, Walsh started his first show on May 23 with the introduction: "I was thinking... if I was gonna listen to the radio, what songs would I like to hear? So I made a list of them." Playing a variety of classic rock, blues and pop songs, Walsh kicked off his first show with "Good Times Bad Times" – the first track of the first Led Zeppelin album.

On one show, the playlist included music by rock acts such as Supertramp, the Who and David Bowie as well as oldies by Huey "Piano" Smith, Johnny Nash and Harold Melvin & The Blue Notes. On another show, Walsh spent two-hours playing his favorite rock and roll classics from the 1950s. Additionally, Walsh frequently offered some of his unconventional wisdom and also interviewed a number of his musician friends, including Linda Ronstadt, Randy Meisner and Brian Johnson of AC/DC. After nine-months behind the microphone, Walsh wanted to return to his normal routine and ended his radio show.

Meanwhile, in February 2021, Walsh revealed his frustration over his inability to go on the road and perform: "That's a monster that needs to be fed. We get disoriented – I haven't played in a year. The Covid experience is a study in human nature. I got time, and I had no choice but to get to know Joe Walsh: not the rock star, but the dumb guy from Ohio.... I think the Eagles, when we get back together and get to work, we're going to talk about the experience that we had and maybe come up with some music." During this period, Walsh participated in a number of virtual events such as Ringo Starr's 80th birthday celebration and the annual VetsAid benefit. Meanwhile, on November 20, 2020, Walsh's stepfather, Robert Newton Walsh, passed away at the age of 94.

* * * * * *

After an 18-month break due to the pandemic, the Eagles resumed their Hotel California Tour in August 2021, beginning with a pair of shows at Madison Square Garden in New York City. Again, all of the members donned their dark suits except for Joe Walsh – the band's eternal showman – who took the stage in a long, dark trenchcoat and black leather pants.

A reviewer in St. Paul wrote: "While Henley is now the major-domo of the Eagles... you would not get the best of the Eagles without Walsh. The resident live wire since 1976, he brought animation, personality and joy to the nearly three-hour program. And great guitar work. He was nasty and uplifting at the same time during 'Life's Been Good,' his tongue-in-cheek solo smash." Amazingly, Joe Walsh and the Eagles were continuing their phenomenal career run with no end in sight.

▶ CLOSING TIME

Joe Walsh once stated: "A philosopher said as we live life, it looks like random anarchy, one event smashing into another. But when you look back, life looks like a finely crafted novel." When Walsh was nearly 60-years-old, he admitted: "I'm very lucky; very blessed. I never thought what it would be like when I got this old. Actually, I never planned on living this long."

Walsh had experienced a series of fortuitous events during his lifetime – he replaced Glenn Schwartz in the James Gang, he was discovered by Bill Szymczyk in Cleveland, he joined a major rock group in 1975, he contributed to classic albums like *Hotel California*, he bounced back from decades of substance abuse and he married Marjorie Bach, which meant he was the brother-in-law of Ringo Starr.

Possessing great talent as both a songwriter and musician, Walsh had a successful career as both a solo artist and a member of a superstar group. And amazingly, the Eagles managed to stay popular, several-decades after the group's formation during the golden age of classic rock in the 1970s. Walsh and the Eagles never had to launch a comeback because they were *never* unpopular.

Instead, the Eagles stayed relevant as their songs were passed down from one generation to another. While touring with the Eagles in 2010, Joe Walsh was asked by a reporter, "Great songs last, don't they?" He responded, "They do. That's why we are still here. We have a whole new audience, a generation of people who come who weren't around when the records were out but they have grown up hearing them because their parents played them. They are coming to see us for the first time and that's tremendous energy to have."

Lastly, there's still a debate whether or not Joe Walsh has actually owned a Maserati at any time of his life. In his press bio, he once stated: "I have absolutely no idea whether I have a Maserati or not... probably. It would seem logical." In interviews, Walsh has answered both "yes" and "no" when asked if he owned a Maserati. In 1987, he protested: "Everybody is obsessed with whether I have a Maserati or not. And they all miss the point. I'm screaming at people not to base reality on the stupid lifestyles that we rock stars have to live, not by choice. No, I don't have a Maserati. Why would anyone in their right mind have a

Maserati?.... I mean I'm not a rock star, I'm just an idiot from Ohio."

However, in 2012, when Walsh appeared at the Troubadour in Los Angeles, he performed a spoken-word version of "Life's Been Good," during which he dissected the lyrics of the song. He stated at the time, "I have one, yes." And again, in 2020, he told *Rolling Stone* that he did in fact own a Maserati, but that he had reached a speed of 140-miles-per-hour, without pushing the car to its limit.

And in 2018, when an extremely rare 1962 Maserati 5000GT was offered for sale, media reports stated that Walsh *reportedly* owned the vehicle. According to RM Sotheby's, the auction gallery overseeing the sale of the vehicle, the Maserati "was understood to have been owned by Joe Walsh." One thing is known for certain – a 1962 Maserati can't go 185-miles-per-hour.

▶ SELECTED BIBLIOGRAPHY

Adams, Deanna R. (2002). *Cleveland's Rock and Roll Roots*. Mount Pleasant, SC: Arcadia Publishing.

Belkin, Fran. (2018). *Rock This Town*. Cleveland: FranProjects.

Bienstock, Richard. (2016, May 19). Joe Walsh: My life in 15 songs. *Rolling Stone* [online].

Blackwood, Nina. (1993, June 6). Joe Walsh: The nutty professor. *Music Connection*.

Brown, Jake. (2014, September/October). The architect of 70's AOR: Bill Szymczyk on recording Joe Walsh, B.B. King, & the Eagles. *Tape Op*.

Casey, Kristin. (2018). *Rock Monster*. Los Angeles: Rare Bird Books.

Clary, Mike. (1975, May 4). The return of Joe Walsh: A rock star comes back to where it all began. *The Akron Beacon Journal Magazine*.

Crowe, Cameron. (1975, February 27). Joe Walsh, child of the silent majority: Ex-James Gangster tends to his garden. *Rolling Stone*.

Crump, Sarah. (1998, August 19). The three Mikes take the mike. *The Cleveland Plain Dealer*.

Daley, Dan. (2004, November). Bill Szymczyk: Producer. *Sound On Sound*.

Di Paolo, Roger. (2009). *Rooted in Kent: 101 Tales From Tree City*. Kent, OH: Kent Historical Society Press.

Edgers, Geoff. (2016, November 29). Don Henley says the Eagles are done – it was always Glenn Frey's band. *The Washington Post*.

Felder, Don. (2009). *Heaven and Hell: My Life in the Eagles (1974-2001)*. Hoboken, NJ: Wiley.

Goldberg, Michael. (1982, September). No bright ones tonight: Richard Thompson shoots out the lights. *Creem*.

Greene, Andy. (2020, August 27). Drummer Joe Vitale on his 50-year saga with CSNY, Joe Walsh, the Eagles, and John Lennon. *Rolling Stone*.

Greene, Andy. (2021, January 14). Drummer Chad Cromwell on his years with Neil Young, Mark Knopfler, and Joe Walsh. *Rolling Stone*.

Grundy, Stuart; & Tobler, John. (1982). *The Record Producers*. New York: St. Martin's Press.

Gundersen, Edna. (2019, November 5). The Eagles' Joe Walsh rocks for veterans. *AARP*.

Halasa, Joyce. (1989, April 20). The James Gang, pt. IV: The good times and sad times with Joe Walsh. *Scene*.

"Halloween comes early." (1964, October 29). *The Montclair Times*.

Heaton, Michael. (2013, July 7). David Spero, artist-manager, talks about what went on behind the scenes with the Eagles – exclusive interview. *The Cleveland Plain Dealer*.

Hedegaard, Eric. (2006, August 24). Joe Walsh rides again. *Rolling Stone*.

Hotten, Jon. (2004, January). Life in the fast lane: The turbulent tale of the Eagles. *Classic Rock*.

Jancik, Wayne. (1998). *The Billboard Book of One-Hit Wonders*. New York: Billboard Books.

Johnson, Richard. (2018, March 7). Eagles singer's ex details his rockstar lifestyle in new book. *The New York Post*.

Kane, Dan. (2013, May 24). The Chylds had radio hits, signed with Warner Bros., opened for the Beach Boys and more. *The Canton Repository*.

Lombardo, John. (2005). *A Fire to Win: The Life and Times of Woody Hayes*. New York: Thomas Dunne Books.

Marsh, Dave [Ed.]; & Swenson, John [Ed.]. (1979). *The Rolling Stone Record Guide*. New York: Random House / Rolling Stone Press.

Martoccio, Angie. (2020, December 3). *Rolling Stone* interview: Special edition' with Joe Walsh. *Rolling Stone* [online].

Marx, Richard. (2021). *Stories to Tell: A Memoir*. New York: Simon & Schuster.

Newman, Melinda. (2012, June 11). Before the fast lane: Eagles guitarist Joe Walsh fondly recalls his Jersey years. *New Jersey Monthly*.

Phillips, Beau. (2014). *I Killed Pink Floyd's Pig*. Seattle: Peanut Butter Publishing.

Prufer, Jason. (2019). *Small Town, Big Music: The Outsized Influence of Kent, Ohio, on the History of Rock and Roll.* Kent, OH: Kent State University Press.
Romero, Dennis. (1991, December 18). The China Club faces a fateful countdown. *The Los Angeles Times.*
Runtagh, Jordan. (2017, September 25). Ringo Starr's wife Barbara Bach first saw her future husband as a teenager at a Beatles concert. *People.*
Schipper, Henry. (1992). *Broken Record: An Inside Story of the Grammy Awards.* New York: Birch Lane Press.
Scott, Jane. (1968, November 25). Airplane soars in Allen concert. *The Cleveland Plain Dealer.*
Scott, Jane. (1969, February 7). The happening. *The Cleveland Plain Dealer.*
Scott, Jane. (1981, June 19). Vitale and Walsh back at Blossom. *The Cleveland Plain Dealer.*
Scott, Jane. (1992, November 2). Rocker campaigns with flag costume. *The Cleveland Plain Dealer.*
Scott, Jane. (1997, March 15). Cleveland shows Texas how it rocks. *The Cleveland Plain Dealer.*
Singular, Stephen. (1997). *The Rise and Rise of David Geffen.* Secaucus, NJ: Birch Lane Press.
Spevak, Jeff. (1993, June 4). Dueling guitars. *The Rochester Democrat and Chronicle.*
Stern, Howard. (2012, June 4). Joe Walsh is an Analog Man. *The Howard Stern Show* (SiriusXM).
Stevenson, Jeff C. (2015). *Fortney Road: Life, Death, and Deception in a Christian Cult.* Minneapolis-St. Paul: Freethought.
"The Eagles find a common thread." (1994, September 16). *The Allentown Morning Call.*
Thomas, Nick. (2017). *The Traveling Wilburys: A Biography.* Green, OH: Guardian Express Media.
Thomas, Nick. (2018). *Tom Petty: A Rock and Roll Life.* Green, OH: Guardian Express Media.
Tobler, John; & Grundy, Stuart. (1984). *The Guitar Greats.* New York: St. Martin's Press.
Vitale, Joe; & Vitale, Susie. (2008). *Backstage Pass.* Canton, OH: Hit Records.
Walsh, Joe. (2018, June 10). Speech, Alcoholics Anonymous: Founder's Day Conference, Akron, OH.
Walsh, Joe. (2018, November 7). Speech, Joint Base Lewis-McChord, Tacoma, WA.
Wardlaw, Matt. (2017, June 11). Tom Petty & the Heartbreakers celebrate their 40th anniversary with a rousing performance at the Q. *Scene.*
Whitburn, Joel. (2001). *Top Pop Albums 1955-2001.* Menomonee Falls, WI: Record Research.
Whitburn, Joel. (2008). *Rock Tracks 1981-2008.* Menomonee Falls, WI: Record Research.
Whitburn, Joel. (2009). *Top Pop Singles 1955-2008.* Menomonee Falls, WI: Record Research.
"Widow of airman killed on Okinawa returns to Wichita." (1949, August 5). *The Wichita Eagle.*
Wolf, Carlo. (2006). *Cleveland Rock & Roll Memories.* Cleveland: Gray & Company.
Woodward, Bob. (1984). *Wired: The Short Life & Fast Times of John Belushi.* New York: Simon & Schuster.

NOTES

INTRODUCTION

1. "I believe my job on..." ~ Holan, Marc. (1986, October 2). Joe Walsh comes home. *Scene.*

CHAPTER 1: HOME IN KANSAS

1. "fortunes were being made in..." ~ Schulman, Daniel. (2014). *Sons of Wichita: How the Koch Brothers Became America's Most Powerful and Private Dynasty.* New York: Grand Central Publishing.
2. "He flew pre-jet, prop planes..." ~ Rose, Joseph. (1975, September). Trains and buses and planes and Joe Walsh. *Hit Parader.*
3. "In the formative years of..." ~ Dorr, Robert F. (1994, August). Lockheed F-80: A star is born. *Air International.*
4. "was teaching a guy to..." ~ Rose, Joseph. (1975, September). Trains and buses and planes and Joe Walsh. *Hit Parader.*
5. "I always felt kind of..." ~ Radke, Brock. (2017, November 14). Talking with the Eagles' Joe Walsh, back at the House of Blues. *The Las Vegas Sun.*
6. "In the early years, I..." ~ Rietmulder, Michael. (2018, November 8). Joe Walsh's VetsAid concert at Tacoma Dome unites rock greats for great cause. *The Seattle Times.*

CHAPTER 2: THE MIDWEST & EAST COAST

1. "vacant lots, BB gun wars..." ~ di Perna, Alan. (1992, May). Joe Walsh discusses his career, gear and new album, 'Analog Man.' *Guitar World.*
2. "It puts me in a..." ~ Woods, Sean. (2012, June). The last word: Joe Walsh. *Men's Journal.*
3. "Some of the happiest times..." ~ Joy, Kevin. (2012, June 28). 'Rocky Mountain Way' rocker returns to his Ohio roots. *The Columbus Dispatch.*
4. "All my influences really existed..." ~ Hislop, Christopher. (2016, July 21). A chat with Joe Walsh: 'Eagles' guitarist plays Casino July 26. *Foster's Daily Democrat.*
5. "On the roof of my..." ~ Hedegaard, Eric. (2006, August 24). Joe Walsh rides again. *Rolling Stone.*
6. "I went with my parents..." ~ Krepack, Benjamin; & Firestone, Rod. (1986). *Start Me Up: The Music Biz Meets the Personal Computer.* Van Nuys, CA: Media Press.
7. "I had, without knowing, attention-deficient..." ~ Walsh, Joe. (2018, October 8). Speech, Facing Addiction and the National Council on Alcoholism and Drug Dependence, New York City.
8. "[I was the] third-chair..." ~ Crowe, Cameron. (1975, February 27). Joe Walsh, child of the silent majority: Ex-James Gangster tends to his garden. *Rolling Stone.*
9. "Cousin Brucie, Scott Muni, Murray..." ~ Resnicoff, Matt. (1988, January). The clown prince of rock guitar. *Guitar World.*
10. "I had a Sears, Roebuck..." ~ Joy, Kevin. (2012, June 28). 'Rocky Mountain Way' rocker returns to his Ohio roots. *The Columbus Dispatch.*
11. "It was like a serial..." ~ Tobler, John; & Grundy, Stuart. (1984). *The Guitar Greats.* New York: St. Martin's Press.
12. "I always wanted an electric..." ~ Gans, David. (1981, July 17). Joe Walsh. *BAM.*
13. "Even though we could hardly..." ~ Crowe, Cameron. (1975, February 27). Joe Walsh, child of the silent majority: Ex-James Gangster tends to his garden. *Rolling Stone.*
14. "Oh it was great, for..." ~ Kutner, Rick. (2006, August 16). James Gang: Interview with Joe Walsh. *The Aquarian.*
15. "I got to get out..." ~ Newman, Melinda. (2012, June 11). Before the fast lane: Eagles guitarist Joe Walsh fondly recalls his Jersey years. *New Jersey Monthly.*
16. "I still have a really..." ~ Tobler, John; & Grundy, Stuart. (1984). *The Guitar Greats.* New York: St. Martin's Press.
17. "I would stand out in..." ~ Hyman, Dan. (2015, September 28). Joe Walsh won't slow down: 'You Know What? I'm Not Done.' *The Village Voice.*

18. "I would go to Manny's..." ~ Newman, Melinda. (2012, June 11). Before the fast lane: Eagles guitarist Joe Walsh fondly recalls his Jersey years. *New Jersey Monthly*.
19. "They had just dumped their..." ~ Crowe, Cameron. (1975, February 27). Joe Walsh, child of the silent majority: Ex-James Gangster tends to his garden. *Rolling Stone*.
20. "The leader of the band..." ~ Cannon, Bob. (2015, September 24). Joe Walsh comes home. *The Montclair Times*.
21. "Back then, you didn't have..." ~ Newman, Melinda. (2012, June 11). Before the fast lane: Eagles guitarist Joe Walsh fondly recalls his Jersey years. *New Jersey Monthly*.
22. "The Nomads made a record..." ~ Tobler, John; & Grundy, Stuart. (1984). *The Guitar Greats*. New York: St. Martin's Press.
23. "The Beatles packed Shea Stadium..." ~ McGee, John; & Moberly, Leeds. (1965, August 16). 55,000 scream for Beatles. *The New York Daily News*.

▶ CHAPTER 3: JOE GOES TO COLLEGE

1. "I fought with my parents..." ~ Crowe, Cameron. (1975, February 27). Joe Walsh, child of the silent majority: Ex-James Gangster tends to his garden. *Rolling Stone*.
2. "My grandfather took me aside..." ~ Woods, Sean. (2012, June). The last word: Joe Walsh. *Men's Journal*.
3. "wanted to go to Vietnam..." ~ "Today." (1982, January 20). *Daily Kent Stater*.
4. "*Playboy* [magazine] called it a..." ~ Crowe, Cameron. (1975, February 27). Joe Walsh, child of the silent majority: Ex-James Gangster tends to his garden. *Rolling Stone*.
5. "Two odors... pervaded Akron when..." ~ White, Timothy. (1995, October 14). Pretenders' Hynde appreciates the *View*. *Billboard*.
6. "One of the biggest thrills..." ~ Halasa, Joyce. (1991, August 22). Sonny Geraci: From Starfires to Outsiders. *Scene*.
7. "I majored in English and..." ~ Varga, George. (2012, February 2). Fact or fiction? With Joe Walsh, you never know. *The San Diego Union-Tribune*.
8. "I became the phantom of..." ~ Rosen, Steven. (1975, June). Joe Walsh: Rock master. *Guitar Player*.
9. "It was a very creative..." ~ "Joe gains honorary Doctorate." (2002, January). *Natural Progressions*.
10. "Kent was a cool university..." ~ Hynde, Chrissie. (2015). *Reckless: My Life as a Pretender*. New York: Doubleday.

▶ CHAPTER 4: THE MEASLES

1. At one point, there were... ~ Montgomery, Theresa. (2007, February 8). Music scene in Kent has rolled with the punches. *Daily Kent Stater*.
2. "If you were in Kent..." ~ Faris, Mark. (1991, September 19). Where the good times roll. *The Akron Beacon Journal*.
3. "I walked in and met..." ~ Rathbun, Keith. (1981, February 5). The bands and clubs agree: Cleveland's the best location in the nation. *Scene*.
4. "Joe worked. We paid them..." ~ Clary, Mike. (1975, May 4). The return of Joe Walsh: A rock star comes back to where it all began. *The Akron Beacon Journal Magazine*.
5. "I studied the blues through..." ~ Resnicoff, Matt. (1988, January). The clown prince of rock guitar. *Guitar World*.
6. "I removed the tone condenser..." ~ Rosen, Steven. (1975, June). Joe Walsh: Rock master. *Guitar Player*.
7. "people treated Joe Walsh like..." ~ Draus, Joanne. (1982, January 12). Veteran Kent musician returns to JB's. *Daily Kent Stater*.

▶ CHAPTER 5: THE JAMES GANG

1. "I was going to Ohio..." ~ Girard, Jim. (1976, October 21). James Gang: 10 years and counting. *Scene*.
2. "So, Ronnie Silverman and I..." ~ Girard, Jim. (1976, October 21). James Gang: 10 years and counting. *Scene*.
3. "There weren't any bands, less..." ~ Girard, Jim. (1976, October 21). James Gang: 10 years and

counting. *Scene.*
4. "I was thirteen-years-old..." ~ Stevenson, Jeff C. (2015). *Fortney Road: Life, Death, and Deception in a Christian Cult.* Minneapolis-St. Paul: Freethought.
5. "Like Hendrix and the Who..." ~ Francis, Thomas. (2004, December 8). Lord of the strings. *Scene.*
6. "People danced to the James..." ~ Rathbun, Keith. (1981, February 5). The bands and clubs agree: Cleveland's the best location in the nation. *Scene.*
7. "Some friends say that Glenn..." ~ Francis, Thomas. (2004, December 8). Lord of the strings. *Scene.*
8. "We were blown away by..." ~ Stevenson, Jeff C. (2015). *Fortney Road: Life, Death, and Deception in a Christian Cult.* Minneapolis-St. Paul: Freethought.
9. "Our last gig with Glenn..." ~ Girard, Jim. (1976, October 21). James Gang: 10 years and counting. *Scene.*
10. "We played with Joe and..." ~ Girard, Jim. (1976, October 21). James Gang: 10 years and counting. *Scene.*
11. "I was joyous and carefree..." ~ Baca, Ricardo. (2006, August 11). After 35 years, Joe Walsh and the James Gang saddle up for another ride. *The Denver Post.*
12. "We were starving, and it..." ~ Greenleaf, Vicki. (1983, December). Exclusive interview with Joe Walsh. *Song Hits Magazine.*
13. "Phil [Giallombardo] was having troubles..." ~ Girard, Jim. (1976, October 21). James Gang: 10 years and counting. *Scene.*
14. "I'd have my dad chauffeur..." ~ Blackwood, Nina. (1993, June 6). Joe Walsh: The nutty professor. *Music Connection.*
15. "In my early 20s, I..." ~ Heath, Chris. (2019, February). Clean: 9 sobers musicians on how they thrive creatively without drugs or booze. *GQ.*

⏵ CHAPTER 6: THE POWER TRIO

1. "We figured we'd pick some..." ~ Kutner, Rick. (2006, August 16). James Gang: Interview with Joe Walsh. *The Aquarian.*
2. "I was one of the..." ~ Davis, Hays. (2016, July 16). Joe Walsh talks about his music before his Richmond appearance at Innsbrook. *The Martinsville Bulletin.*
3. "We thought 'oh well this'll..." ~ Valentine, Penny. (1970, October 17). The James Gang. *Sounds.*
4. "Each time we played another..." ~ Girard, Jim. (1976, October 21). James Gang: 10 years and counting. *Scene.*
5. "When we came off the stage..." ~ Girard, Jim. (1976, October 21). James Gang: 10 years and counting. *Scene.*
6. "A three-piece group is a..." ~ Greenleaf, Vicki. (1983, December). Exclusive interview with Joe Walsh. *Song Hits Magazine.*
7. "People were doing a lot..." ~ Petkovic, John. (2018, November 4). Rock legend and guitarist Glenn Schwartz dies at 78. *The Cleveland Plain Dealer.*

⏵ CHAPTER 7: THE JAMES GANG GET SIGNED

1. "I'm a professional listener. I..." ~ Daley, Dan. (2004, November). Bill Szymczyk: Producer. *Sound On Sound.*
2. "It was the height of..." ~ Daley, Dan. (2004, November). Bill Szymczyk: Producer. *Sound On Sound.*
3. "If anyone taught me how..." ~ Daley, Dan. (2004, November). Bill Szymczyk: Producer. *Sound On Sound.*
4. "The energy was there. B.B..." ~ Daley, Dan. (2004, November). Bill Szymczyk: Producer. *Sound On Sound.*
5. "I had a friend of..." ~ Brown, Jake. (2014, September/October). The architect of 70's AOR: Bill Szymczyk on recording Joe Walsh, B.B. King, & the Eagles. *Tape Op.*
6. "died a death it deserved..." ~ "Michael Stanley fights fashion... & wins!" (1984, March/April). *RockLine.*
7. "I must have lived in..." ~ Scott, Jane. (1983, June 29). Joe Walsh reunited with rock. *The Cleveland Plain Dealer.*

8. "Walsh was getting into more..." ~ Scott, Jane. (1977, November 4). T-N-T promotes teen power. *The Cleveland Plain Dealer.*
9. "Cleveland's own James Gang is..." ~ Scott, Jane. (1969, October 10). The happening. *The Cleveland Plain Dealer.*
10. "The fun for me was..." ~ di Perna, Alan. (1992, May). Joe Walsh discusses his career, gear and new album, 'Analog Man.' *Guitar World.*
11. "We went to L.A. with..." ~ Halasa, Joyce. (1989, April 20). The James Gang, pt. IV: The good times and sad times with Joe Walsh. *Scene.*
12. "It was hot; it was..." ~ Kutner, Rick. (2006, August 16). James Gang: Interview with Joe Walsh. *The Aquarian.*
13. "The James Gang played regularly..." ~ Hynde, Chrissie. (2015). *Reckless: My Life as a Pretender.* New York: Doubleday.

⏵ CHAPTER 8: MAY 4TH AT KENT STATE

1. "was enthralled by Joe Walsh..." ~ Barham, Andrea. (1970, April 7). Audience digs James Gang. *Daily Kent Stater.*
2. "Kent had its first political..." ~ Hildebrand, William H. (2009). *A Most Noble Enterprise: The Story of Kent State University, 1910-2010.* Kent, OH: Kent State University Press.
3. "One irate motorist gunned his..." ~ "At war with war." (1970, May 18). *Time.*
4. "Saturday began quietly. Black student..." ~ "At war with war." (1970, May 18). *Time.*
5. "Without bothering to consult Kent..." ~ "At war with war." (1970, May 18). *Time.*
6. "On Sunday, Governor Rhodes arrived..." ~ "At war with war." (1970, May 18). *Time.*
7. "It seemed that the campus..." ~ "At war with war." (1970, May 18). *Time.*
8. "We had no idea there..." ~ "10 questions for... Devo's Gerald Casale." (2006, December 8). *Goldmine.*
9. "The grassy, rolling common was..." ~ Hynde, Chrissie. (2015). *Reckless: My Life as a Pretender.* New York: Doubleday.
10. "Everybody stopped dead in their..." ~ Crowe, Cameron. (1975, February 27). Joe Walsh, child of the silent majority: Ex-James Gangster tends to his garden. *Rolling Stone.*
11. "When I first went to..." ~ Shears, Jake. (2006, November 12). When Elton met Jake. *The Observer.*
12. "After that, I didn't look..." ~ Varga, George. (2012, February 2). Fact or fiction? With Joe Walsh, you never know. *The San Diego Union-Tribune.*

⏵ CHAPTER 9: JOE RIDES AGAIN

1. "The Who played its one..." ~ Mervis, Scott. (2016, March 10). The Who: A look back at the British Invasion band's 50 years in Pittsburgh. *The Pittsburgh Post-Gazette.*
2. "The Who came in before..." ~ Halasa, Joyce. (1989, April 20). The James Gang, pt. IV: The good times and sad times with Joe Walsh. *Scene.*
3. "If Dale hadn't been walked..." ~ Wolf, Carlo. (2006). *Cleveland Rock & Roll Memories.* Cleveland: Gray & Company.
4. "Sure we all listened to..." ~ Rosenfelt, Philip; & Beller, Andrea. (1967, June). Interview: The James Gang. *Action World.*
5. "Joe Walsh is definitely one..." ~ Townshend, Pete. (1970, August 22). The Pete Townshend Page #1. *Melody Maker.*
6. "We were supposed to be..." ~ Young, Charles. (1979, November 29). The Eagles: Hell is for heroes. *Rolling Stone.*
7. "Keith Moon decided that he..." ~ Makowsko, Peter. (2012, July). Interview: Joe Walsh on rock 'n' roll excess and running for president. *Classic Rock.*
8. "The Who's perpetual-motion machine..." ~ Jones, Dylan. (2018, July). Roger Daltrey: 'Keith Moon lived his entire life as a fantasy.' *GQ.*
9. "I decided my hotel room..." ~ Pang, May; & Edwards, Henry. (1983). *Loving John: The Untold Story.* New York: Warner Books.
10. "I have fond memories of..." ~ Fletcher, Tony. (1999). *Moon: The Life and Death of a Rock Legend.* New York: Spike.

11. "At around 8 a.m. I..." ~ Valentine, Penny. (1970, October 17). The James Gang. *Sounds.*
12. "I'll be honest, though. We..." ~ Hollingworth, Roy. (1971, August 14). Home James: The James Gang. *Melody Maker.*
13. "Europe made me a little..." ~ Tobler, John; & Grundy, Stuart. (1984). *The Guitar Greats.* New York: St. Martin's Press.
14. "Led by Joe Walsh.... they..." ~ Mendelssohn, John. (1970, December 1). The Steve Miller Band, James Gang: Civic Auditorium, Pasadena and Santa Monica, CA. *The Los Angeles Times.*

▶ CHAPTER 10: THIRDS: A FINALE

1. "For so many years we..." ~ Green, Richard. (1971, July 24). James Gang ride on their own. *New Musical Express.*
2. "We're big Elvis Presley fans..." ~ Green, Richard. (1971, July 24). James Gang ride on their own. *New Musical Express.*
3. "By no exertion of the..." ~ Mendelsohn, J. (1971, July 22). Records: *Thirds*, James Gang. *Rolling Stone.*
4. "The way that Joe left..." ~ Girard, Jim. (1976, October 21). James Gang: 10 years and counting. *Scene.*
5. "Pete Townshend told us to..." ~ Hedegaard, Erik. (2006, August 24). Joe Walsh rides again. *Rolling Stone.*
6. "So there we were with..." ~ Shirley, Jerry. (2011). *Best Seat in the House: Drumming in the '70s with Marriott, Frampton, and Humble Pie.* Alma, MI: Rebeats.
7. "That was something I really..." ~ Tobler, John; & Grundy, Stuart. (1984). *The Guitar Greats.* New York: St. Martin's Press.
8. "[Walsh] was very, very tired..." ~ Swenson, John. (1972, November 30). The James Gang. *Beetle.*
9. "When I left the James..." ~ di Perna, Alan. (1992, May). Joe Walsh discusses his career, gear and new album, 'Analog Man.' *Guitar World.*
10. "We found he was more..." ~ Pantsios, Anastasia. (1974, September 6). The James Gang rides recording success trail again. *The Cleveland Plain Dealer.*
11. "I think the James Gang..." ~ Ferris, D.X. (2006, August 9). Back in the saddle: After 35 years, the James Gang rides again. *Scene.*
12. "I like to give people..." ~ di Perna, Alan. (1992, May). Joe Walsh discusses his career, gear and new album, 'Analog Man.' *Guitar World.*
13. "I never really got into..." ~ Brooks, Michael. (1972, May/June). Peter Townshend. *Guitar Player.*
14. "I said, 'Great, cheers, man..." ~ Brooks, Michael. (1972, May/June). Peter Townshend. *Guitar Player.*
15. "I used that guitar on..." ~ Brooks, Michael. (1972, May/June). Peter Townshend. *Guitar Player.*
16. "Pete always seems to smash..." ~ Jisi, Chris. (1982, May). The return of Thunderfingers: John Entwistle. *Guitar Player.*
17. "When the first [Led Zeppelin]..." ~ di Perna, Alan. (1992, May). Joe Walsh discusses his career, gear and new album, 'Analog Man.' *Guitar World.*
18. "In those days, Les Pauls..." ~ Meeker, Ward. (2012, August). Joe Walsh: Life's still good. *Vintage Guitar.*

▶ CHAPTER 11: ROCKY MOUNTAIN WAY

1. "That was not fun at..." ~ Kane, Dan. (2013, May 24). The Chylds had radio hits, signed with Warner Bros., opened for the Beach Boys and more. *The Canton Repository.*
2. "It was the greatest day..." ~ Kane, Dan. (2013, May 24). The Chylds had radio hits, signed with Warner Bros., opened for the Beach Boys and more. *The Canton Repository.*
3. "We had to turn down..." ~ Kane, Dan. (2013, May 24). The Chylds had radio hits, signed with Warner Bros., opened for the Beach Boys and more. *The Canton Repository.*
4. "He was disgusted by the..." ~ Scott, Jane. (1981, June 19). Vitale and Walsh back at Blossom. *The Cleveland Plain Dealer.*
5. "We'd both be playing in..." ~ Scott, Jane. (1979, October 26). Stars shine unexpectedly on Cleveland scene. *The Cleveland Plain Dealer.*
6. "I sure lost a lot..." ~ Flans, Robyn. (1982, June). Joe Vitale: Full spectrum. *Modern Drummer.*

7. "I had spoken to Ted..." ~ Lisko, B.J. (2020, September 9). Hey Joe!: Catching up with legendary drummer Joe Vitale. *The Canton Repository.*
8. "They'd unionized the studios. I..." ~ Brown, Mark. (2008, January 26). Reliving the ranch. *Rocky Mountain News.*
9. "In 1968 I had been..." ~ Brown, Mark. (2008, January 26). Reliving the ranch. *Rocky Mountain News.*
10. "We were on our own..." ~ Brown, Mark. (2008, January 26). Reliving the ranch. *Rocky Mountain News.*

▶ CHAPTER 12: ARRIVAL OF BARNSTORM

1. "We were playing pretty much... ~ Tobler, John; & Grundy, Stuart. (1984). *The Guitar Greats.* New York: St. Martin's Press.
2. "running the affairs of eighty-six..." ~ Crowe, Cameron. (1978, June 15). They call him Big Shorty. *Rolling Stone.*
3. "Out of nowhere, Irving [Azoff]..." ~ Crowe, Cameron. (1978, June 15). They call him Big Shorty. *Rolling Stone.*
4. "He's Napoleon with a heart..." ~ Crowe, Cameron. (1978, June 15). They call him Big Shorty. *Rolling Stone.*
5. "People keep saying I'm just..." ~ Palmer, Robert. (1981, July 6). U. of I. dropout now rock tycoon. *The St. Louis Post-Dispatch.*

▶ CHAPTER 13: THE SMOKER YOU DRINK

1. "The experience of recording in..." ~ Seraphine, Danny. (2011). *Street Player: My Chicago Story.* Hoboken, NJ: John Wiley & Sons.
2. "We loved the mountains but..." ~ Putman, Norbert. (2017). *Music Lessons, Volume One.* Nashville: Thimbleton House Media.
3. "The Neve boards were considered..." ~ Block, Melissa. (2013, March 8). Dave Grohl finds music's human element – in a machine. *All Things Considered.* Philadelphia: NPR.
4. "kinda laughed about album titles..." ~ Morsch, Mike. (2014). *The Vinyl Dialogues.* Grandview Heights, OH: Biblio Publishing.
5. "Duane Allman had showed me..." ~ di Perna, Alan. (1992, May). Joe Walsh discusses his career, gear and new album, 'Analog Man.' *Guitar World.*
6. "It was the first recording..." ~ Morsch, Mike. (2014). *The Vinyl Dialogues.* Grandview Heights, OH: Biblio Publishing.
7. "[We] had our first falling..." ~ Grundy, Stuart; & Tobler, John. (1982). *The Record Producers.* New York: St. Martin's Press.
8. "I always felt 'Rocky Mountain..." ~ Brown, G. (2004). *Colorado Rocks!: A Half-Century of Music in Colorado.* Boulder, CO: Pruett Publishing.
9. "I taught Peter how to..." ~ Resnicoff, Matt. (1988, January). The clown prince of rock guitar. *Guitar World.*
10. "He got out this metal..." ~ Frampton, Peter; & Light, Alan. (2020). *Do You Feel Like We Do?: A Memoir.* New York: Hachette.
11. "After I'd learned how to..." ~ Frampton, Peter; & Light, Alan. (2020). *Do You Feel Like We Do?: A Memoir.* New York: Hachette.
12. "Several hours before showtime, Joe..." ~ Crowe, Cameron. (1973, August 16). Joe Walsh and Barnstorm: Winterland, July 7th, 1973. *Rolling Stone.*
13. "Walsh's guitar wailed and his..." ~ Crowe, Cameron. (1973, August 16). Joe Walsh and Barnstorm, Winterland. *Rolling Stone.*
14. "I've always loved that song..." ~ Scott, Jane. (1985, July 13). Joe Walsh proves rarity – an Indian fan. *The Cleveland Plain Dealer.*
15. "Cleveland's most talented native son..." ~ "50/50 vision: A look back at the 50 best concerts in Cleveland from the past 50 years." (2021, October 20). *Scene.*
16. "In 1974, Mark [Mothersbaugh] and..." ~ Nagy, Evie. (2015). 33 1/3: *Devo, Freedom of Choice.* New York: Bloomsbury Academic.
17. "At the hospital, there were..." ~ Hedegaard, Eric. (2006, August 24). Joe Walsh rides again.

Rolling Stone.
18. "The accident kind of did..." ~ Taylor, Carol. (2010, October 24). Emma's fountain lives long after rock 'n' roll tragedy. *The Daily Camera.*
19. "I'm not afraid to die..." ~ Bishop, Pete. (1985, September 5). Joe Walsh keeps it lean and gritty. *The Pittsburgh Press.*
20. "I was totally down and..." ~ Crowe, Cameron. (1978, June 15). They call him Big Shorty. *Rolling Stone.*
21. "It was great out in..." ~ Pantsios, Anastasia. (1974, September 13). Ex-Barnstormer Joe Vitale returns to Canton to record. *The Cleveland Plain Dealer.*

CHAPTER 14: JOE SAYS SO WHAT
1. "As he's moved westward – from..." ~ Scoppa, Joe. (1975, April 24). So What: Joe Walsh. *Rolling Stone.*
2. "It's really strange because we..." ~ Rosen, Steve. (1975). Joe Walsh's 'So What' – beyond fact, fiction, and Barnstorm. *Raves.*
3. "I just used to sit..." ~ "Guitarist claims superstar will take mod music out of rut." (1975, March 24). *The Pomona Progress Bulletin.*
4. "Jimmy came down to the..." ~ Rosen, Steve. (1975). Joe Walsh's 'So What' – beyond fact, fiction, and Barnstorm. *Raves.*
5. "interfering with the management relationship..." ~ "Belkin names ABC & execs in $1Mil James Gang action." (1974, October 26). *Billboard.*
6. "You'd get something done for..." ~ Fletcher, Tony. (1999). *Moon: The Life and Death of a Rock Legend.* New York: Spike.
7. "Here was this really humble..." ~ Walsh, Joe. (2007, December 17). Interview, *Larry King Live* (CNN).
8. "It was a perfect match, working..." ~ Rensin, David. (1975, March 13). Dan Fogelberg: Home Free at last. *Rolling Stone.*
9. "Bill and I got very..." ~ Uhelszki, Jaan. (1975) Joe Walsh: Lonely in the spotlight. *Creem.*

CHAPTER 15: THE RISE OF THE EAGLES
1. "an educated redneck" ~ Lester, Paul. (2015, October 1). Don Henley: 'There's no partying, no alcohol, it's like a morgue backstage.' *The Guardian.*
2. "I went to Ahmet again..." ~ Smith Joe. (1988). *Off the Record: An Oral History of Popular Music.* New York: Warner Books.
3. "As it happened, [J.D.] Souther..." ~ Smith Joe. (1988). *Off the Record: An Oral History of Popular Music.* New York: Warner Books.
4. "One night I was lingering..." ~ Martin, Steve. (2007). *Born Standing Up: A Comic's Life.* New York: Scribner.
5. "About eight people came each..." ~ Sebastian, Matt. (2016, January 19). Glenn Frey and the Eagles a storied part of Boulder's music history. *The Daily Camera.*
6. "We had it all planned..." ~ Brown, G. (2004). *Colorado Rocks!: A Half-Century of Music in Colorado.* Boulder, CO: Pruett Publishing.
7. "It was hell from the..." ~ Young, Charles. (1979, November 29). The Eagles: Hell is for heroes. *Rolling Stone.*
8. "Some of it you can't..." ~ Everley, Dave. (2018, December). California Dreaming. *Classic Rock.*
9. "Geffen told the Eagles they..." ~ Crowe, Cameron. (1978, June 15). They call him Big Shorty. *Rolling Stone.*
10. "I didn't mind him pointing..." ~ Crowe, Cameron. (1975, September 25). The Eagles: Chips off the old buffalo. *Rolling Stone.*
11. "Glenn and Don wanted a..." ~ Johns, Glyn. (2014). *Sound Man.* New York: Blue Rider Press.
12. "The Eagles were interviewing producers..." ~ Szymczyk, Bill. (2017, January 28). Glenn had this all laid out. *Billboard.*
13. "Walsh told me I should..." ~ Charone, Barbara. (1976, March 27). The Eagles: Desperados in blue jeans and sneakers. *Sounds.*
14. "They started the third record..." ~ Daley, Dan. (2004, November). Bill Szymczyk: Producer.

Sound On Sound.
15. "Working with the Eagles was..." ~ Charone, Barbara. (1976, March 27). The Eagles: Desperados in blue jeans and sneakers. *Sounds.*
16. "I was blown away that..." ~ Young, Charles. (1979, November 29). The Eagles: Hell is for heroes. *Rolling Stone.*
17. "I went to Glyn's house..." ~ Grundy, Stuart; & Tobler, John. (1982). *The Record Producers*. New York: St. Martin's Press.
18. "They returned to America with..." ~ Johns, Glyn. (2014). *Sound Man.* New York: Blue Rider Press.

▶ CHAPTER 16: BEFORE JOE JOINED

1. "Joe Walsh is coming back..." ~ Hudson, Buckwheat. (1975, March 13). Walsh 'comes home' in KSU concert stand. *Daily Kent Stater.*
2. "Basically I'm the same dude." ~ "Walsh recalls 'crazy days' in Kent." (1975, March 14). *Daily Kent Stater.*
3. "Sometimes it feels like a..." ~ Clary, Mike. (1975, May 4). The return of Joe Walsh: A rock star comes back to where it all began. *The Akron Beacon Journal Magazine.*
4. "You could tell it was..." ~ Pantsios, Anastasia. (1975, March 21). Joe Walsh gave threadbare reply to Kent's red carpet. *The Cleveland Plain Dealer.*
5. "Walsh appeared on stage in..." ~ Clary, Mike. (1975, May 4). The return of Joe Walsh: A rock star comes back to where it all began. *The Akron Beacon Journal Magazine.*
6. "Then came the song the..." ~ Hudson, Alex. (1975, May 6). Eagles concert 'suburb' despite amplifier woes. *Kent Stater.*
7. "A light plane bound for..." ~ Kissell, E. J. (1975, March 15). 6 die as storm rakes Ohio. *The Cleveland Plain Dealer.*
8. "We were in a Twin..." ~ Rose, Joseph. (1975, September). Trains and buses and planes and Joe Walsh. *Hit Parader.*
9. "The audience response was incredibly..." ~ Kubernik, Harvey. (1975, May 10). Joe Walsh: Shrine Auditorium, Los Angeles CA. *Melody Maker.*
10. "I had a chain saw..." ~ Heath, Chris. (2019, February). Clean: 9 sobers musicians on how they thrive creatively without drugs or booze. *GQ.*
11. "Good live set that captures..." ~ Kirsch, Bob (Ed.). (1976, April 3). *Billboard's* top album picks. *Billboard.*

▶ CHAPTER 17: JOE JOINS THE EAGLES

1. "When we brought Joe in..." ~ Flanagan, Bill. (1989, October). Don Henley: The end of the innocent act. *Musician.*
2. "I had very little to..." ~ Grundy, Stuart; & Tobler, John. (1982). *The Record Producers*. New York: St. Martin's Press.
3. "We knew a year before..." ~ Charone, Barbara. (1977, April). One of these nightmares. *Crawdaddy.*
4. "I kept asking: 'Are we..." ~ Hotten, Jon. (2004, January). Life in the fast lane: The turbulent tale of the Eagles. *Classic Rock.*
5. "Those guys were about as..." ~ Linafelt, Tom. (1992, September 28). Rocker Walsh to run for vice president. *The Bangor Daily News.*
6. "In some ways we were..." ~ Sharp, Ken. (2006, September). Randy Meisner: Takes it to the limit one more time. *Discoveries.*
7. "I joined their band. They..." ~ Young, Charles M. (2007, May 29). How the kings of Seventies California rock stopped feuding, recorded their first album in 30 years and landed at the top of the charts. *Rolling Stone.*
8. "There were two groups that..." ~ Fey, Barry; Alexander, Steve; & Wolfe, Rich. (2011). *Backstage Past.* Overland Park, KS: Lone Wolfe Press.
9. "We went to Australia. Boy..." ~ Campbell, Mary. (October 4, 1985). Former Eagles guitarist Walsh staying busy with solo work. *The Victoria Advocate.*
10. "The Eagles is a certain..." ~ Baca, Ricardo. (2010, September 1). Walsh, Frey are headed Rocky

Mountain way. *The Denver Post.*
11. "Though Walsh's guitar work, particularly..." ~ Hilburn, Robert. (1976, October 21). The Eagles have landed. *The Los Angeles Times.*
12. "In Joe Walsh, replacing Bernie..." ~ Silvert, Conrad. (1976, August 21). Talent in action: Eagles, Linda Rondstadt, Loggins & Messina, Oakland Stadium. *Billboard.*

▶ CHAPTER 18: HOTEL CALIFORNIA

1. "[The] thing I'm proudest about..." ~ Graham, Samuel. (1983, October). Joe Walsh goes back to barn-storming. *Musician.*
2. "Chris Stone, a businessman, and..." ~ Kooper, Al. (2008). *Backstage Passes & Backstabbing Bastards.* New York: Backstreet Books.
3. "The Eagles were recording next... ~ Pinnock, Tom. (2014, July). Black Sabbath: "The Eagles were recording next door, but we were too loud for them." *Uncut.*
4. "'Pretty Maids In A Row'..." ~ Brinkley, Douglas. (2020, June 12). Bob Dylan has a lot on his mind. *The New York Times.*
5. "I had this lick that..." ~ Walsh, Joe. (2019, September 15). *Paul Shaffer Plus One* (AXS TV).
6. "This business makes it easy..." ~ Hilburn, Robert. (1979, February 24). Rock stars own enemies. *The Victoria Advocate.*
7. "I played keyboards on 'New..." ~ Resnicoff, Matt. (1988, January). The clown prince of rock guitar. *Guitar World.*
8. "So we sat down in..." ~ McCormick, Neil. (2013, May 6). The Eagles: Documentary reveals band's journey from naive kids to 1970s superstars. *The Windsor Star.*

▶ CHAPTER 19: CHECKING OUT OF THE HOTEL

1. "This album will sell by..." ~ Irwin, Colin. (1976, December 11). The Eagles: Hotel California. *Melody Maker.*
2. "Walsh's exact effect isn't always..." ~ Walters, Charley. (1977, February 24). Records: Hotel California, Eagles. *Rolling Stone.*
3. "I was a little disappointed..." ~ Gilmore, Mikal. (1987, November 5). Don Henley. *Rolling Stone.*
4. "Nobody was from California. Everybody..." ~ Walsh, Joe. (2010). *Top 2000 A Gogo* (Dutch Public Television).
5. "you might as well bill..." ~ Grundy, Stuart; & Tobler, John. (1982). *The Record Producers.* New York: St. Martin's Press.
6. "Walsh would be worth watching..." ~ Scott, Jane. (1977, April 2). Rock: Eagles are uplighting. *The Cleveland Plain Dealer.*
7. "[There's] neon Hotel California signs..." ~ Evans, Jim. (1977, April 30). One of these nights. *Record Mirror.*
8. "a dominant member of the..." ~ Evans, Jim. (1977, April 30). One of these nights. *Record Mirror.*
9. "The decision to include Walsh..." ~ Smith, Ramsay. (1977, May 4). It's the 5-star Eagles. *The Aberdeen Evening Express.*
10. "We've been out for a..." ~ Eliot, Marc. (1998). *To the Limit: The Untold Story of the Eagles.* Boston: Little, Brown & Company.
11. "When the tour ended, I..." ~ Eliot, Marc. (1998). *To the Limit: The Untold Story of the Eagles.* Boston: Little, Brown & Company.
12. "I'd been singing mostly background..." ~ Zimmer, Dave. (1980) Randy Meisner: Ex-Eagle flies high solo. *BAM.*
13. "I had a forty-one-foot..." ~ Crosby, David; & Gottlieb, Carl. (1988). *Long Time Gone: The Autobiography of David Crosby.* New York: Doubleday.
14. "The talent lineup for the..." ~ Schipper, Henry. (1992). *Broken Record: An Inside Story of the Grammy Awards.* New York: Birch Lane Press.
15. "would perform after all, without..." ~ Schipper, Henry. (1992). *Broken Record: An Inside Story of the Grammy Awards.* New York: Birch Lane Press.
16. "We thought the competition was..." ~ "Top disc stars feted." (1978, February 24). *The Oakland Tribune.*

⯈ CHAPTER 20: THE LONG RUN

1. "It made us paranoid. People..." ~ Hilburn, Robert. (1980, March 21). Eagles challenged by 'Hotel' success. *The Eugene Register-Guard*.
2. "Don and I did not..." ~ Yarbrough, Jeff. (1986, April). Interview: Glenn Frey. *Interview*.
3. "The thing that eventually became..." ~ Graham, Samuel. (1983, October). Joe Walsh goes back to barn-storming. *Musician*.
4. "He's a wonderful guy. He's..." ~ Glazer, Mitchell. (1983, July). Don Henley & Danny Kortchmar, the recording team of the 80s. *Musician*.
5 "As one fifth of the..." ~ Radel, Cliff. (1978, August 17). Rock makes big splash in Riverfront. *The Cincinnati Enquirer*.
6 "We only hear from them..." ~ Young, Charles. (1979, November 29). The Eagles: Hell is for heroes. *Rolling Stone*.
7 "We couldn't even show up..." ~ Resnicoff, Matt. (1988, January). The clown prince of rock guitar. *Guitar World*.
8. "Joe and I were friends and..." ~ Hyman, Dan. (2015, September 8). Meet the men behind the distinctive soundtrack of 'The Warriors.' *The Village Voice*.
9. "was made about gang-type..." ~ Interview. (1981). Joe Walsh (BBC).
10. "So I brought ['In the..." ~ Hyman, Dan. (2015, September 8). Meet the men behind the distinctive soundtrack of 'The Warriors.' *The Village Voice*.

⯈ CHAPTER 21: BUT SERIOUSLY FOLKS

1. "We spent a week down..." ~ Brown, Jake. (2014, September/October). The architect of 70's AOR: Bill Szymczyk on recording Joe Walsh, B.B. King, & the Eagles. *Tape Op*.
2. "We got back to my..." ~ Brown, Jake. (2014, September/October). The architect of 70's AOR: Bill Szymczyk on recording Joe Walsh, B.B. King, & the Eagles. *Tape Op*.
3. "I never thought that would..." ~ Resnicoff, Matt. (1988, January). The clown prince of rock guitar. *Guitar World*.
4. "a satirical statement on the..." ~ Madden, Mark. (1988, February 5). 18 years of Joe Walsh. *The Pittsburgh Post-Gazette*.
5. "I was on stage one..." ~ Sewald, Jeff. (1985, September 5). Ex-Eagle Joe Walsh is still living music. *The Pittsburgh Post-Gazette*.

⯈ CHAPTER 22: RELEASING THE LONG RUN

1. "Toward the end of August..." ~ Young, Charles M. (2007, May 29). How the kings of Seventies California rock stopped feuding, recorded their first album in 30 years and landed at the top of the charts. *Rolling Stone*.
2. "One first listening *The Long...*" ~ White, Timothy. (1979, November 15). The Eagles: Last tycoons in a lost lotusland. *Rolling Stone*.
3. "a brittle but forceful rocker" ~ White, Timothy. (1979, November 15). The Eagles: Last tycoons in a lost lotusland. *Rolling Stone*.
4. "*Long Run* is a finely..." ~ Hilburn, Robert. (1979, September 30). The Eagles' 'Long Run:' Survival in the fast lane. *The Los Angeles Times*.
5. "I couldn't possibly figure out..." ~ Flans, Robyn. (1982, June). Joe Vitale: Full spectrum. *Modern Drummer*.
6. "If I'm elected, I'll make..." ~ Scott, Jane. (1979, October 22). Eagles, Joe Walsh soar at Coliseum. *The Cleveland Plain Dealer*.
7. "Walsh is the only one..." ~ Young, Charles. (1979, November 29). The Eagles: Hell is for heroes. *Rolling Stone*.
8. "When we walked into the..." ~ Hilburn, Robert. (1980, July 29). The Eagles return to the Civic. *The Los Angeles Times*.

⯈ CHAPTER 23: JOE AND JOHN

1. "Joe is the hardest person..." ~ Young, Charles. (1979, November 29). The Eagles: Hell is for heroes. *Rolling Stone*.
2. "I've come to think of..." ~ Raymond, Joe. (1981, June 7). The Walsh plan for urban renewal. *The*

South Bend Tribune.
3. "efficient at wrecking hotel rooms" ~ Young, Charles. (1979, November 29). The Eagles: Hell is for heroes. *Rolling Stone.*
4. "So, I'll be sitting in..." ~ Gans, David. (1981, July 17). Joe Walsh. *BAM.*
5. "I'm not even hungry, but..." ~ Walsh, Joe. (2016). Interview on *Big Jim's House* (WCSX, Detroit).
6. "John broke a glass and..." ~ DeVault, Russ. (1991, May 24). Walsh leaves behind wild, hazy days behind him. *The Atlanta Constitution.*
7. "Belushi – you couldn't say 'no'..." ~ Walsh, Joe. (2016). Interview on *Big Jim's House* (WCSX, Detroit).
8. "I went to Benihana once..." ~ Walsh, Joe. (2017, August 2). Interview. *The Late Show With Stephen Colbert* (CBS).
9. "John had a party house..." ~ Felder, Don. (2008). *Heaven and Hell: My Life in the Eagles (1974-2001).* Hoboken, NJ: John Wiley & Sons.

▶ CHAPTER 24: THE EAGLES BREAK UP

1. "Towards the end, we just..." ~ Bradley, Lloyd. (1992, July 1). Interview: Eagle lands: Glenn Frey tells Lloyd Bradley about life after the Eagles. *The Independent.*
2. "The romance had gone of..." ~ Gilmore, Mikal. (1987, November 5). Don Henley. *Rolling Stone.*
3. "You're welcome... I guess." ~ Felder, Don. (2008). *Heaven and Hell: My Life in the Eagles (1974-2001).* Hoboken, NJ: John Wiley & Sons.
4. "I'm going to kick your..." ~ Felder, Don. (2008). *Heaven and Hell: My Life in the Eagles (1974-2001).* Hoboken, NJ: John Wiley & Sons.
5. "I remembered something Joe [Walsh]..." ~ Felder, Don. (2008). *Heaven and Hell: My Life in the Eagles (1974-2001).* Hoboken, NJ: John Wiley & Sons.
6. "Everybody picked that night to..." ~ Schruers, Fred. (1982, November 1). They soared in the seventies but the Eagles are now following separate flight plans. *People.*
7. "I just told Irving [Azoff]..." ~ Schruers, Fred. (1982, November 1). They soared in the seventies but the Eagles are now following separate flight plans. *People.*
8. "'usually articulate' senior senator 'seemed..." ~ Robinson, Judith. (2008). *Alan Cranston: Senator from California – Making a 'Dent in the World,' Volume II.* San Francisco: Telegraph Hill Press.
9. "The Eagles talked about breaking..." ~ Hilburn, Robert. (1982, May 21). The Eagles – a long run is over. *The Los Angeles Times.*
10. "A band is supposed to..." ~ Baird, Jock. (1984, October). Glenn Frey's benign dictatorship. *Musician.*
11. "We were together for almost..." ~ Cassata, Mary Anne. (1985, July). Don Henley's solo flight. *Rock.*
12. "There'll never be a 'Greed..." ~ Hilburn, Robert. (1994, July 22). The road to resumption. *The Gainesville Sun.*
13. "Even when we were broken..." ~ Everley, Dave. (2018, December). California dreaming. *Classic Rock.*
14. "My Eagles commitment is first..." ~ Grein, Paul. (1981, September 5). Solo LPs by group members growing. *Billboard.*
15. "I didn't know what to..." ~ Kruger, Debbie. (2013) The Eagles: Birds of pray. *Rhythms.*
16. "There were all these people..." ~ Bishop, Pete. (1983, June 27). Joe Walsh, ex-Eagles guitarist, flying solo again. *The Pittsburgh Press.*
17. "If you're looking for someone..." ~ Belushi Pisano, Judith; & Colby, Tanner. (2005). *Belushi: A Biography.* New York: Rugged Land.
18. "If I don't do something..." ~ Zeman, Ned. (2013, January). Soul men: The making of the Blues Brothers. *Vanity Fair.*
19. "There was a song that..." ~ Belushi Pisano, Judith; & Colby, Tanner. (2005). *Belushi: A Biography.* New York: Rugged Land.

▶ CHAPTER 25: JOE GOES SOLO AGAIN

1. "is why kids can't read..." ~ Linafelt, Tom. (1992, September 28). Rocker Walsh to run for vice president. *The Bangor Daily News.*

2. "It's the first time I've..." ~ Lloyd, Jack. (1981, June 21). Eagle on the loose. *The Philadelphia Inquirer.*
3. "characteristic wry humor with his..." ~ "Top album picks." (1981, May 9). *Billboard.*
4. "It didn't make it in..." ~ Chelstowski, Ray. (2021, April). Forty-year-old *Neighborhood. Goldmine.*
5. "Walsh goes for a large..." ~ Pantsios. Anastasia. (1981, June 20). Joe Walsh comes back in triumph. *The Cleveland Plain Dealer.*
6. "Sunday night at the Oakland..." ~ Kelp, Larry. (1981, July 21). Rock's been good to him, and vise versa. *The Oakland Tribune.*
7. "I'm actually pleased with the..." ~ Campbell, Mary. (1981, October 16). The Who's bassist breaks from 'black humor.' *The San Pedro News-Pilot.*
8. "a hard rock album that's..." ~ Denselow, Robin. (1981, November 27). Talking head speaks for himself. *The Guardian.*
9. "a reasonable album... I don't..." ~ Holt, Peter. (1983, December 1). Poor Ringo – the falling Starr. *The Evening Standard.*
10. "How do you think I..." ~ Davies, Hunter. (1996). *The Beatles.* New York: W. W. Norton & Company.
11. "Yeah, which position do you..." ~ Harrell, Jeff. (2001, February 8). A rocky Montclair way in 1982. *The Montclair Times.*

▶ CHAPTER 26: JOE AND STEVIE

1. "They were *not* supportive when..." ~ Rogers, Ray. (1988, July). A storm called Stevie. *Interview.*
2. "Believe it or not, people..." ~ "Believe it or not, people..." ~ Hiatt, Brian. (2015, January 29). Magic & loss. *Rolling Stone.*
3. After completing a grueling but... ~ Harris, Carol Ann. (2007). *Storms: My Life With Lindsey Buckingham and Fleetwood Mac.* Chicago: Chicago Review Press.
4. "Joe Walsh opened the show..." ~ Thornton, Linda R. (1983, November 7). Review: Nicks' vocals fall flat. *The Miami Herald.*
5. "I fell in love with..." ~ Brown, Mick. (2007, September 8). Stevie Nicks: A survivor's story. *The Telegraph.*
6. "I remember thinking, I can..." ~ Davis, Stephen. (2017). *Gold Dust Woman: The Biography of Stevie Nicks.* New York: St. Martin's Press. Interview, BBC Radio 1.
7. "I took really good care..." ~ Horne, Nicky. (1991, August 27). Interview, BBC Radio.
8. "I guess I had been..." ~ Nicks, Stevie. (1991). Booklet from *Time Space: The Best Of.* Los Angeles: Modern Records.
9. "We used an old API..." ~ Graham, Samuel. (1983, October). Joe Walsh goes back to barn-storming. *Musician.*
10. "I'm gonna get killed for..." ~ Graff, Gary. (1983, July 18). Joe Walsh: He's just having fun. *The Detroit Free Press.*
11. "As far as I'm concerned..." ~ Kaye, Roger. (1983, September). Joe Walsh tours again for fun and little profit. *The Fort Worth Star-Telegram.*
12. "I was woken up at..." ~ Stewart, Dave. (2016). *Sweet Dreams Are Made of This.* New York: New American Library.
13. "One day my friend Sharon..." ~ McNair, James. (2013, December). The Texas kid who became a rock star. *Mojo.*
14. "Tell Stevie I'm going because..." ~ Iley, Chrissy. (2013, October). In conversation with the real rebel. *Elle UK.*
15. "a lecture Tom Petty gave..." ~ Tannenbaum, Rob. (2014, October 4). Stevie Nicks admits past pregnancy with Don Henley and more about her wild history. *Billboard.*
16. "There was no closure, so..." ~ McNair, James. (2013, December). The Texas kid who became a rock star. *Mojo.*
17. "I don't know what my..." ~ Iley, Chrissy. (2013, October). In conversation with the real rebel. *Elle UK.*
18. "We were probably the perfect.." ~ Davis, Stephen. (2017). *Gold Dust Woman: The Biography of Stevie Nicks.* New York: St. Martin's Press.
19. "I was flattered when I..." ~ Koha, Nui Te. (2010, June 20). Eagles detour into life in slow lane.

The Melbourne Sunday Herald Sun.
20. "We were seeking refuge – kind..." ~ Walsh, Joe. (c. 2002). Interview, *The Howard Stern Show.*
21. "Out of a clear blue..." ~ Creswell, Toby. (1984, December 7). Guess where the Eagle has landed. *The Sydney Morning Herald.*
22. "de-Eagleising therapy." ~ Creswell, Toby. (1984, December 7). Guess where the Eagle has landed. *The Sydney Morning Herald.*
23. "thrown out" ~ Howlett, Scott. (1984, December 9). Rock of ages. *The Sydney Morning Herald.*
24. "Why should I? So people..." ~ Howlett, Scott. (1984, December 9). Rock of ages. *The Sydney Morning Herald.*

CHAPTER 27: THE CONFESSOR

1. "I decided not to be..." ~ Schuller, Geoff. (1985, September 12). Rocker tries to restore music's artistry. *Daily Kent Stater.*
2. "This is the best album..." ~ Henke, James. (1985, June 30). R.E.M. gets into gear while on familiar track. *The Cleveland Plain Dealer.*
3. "as mundane as brushing your..." ~ Bishop, Pete. (1985, September 5). Joe Walsh keeps it lean and gritty. *The Pittsburgh Press.*
4. "I do a good 40-minute..." ~ Bishop, Pete. (1985, September 5). Joe Walsh keeps it lean and gritty. *The Pittsburgh Press.*
5. "Can you bring Joe Walsh..." ~ Hoynes, Paul. (1985, July 15). Needing a break. *The Cleveland Plain Dealer.*
6. "As Randy was leaving the..." ~ Marx, Richard. (2021). *Stories to Tell: A Memoir.* New York: Simon & Schuster.
7. "I sat anxiously inside Studio..." ~ Marx, Richard. (2021). *Stories to Tell: A Memoir.* New York: Simon & Schuster.

CHAPTER 28: GOT ANY GUM IN MEMPHIS?

1. "I wasn't getting much done..." ~ Nager, Larry. (1995, January 29). Soaring Eagles: Shaped-up Walsh returns to Memphis. *The Memphis Commercial Appeal.*
2. "Lisa was a gorgeous-looking..." ~ Rees, Paul. (2020). *The Ox.* London: Constable.
3. "Deep down, she was a..." ~ Rees, Paul. (2020). *The Ox.* London: Constable.
4. "Gary asked if I would..." ~ Mehr, Bob. (2016, August 10). 'They're really pushing me,' Joe Walsh says of new band. *The Memphis Commercial Appeal.*
5. "It was a real kick..." ~ Nager, Larry. (1995, January 29). Soaring Eagles: Shaped-up Walsh returns to Memphis. *The Memphis Commercial Appeal.*
6. "I don't particularly want a..." ~ King, Peter B. (1988, February 4). Joe Walsh brings social consciousness, rock savvy into Syria Mosque. *The Pittsburgh Press.*
7. "A bum came up to..." ~ Madden, Mark. (1988, February 5). 18 years of Joe Walsh. *The Pittsburgh Post-Gazette.*
8. "There is absolutely nothing wrong..." ~ Long, Tom. (1987, July 10). Stuck in the '70s again with rocker Joe Walsh. *The Santa Cruz Sentinel.*
9. "So, from CYO dances at..." ~ Heaton, Michael. (1987, September 7). Guitarist fires up amps, Blossom crowd. *The Cleveland Plain Dealer.*
10. "Clearly, Walsh remains a fan..." ~ McTavish, Brian. (1987, September 10). Joe Walsh's hardy spirit defies rain. *The Kansas City Star.*
11. "I've been rich a couple..." ~ King, Peter B. (1988, February 4). Joe Walsh brings social consciousness, rock savvy into Syria Mosque. *The Pittsburgh Press.*
12. "I don't see it ever..." ~ Kay, Roger. (1987, December 5). Eagle eager for reunion but isn't counting on it. *The Fort Worth Star-Telegram.*
13. "Never much interested in cars..." ~ Townshend, Pete. (2017). *Who I Am: A Memoir.* New York: Harper.
14. "He was definitely cute – nice..." ~ Casey, Kristin. (2020). *Rock Monster: My Life With Joe Walsh.* Los Angeles: Rare Bird Books.

⯈ CHAPTER 29: THE ALL-STARR TOUR

1. "One Friday afternoon [I] was..." ~ Roper, Matt. (2020, July 7). Ringo Starr thought he killed wife Barbara Bach after boozy bender in the 80s. *The Mirror*.
2. "I had a second, maybe..." ~ Hibbert, Tibbert. (1992, June). Who the hell does RINGO STARR think he is? *Q*.
3. "I landed drunk as a..." ~ Dougherty, Steve; Balfour, Victoria. (1989, August 28). Ringo on the rebound. *People*.
4. "At some point, you realize..." ~ Kozinn, Allan. (1989, August 2). Ringo Starr, back on the road. *The New York Times*.
5. "David did a very smart..." ~ Wild, David. (1989, August 24). A Starr is reborn. *Rolling Stone*.
6. "In the mathematics of the..." ~ Wild, David. (1989, August 24). A Starr is reborn. *Rolling Stone*.
7. "After Joe told me yes..." ~ Sandall, Robert. (1991, January) Ringo Starr. *Q*.
8. "The first three days of..." ~ Kozinn, Allan. (1989, August 2). Ringo Starr, back on the road. *The New York Times*.
9. "Vodka was what worked for..." ~ Heath, Chris. (2019, February). Clean: 9 sobers musicians on how they thrive creatively without drugs or booze. *GQ*.
10. "I had a moment of..." ~ Kaulessar, Ricardo. (2004, October 8). Sex, drugs & life advice. *The Montclair Times*.
11. "Joe suggested him. Mac speaks..." ~ Sandall, Robert. (1991, January). Ringo Starr. *Q*.
12. "When I called them originally..." ~ Sandall, Robert. (1991, January). Ringo Starr. *Q*.
13. "It's great to be here..." ~ Warren, Jill. (1989, July 27). Ringo's concert one of the best. *The Indianapolis Star*.
14. "Ringo's always been surrounded by..." ~ Smith, George. (1990, March 31). For Joe Walsh, it's still jest rock 'n' roll. *The Allentown Morning Call*.
15. "I played 'Desperado' in rehearsal..." ~ Smith, George. (1990, March 31). For Joe Walsh, it's still jest rock 'n' roll. *The Allentown Morning Call*.
16. "That's not his song to..." ~ Van Matre, Lynn. (1989, August 9). Lone Eagle. *The Chicago Tribune*.
17. "I didn't want to talk..." ~ Van Matre, Lynn. (1989, August 9). Lone Eagle. *The Chicago Tribune*.
18. "Walsh arrived at the studio..." ~ Coletti, Alex (Ed.); Hinckley, David (Ed.); & Malarkey, Sarah (Ed.). (1995). *MTV Unplugged*. New York: MTV Books / Pocket Books.
19. "Don Henley kept an audience..." ~ Marks, Craig; & Tannenbaum, Rob. (2011). *I Want My MTV: The Uncensored History of the Music Video Revolution*. New York: Dutton.

⯈ CHAPTER 30: EAGLE RUMBLINGS

1. "Glenn showed up at a..." ~ McCambridge, Michael. (1990, January 20). Eagles reunion is in talking stage. *The Cleveland Plain Dealer*.
2. "I wouldn't call what you..." ~ Drozdowski, Ted. (2000, March). Eagles reunite for concert and album. *Musician*.
3. "Walsh's manner was odd – his..." ~ King, Peter B. (1990, March 30. Joe Walsh leaves fans disappointed. *The Pittsburgh Press*.

⯈ CHAPTER 31: ORDINARY AVERAGE JOE

1. "We were lucky with good..." ~ Scott, Jane. (1995, January 18). TV-5 goes 'Upbeat' for an hour tonight. *The Cleveland Plain Dealer*.
2. "He'd call me up and..." ~ Olszewski, Mike. (2003). *Radio Daze: Stories From the Front in Cleveland's Radio Wars*. Kent, OH: Kent State University Press.
3. "Spero was shocked. While Walsh..." ~ Heaton, Michael. (2013, July 7). David Spero, artist-manager, talks about what went on behind the scenes with the Eagles – exclusive interview. *The Cleveland Plain Dealer*.
4. "Meanwhile the answering machine is..." ~ Budin, David. (1994, February 13). David Spero rock around the block. *The Cleveland Plain Dealer*.
5. "Since the break-up of..." ~ Graff, Gary. (1991, May 18). Joe Walsh stronger on new release. *The Bangor Daily News*.
6. "During the tour, the Doobie..." ~ "Joe Vitale Jr.: What's in a name?" (2014, May 9). *Pure Times*

Entertainment Magazine.
7. "It was funny the way..." ~ Davis, Ken. (1991, July 28). Grand-slam guitarists. *The South Bend Tribune.*
8. "His guitar licks are hotter..." ~ Davis, Sandi. (1991, August 25). Walsh entertains zoo crowd with hits of old, new. *The Oklahoman.*
9. "At 43, the wizened musician..." ~ McShane, Larry. (1991, August 23). Is life still good? Joe Walsh has doubts. *The Charlotte Observer.*
10. "Joe had been on the..." ~ Phillips, Beau. (2014). *I Killed Pink Floyd's Pig.* Seattle: Peanut Butter Publishing.

▶ CHAPTER 32: JOE AND GLENN

1. "This band has a different..." ~ Hinkley, David. (1992, May 24). Starr ready to hit the road again. *The Wichita Eagle.*
2. "Joe's brilliant. A lovely man..." ~ Booth, Philip. (1992, June 5). It's Starr time for rock vets. *The Tampa Tribune.*
3. "We're leaving the airport and..." ~ Budin, David. (1994, February 13). David Spero rock around the block. *The Cleveland Plain Dealer.*
4. "It wasn't just a concert..." ~ Scott, Jane. (1992, November 2). Rocker campaigns with flag costume. *The Cleveland Plain Dealer.*
5. "I don't want to get..." ~ Graff, Gary. (1993, June 23). Glenn Frey, Joe Walsh touring again. *The Beaver County Times.*
6. "Frey complained that he had..." ~ Heaton, Michael. (2013, July 7). David Spero, artist-manager, talks about what went on behind the scenes with the Eagles – exclusive interview. *The Cleveland Plain Dealer.*
7. "Glenn was giving me the..." ~ Heaton, Michael. (2013, July 7). David Spero, artist-manager, talks about what went on behind the scenes with the Eagles – exclusive interview. *The Cleveland Plain Dealer.*
8. "I said, 'Would you do..." ~ Morse, Steve. (1993, June 13). Ex-Eagles Glenn Frey, Joe Walsh team up and hit the road. *The San Bernardino County Sun.*
9. "The Eagles are like a..." ~ Morse, Steve. (1993, June 13). Ex-Eagles Glenn Frey, Joe Walsh team up and hit the road. *The San Bernardino County Sun.*
10. "That stood for No Blow..." ~ Heaton, Michael. (2013, July 7). David Spero, artist-manager, talks about what went on behind the scenes with the Eagles – exclusive interview. *The Cleveland Plain Dealer.*
11. "Joe and I individually are..." ~ Morse, Steve. (1993, June 13). *The San Bernardino County Sun.*
12. "Glenn plays a couple and..." ~ Eberhart, John Mark. (1993, June 4). Ex-Eagles Glenn Frey, Joe Walsh resumed playing together on a lark. *The Kansas City Star.*
13. "It was Frey who wound..." ~ Scott, Jane. (1993, July 13). Former Eagles soar at Nautica show. *The Cleveland Plain Dealer.*
14. "Walsh looked like he should..." ~ Johnson, Dean. (1993, June 7). Ex-Eagles duo flies high at Great Woods Glenn Frey and Joe Walsh at Great Woods. *The Boston Herald.*

▶ CHAPTER 33: HELL DOES FREEZE OVER

1. "That's when we were all..." ~ "The Eagles find a common thread." (1994, September 16). *The Allentown Morning Call.*
2. "We all did our solo..." ~ "The Eagles find a common thread." (1994, September 16). *The Allentown Morning Call.*
3. "We've all grown up a..." ~ Hilburn, Robert. (1994, May 22). They can tell you why: Welcome back to Hotel California: After a split-up that left anything but peaceful, easy feelings, the Eagles are together again, Don Henley and Glenn Frey are writing songs – and they promise it's *not* just a money thing. *The Los Angeles Times.*
4. After achieving sobriety, Walsh tried... ~ Stern, Howard. (2012, June 4). Joe Walsh is an Analog Man. *The Howard Stern Show* (SiriusXM).
5. "Some people say, 'Up yours..." ~ Stern, Howard. (2012, June 4). Joe Walsh is an Analog Man. *The Howard Stern Show* (SiriusXM).

6. "The Eagles heading out on..." ~ Staunton, Terry. (2012, September). Life's been good... eventually. *Record Collector.*

▶ CHAPTER 34: THE REUNION

1. "We were told by MTV..." ~ Russell, Deborah. (1994, May 14). Secrets & school buses; experiencing the Eagles. *Billboard.*
2. "It was terrifying going onstage..." ~ McCormick, Neil. (2013, May 6). The Eagles: Documentary reveals band's journey from naive kids to 1970s superstars. *The Windsor Star.*
3. "It's being called a resumption..." ~ DeYoung, Bill. (1994, July 22). Hell freezes over for the Eagles. *The Ocala Star-Banner.*
4. "Managing the Eagles had to..." ~ Fey, Barry; Alexander, Steve; & Wolfe, Rich. (2011). *Backstage Past.* Overland Park, KS: Lone Wolfe Press.
5. "says he was told by Eagles..." ~ Heaton, Michael. (2013, July 7). David Spero, artist-manager, talks about what went on behind the scenes with the Eagles – exclusive interview. *The Cleveland Plain Dealer.*
6. "It was evident why the..." ~ DiMartino, Dave. (1994, August). The Eagles: Irvine Meadows Amphitheatre, California. *Mojo.*
7. "I love playing Don's 'Dirty..." ~ Scott, Jane. (1994, July 8). Walsh enjoys regrouping of Eagles. *The Cleveland Plain Dealer.*
8. "You had five guys with..." ~ Heaton, Michael. (2013, July 7). David Spero, artist-manager, talks about what went on behind the scenes with the Eagles – exclusive interview. *The Cleveland Plain Dealer.*
9. "The tour seemed so spiritless..." ~ Casey, Kristin. (2020). *Rock Monster: My Life With Joe Walsh.* Los Angeles: Rare Bird Books.
10. "When we coexist and stay..." ~ Zuel, Bernard. (2010, November 19). The Eagles share their tips for longevity. *The Sydney Morning Herald.*
11. "We made a deal with..." ~ Everley, Dave. (2018, December). California dreaming. *Classic Rock.*
12. "We discovered sleep. That's a..." ~ Walsh, Joe. (2005, May 17). Interview. *Late, Late Show with Craig Ferguson* (NBC).
13. "I would feel embarrassed charging..." ~ Hiatt, Brian. (2005, August 11). Petty rules road. *Rolling Stone.*
14. "What they do in terms..." ~ Lindquist, David. (2002, February 17). American dreamers. *Indianapolis Star.*
15. "I'm not going to name..." ~ Levy, Piet. (2013, July 4). Don Henley hints at end of an era for the Eagles. *Milwaukee Journal Sentinel.*
16. "If people can't afford to..." ~ DeYoung, Bill. (1994, July 22). Eagles' Orlando show takin' it to the limit. *The Ocala Star-Banner.*
17. "You can't be more naked..." ~ "The Scene." (1995, October 27). *The Cleveland Plain Dealer.*
18. "I like the way life..." ~ Norman, Bud. (1995, August 24). Joe Walsh pulls out of the fast lane. *The Wichita Eagle.*
19. "It's the coolest thing I've..." ~ Norman, Michael. (1995, June 18). Anthology spins out appreciation of Joe Walsh. *The Cleveland Plain Dealer.*
20. "I was at that final..." ~ Stone, Pam. (2020, May 18). Good gosh almighty. *The Greenwood Index-Journal.*
21. "Walsh sang and played hard..." ~ Pantsios, Anastasia. (1997, July 3). Show just scratches of superb career. *The Cleveland Plain Dealer.*
22. "I was going into the..." ~ Beal, Jim Jr. (1997, July 18). The Eagle has landed – Joe Walsh won't wait for hell to freeze over again. *The San Antonio Express-News.*

▶ CHAPTER 35: THE INDUCTION

1. "Walsh had come to play..." ~ Heaton, Michael. (1998, May 1). The Minister experiences a state of rock 'n' roll bliss at a show by guitar whizzes Glenn Schwartz and his special friend. *The Cleveland Plain Dealer.*
2. "I think it's going to..." ~ Dufala, Denise. (1998, August 16). The guys in Drew's band. *The Cleveland Plain Dealer.*

3. "I guess I'm going to..." ~ "Woody Allen blasts New York Times reporter for reviews." (1998, August 26). *The Cedar Rapids Gazette.*
4. "I was sitting next to..." ~ Sessa, Sam. (2009, July 30). Sweet surrender. *The Baltimore Sun.*

▶ CHAPTER 36: FELDER DEPARTS

1. "The more successful the band..." ~ Farber, Jim. (2008, April 25). Eagle Don Felder has landed. *The New York Daily News.*
2. "To be honest, I've tried..." ~ Bream, Jon. (2008, September 26). Life's been good: After making their first studio album in 28 years, the ever-bickering Eagles are getting along better than ever, says guitarist Joe Walsh. *The Star Tribune.*
3. "Some people have teased me..." ~ Youhana, Jaclyn. (2001, October 2). Joe Walsh to receive honorary KSU degree. *Daily Kent Stater.*
4. "I've been a junior for..." ~ Guziak, Deborah. (2001, December 16). Graduation day at KSU – Call him Dr. Walsh. *The Kent Record Courier.*
5. "Rocker Joe Walsh is in..." ~ "Still in the works." (2000, November 2). *The Cleveland Plain Dealer.*
6. "[I] have a healthy friendship..." ~ Soeder, John. (2001, February 16). Back in the saddle: The James Gang climbs aboard some old warhorses to ride once more. *The Cleveland Plain Dealer.*
7. "I spent a while with..." ~ Rees, Paul. (2020). *The Ox: The Authorized Biography of the Who's John Entwistle.* New York: Hachette Books.
8. "Management asked all of us..." ~ Lutz, Bob. (2002, July 2). The long run – the Eagles come to Wichita on Wednesday as part of their 32-city tour. *The Wichita Eagle.*
9. "The wildly enthusiastic crowd... ended..." ~ Kershner, Jim. (2002, June 18). Audience soars with the Eagles. *The Spokane Spokesman-Review.*
10. "Walsh was faced with the..." ~ Hedegaard, Eric. (2006, August 24). Joe Walsh rides again. *Rolling Stone.*
11. "This is my hobby. I'm..." ~ Hedegaard, Eric. (2006, August 24). Joe Walsh rides again. *Rolling Stone.*
12. "He's a little like an..." ~ Blackwood, Nina. (1993, June 6). *Joe Walsh: The nutty professor.*
13. "Known for its sparse sets..." ~ Newman, Melinda. (2003, May 31). Eagles stage elaborate 'farewell' tour. *Billboard.*
14. "A lot of guys have..." ~ Miller, Michael. (2003, August 7). Walsh: A god for guitar groupies, and grandmas. *The North County Times.*

▶ CHAPTER 37: JAMES GANG REUNION

1. "We're the James Gang from..." ~ Hagan, Jeff. (2005, June 27). No new ground for native gang, but just fun on familiar turf. *The Cleveland Plain Dealer.*
2. "The three of us went..." ~ Soeder, John. (2006, August 11). Band won't walk away, hits trail for first time in three decades. *The Cleveland Plain Dealer.*
3. "When we finished those shows..." ~ Abram, Malcolm X. (2006, August 10). The Gang's all here – Cleveland power trio Joe Walsh, Jim Fox, Dale Peters ride again on first tour in 30 years. *The Akron Beacon Journal.*
4. "I've been in a very..." ~ Pullen, Doug. (2006, August 13). Joe Walsh reunites with James Gang for tour as Eagles land for a while. *The Flint Journal.*
5. "We never know what to..." ~ Clear, Marty. (2006, August 25). Joe Walsh and James Gang ride again – much to their surprise. *The Sarasota Herald-Tribune.*
6. "We're the James Gang, from..." ~ Abram, Malcolm X. (2006, August 17). Joe Walsh, Gang bring classic hits back to life. *The Akron Beacon Journal.*

▶ CHAPTER 38: LONG ROAD OUT OF EDEN

1. "He gave me a big..." ~ Vaziri, Aidin. (2009, July 12). Pop quiz: Kenny Chesney. *The San Francisco Gate.*
2. "Song selection wasn't difficult, song..." ~ Dansby Andrew. (2008, September 9). Copyright 2008 Q&A: Henley casts eye on the past, present, future. *The Houston Chronicle.*
3. "When the record was done..." ~ Brown, Jake. (2014, September/October). The architect of 70's

AOR: Bill Szymczyk on recording Joe Walsh, B.B. King, & the Eagles. *Tape Op.*
4. "Do you want to make..." ~ Smith, Ethan. (2009, February 21). Can He Save Rock 'n' Roll? – Irving Azoff wants to concentrate power in the music world like never before; Bruce Springsteen objects. *The Wall Street Journal.*
5. "When all those record companies..." ~ Young, Charles M. (2007, May 29). How the kings of Seventies California rock stopped feuding, recorded their first album in 30 years and landed at the top of the charts. *Rolling Stone.*
6. "I can't sit here and..." ~ Quan, Denise. (2007, November 7). Don Henley: 'Let the chips fall where they may.' CNN.
7. "When I was little, everyone..." ~ Koha, Nui Te; & Wigney, James. (2007, October 28). Rod and Joe join forces. *The Melbourne Sunday Herald Sun.*
8. "When I'm with the band..." ~ Salkin, Judith. (2007, July 27). Life's been good so far. *The Desert Sun.*
9. "People ask 'Why are you..." ~ Eagles chart a new course." (2007, December). *The Tampa Bay Times.*

▶ CHAPTER 39: THE LONG ROAD GOES ON

1. "We rarely fight or disagree..." ~ Koha, Nui Te. (2010, June 20). Eagles detour into life in slow lane. *The Melbourne Sunday Herald Sun.*
2. "The core of everyone's personality..." ~ Young, Charles M. (2007, May 29). How the kings of Seventies California rock stopped feuding, recorded their first album in 30 years and landed at the top of the charts. *Rolling Stone.*
3. "I don't know exactly why..." ~ Bream, Jon. (2008, September 30). The Eagles: Life's been good. *The Minneapolis Star Tribune.*
4. "For much of the show..." ~ McDonnell, Brandy. (2008, November 12). Concert review: The Eagles soar back to Tulsa. *The Oklahoman.*
5. "I was at the Beatles'..." ~ Varga, George. (2016, May 14). Joe Walsh talks music, politics & artistic seniority. *The San Diego Union-Tribune.*
6. "When I'm flustered by something..." ~ Shriver, Jerry. (2010, January 19). Ringo to turn 70 with gusto. *The Shreveport Times.*
7. "The biggest downside of Joe..." ~ Shriver, Jerry. (2010, January 19). Ringo to turn 70 with gusto. *The Shreveport Times.*
8. "Only Joe Walsh... brought the..." ~ Dalton, Stephen. (2009, July). The Eagles: NIA, Birmingham. *The Times of London.*
9. "I had hoped that we..." ~ McRanor, Graeme. (2010, May 8). Eagles go out on a high. *The Vancouver Sun.*

▶ CHAPTER 40: ANALOG JOE

1. "I didn't particularly feel in..." ~ Soeder, John. (2011, October 21). 'Analog Man' Joe Walsh sizes up the digital world. *The Cleveland Plain Dealer.*
2. "What Jeff did interfaced really..." ~ Soeder, John. (2011, October 21). 'Analog Man' Joe Walsh sizes up the digital world. *The Cleveland Plain Dealer.*
3. "I was listening to what's..." ~ Staunton, Terry. (2012, September). Life's been good... eventually. *Record Collector.*
4. "The last album I made..." ~ Hurwitz, Matt. (2012, August). Joe Walsh meets 2012. *Mix.*
5. "Joe is definitely an 'analog..." ~ Hurwitz, Matt. (2012, August). Joe Walsh meets 2012. *Mix.*
6. "Bruce would come over and..." ~ Hurwitz, Matt. (2012, August). Joe Walsh meets 2012. *Mix.*
7. "It's an observation, not a..." ~ di Perna, Alan. (1992, May). Joe Walsh discusses his career, gear and new album, 'Analog Man.' *Guitar World.*
8. "He needed somebody to play..." ~ Rodman, Sarah. (2012, July 30). Joe Walsh is keeping his mojo alive. *The Boston Globe.*
9. "Records, record stores, record sales..." ~ Hall, Daryl. (2012, November 15). *Live From Daryl's House* [Viacom].

⊡ CHAPTER 41: HISTORY OF THE EAGLES

1. "Some of the archival footage..." ~ Yarborough, Chuck. (2013, July 7). The Eagles' story finds truth in mix of laughs and pain. *The Cleveland Plain Dealer*.
2. "Most of it was about..." ~ Ruggiero, Bob. (2014, May 16). Don Felder surprised at ex-Eagles mates' ill will toward him. *The Houston Press*.
3. "The bitter fighting that the..." ~ Moody, Nekesa Mumbi. (2013, January 25). Eagles talk about new Showtime documentary. *The Daily Oklahoman*.
4. "I don't know why [Starr]..." ~ Smith, Troy L. (2015, April 18). Ringo Starr and Joe Walsh talk about the Beatles drummer's Rock Hall induction. *The Cleveland Plain Dealer*.
5. "I went back and went..." ~ Graff, Gary. (2015, September 17). Sound check: Joe Walsh is digging deep on latest solo tour. *The Macomb Daily*.
6. "would have to tape his..." ~ Edgers, Geoff. (2016, November 29). Don Henley says the Eagles are done – it was always Glenn Frey's band. *The Washington Post*.

⊡ CHAPTER 42: FAREWELL TO GLENN FREY

1. "None of us realized how..." ~ McCormick, Neil. (2017, February 23). Take it to the limit. *The Windsor Star*.
2. "He had a medical condition..." ~ Lynch, Bill. (2016, July 14). Iconic rocker Joe Walsh keeps busy with solo tour, politics. *The Charleston Gazette-Mail*.
3. "Glenn never thought of himself..." ~ Glazer, Mitchell. (1983, July). Don Henley & Danny Kortchmar, the recording team of the 80s. *Musician*.
4. "I had always hoped somewhere..." ~ Italie, Hillel. (2016, January 19). Former Eagle Don Felder mourns death of Glenn Frey. *The San Diego Union-Tribune*.
5. "The Eagles couldn't be the..." ~ McCormick, Neil. (2017, February 23). Take it to the limit. *The Windsor Star*.
6. "I don't know how to..." ~ Mehr, Bob. (2016, August 10). 'They're really pushing me,' Joe Walsh says of new band. *The Memphis Commercial Appeal*.
7. "He was my guitar hero..." ~ Graff, Gary. (2020, July). Black Keys. *Music Connection*.
8. "I got wind that Bad..." ~ Biese, Alex. (2016, June 9). Joe Walsh comes home for New Jersey shows. *The Daily Record*.
9. "We definitely crossed paths. I..." ~ Sculley, Alan. (2016, June 10). Bad Company's plan B finds good company. *The Allentown Morning Call*.
10. "We'd announced the tour and..." ~ Graff, Gary. (2016, June 20). Sound Check: Joe Walsh, Bad Company make good summer tourmates. *The Royal Oak Daily Tribune*.
11. "Walsh will be 69 in..." ~ Yarborough, Chuck. (2016, June 27). Joe Walsh and Bad Company turn back the clock at Blossom Music Center. *The Cleveland Plain Dealer*.
12. "By the end of the..." ~ Hislop, Christopher. (2016, July 21). A chat with Joe Walsh: 'Eagles' guitarist plays Casino July 26. *Foster's Daily Democrat*.
13. "I had seen Walsh perform..." ~ Grant, James. (2016, August 4). Even without the Eagles, Joe Walsh soared in Foellinger concert. *The Fort Wayne News-Sentinel*.
14. "We don't have a lot..." ~ Graff, Gary. (1996, September 26). Joe Walsh explores 'No Man's Land' on song for Afghan war doc: Exclusive. *Billboard*.

⊡ CHAPTER 43: JOE AND TOM

1. "Petty spent the entire 53-date..." ~ Browne, David. (2018, July). Music's Fentanyl crisis. *Rolling Stone*.
2. "We watched them every night..." ~ Lisko, B.J. (2020, September 10). Hey Joe!: Catching up with legendary drummer Joe Vitale: *The Canton Repository*.
3. "The last night, we walked..." ~ Simmons, Sylvie. (2018, February). The dream is fulfilled. *Mojo*.
4. "I looked at Willie Nelson..." ~ Graff, Gary. (2017, July 25). Joe Walsh talks first VetsAid charity concert & Eagles' future: 'We're just going to take it slow.' *Billboard*.

⊡ CHAPTER 44: EAGLES RETURN

1. "After Glenn passed away, none..." ~ Everley, Dave. (2018, December). California Dreaming. *Classic Rock*.

2. "Obviously a reunion was the..." ~ Everley, Dave. (2018, December). California Dreaming. *Classic Rock.*
3. "Well, I always knew how..." ~ Bosso, Joe. (2019, November). Vince Gill: "I reached the point where I said, 'I'm just going to play what's necessary.'" *Guitar World.*
4. "No, we didn't know if..." ~ Everley, Dave. (2018, December). California Dreaming. *Classic Rock.*
5. "We rehearsed and I was..." ~ Radke, Brock. (2017, November 14). Talking with the Eagles' Joe Walsh, back at the House of Blues. *The Las Vegas Sun.*
6. "He could play the songs..." ~ McMahon, Barbara. (2018, December 21). New kid in town: The Eagles embrace Glenn Frey's son into the band ahead of their first UK tour since the singer's tragic death in 2016. *The Sun.*
7. "There's not a lot of..." ~ McClain, Buzz . (2021, April). The Eagles' Steuart Smith keeps his rockstar title private. *Northern Virginia.*
8. "Young Frey was featured early..." ~ Yarborough, Chuck. (2018, October 21). New kid in town does his dad proud with Eagles. *The Cleveland Plain Dealer.*
9. "It was really fun and..." ~ "Vitale joins Joe Walsh in Colorado Music Hall of Fame. (2017, August 20). *The Canton Repository.*
10. "It's great to watch. I..." ~ Radke, Brock. (2017, November 14). Talking with the Eagles' Joe Walsh, back at the House of Blues. *The Las Vegas Sun.*

▶ CHAPTER 45: A PANDEMIC BREAK

1. "By sheer force of personality..." ~ Pappademas, Alex. (2019, October 1). Time flies, and the Eagles soar with it. *The Los Angeles Times.*
2. "While people are coming into..." ~ Doerschuk, Bob. (2020, February 5). Ahead of Hotel California tour, Eagles' Don Henley reflects on the iconic band's 'creative peak.' *USA Today.*
3. "That's a monster that needs..." ~ Ryan, Patrick. (2021, January 27). Joe Walsh talks VetsAid 2020 grant recipients, teases new Eagles music. *USA Today.*
4. "While Henley is now the..." ~ Bream, Jon. (2021, October 1). The Eagles revisit 'Hotel California' in St. Paul. *Star Tribune.*

▶ CHAPTER: CLOSING TIME

1. "A philosopher said as we..." ~ Woods, Sean. (2012, June). The last word: Joe Walsh. *Men's Journal.*
2. "I'm very lucky; very blessed..." ~ "Life continues to be good for Joe Walsh." (2007, August 23). *The Charleston Post and Courier.*
3. "I'd like to go down..." ~ Varga, George. (2012, February 2). Fact or fiction? With Joe Walsh, you never know. *The San Diego Union-Tribune.*
4. "I believe my job on..." ~ Holan, Marc. (1986, October 2). Joe Walsh comes home. *Scene.*
5. "Great songs last, don't they?..." ~ Mengel, Noel. (2010, September 2). Golden Eagles. *The Brisbane Courier Mail.*
6. "I have absolutely no idea..." ~ Lyons, Dee. (1987, November 20). Joe Walsh – Life's been good, so far. *The Dallas Morning News.*
7. According to RM Sotheby's, the... ~ https://rmsothebys.com/en/auctions/LF18/London/lots/r0003-1962-maserati-5000-gt-by-allemano/674767.

Printed in the USA
CPSIA information can be obtained
at www.ICGtesting.com
LVHW020900190923
758538LV00007B/349